To Sally,
With all my
love!

Dottie Demaratus

THE *Force* OF A *Feather*

...an interesting reminiscence occur...
me at the moment. In the year 18...
Los Angeles, with "public opinion" ag...
me, I tried the case of fourteen ne...
claiming the protection of the writ of Ha...
Corpus. I discharged them, as entitle...
freedom. I was denounced as — ...
abolitionist! For declaring a sim...
proposition of law — for granting a c...
constitutional right! Even at Sacra...
I was "da... *free forever*...
me.) A month passed: one day...
little boy from a buggy, under...

THE *Force* OF A *Feather*

THE SEARCH FOR A LOST STORY OF SLAVERY AND FREEDOM

DeEtta Demaratus

The University of Utah Press
Salt Lake City

LIBRARY OF CONGRESS CATALOGING-IN-PUBLICATION DATA

Demaratus, DeEtta, 1941–
    The force of a feather : the search for a lost story of slavery and freedon /
DeEtta Demaratus.
    p. cm.
Includes bibliographical references.
    ISBN 0–87480–714–X
    1. Mason, Biddy, 1818–1891. 2. Mason, Biddy, 1818–1891—Trials, liti-
gation, etc. 3. Habeas corpus—California—Los Angeles County. 4. Women
slaves—United States—Biography. 5. Slaves—United States—Biography.
6. Freedmen—United States—Biography. 7. African American women—
Biography. 8. Women philanthropists—California—Los Angeles County—
Biography. I. Title.
    E444.M38 D46 2002
    306.6'62'092—dc21   2001006782

Printed on acid-free paper

06 05 04 03 02 01 00
5   4   3   2   1

A few names and details in the personal narrative chapters of this
book have been changed to protect the privacy of certain
individuals.

For B. I. H.

CONTENTS

PREFACE

In January 1856, a habeas corpus case was heard in the First District Court of the State of California, County of Los Angeles. Because court was not in session at the time, the case was heard on an emergency basis before the district judge, Benjamin Ignatius Hayes. The charge was that a southerner, Robert Mays Smith, had held two women and eleven children of color in slavery and was now about to remove them from California, a free state, and transport them to Texas, a slave state. The petition for a writ of habeas corpus had been presented to Judge Hayes to prevent Smith from leaving with his slaves. After the judge approved the writ, the women and children were taken into protective custody and held in the county jail, pending trial.

The trial that followed became a public spectacle in Los Angeles and attracted national notice. Several factors made the case conspicuous and incendiary compared to other California emancipation trials. First, there was confusion about the status and relationships of the people involved. Were these women and children in fact slaves or, as Smith asserted, members of his family? Was he forcing them to accompany him, or were they going willingly? Was one of the women a blood relative of Smith's wife? Did Smith father children by either of the women of color?

Smith's relationship to the Church of Jesus Christ of Latter-day Saints—whose members are commonly known as Mormons—was no less fraught and ambiguous. Robert Smith and his wife, Rebecca Smith, had formerly lived in Mississippi, a slave state. There they had converted to Mormonism. In 1848, the Smiths and their slaves joined the westward exodus of Mormons fleeing persecution after the church's martyred leader, Joseph Smith, was shot and killed in Nauvoo, Illinois. This early migration of Mormons established a colony near Great Salt Lake in what would become, in 1896, the state of Utah. But the Smiths did not remain long in Utah Territory. When the Mormons founded another colony in San Bernardino, California—which had entered the Union as a free state under the Compromise of 1850—Robert Mays Smith moved his family and slaves there.

After several years in California, Smith suffered a financial setback for which he blamed the Mormon Church. He severed ties with that religious body and began making plans to move on to Texas. Could the writ of habeas corpus have been an act of vengeance against Smith by members of the church?

Finally, the role of the judge presiding over the Smith case was controversial. Benjamin Hayes was southern-born, had himself been a slave owner, and had political ambitions that depended upon the support of both those who supported the southern cause in the impending civil war and the Mormons who formed a powerful voting bloc. His verdict in the habeas corpus case was bound to alienate some of his constituents: southerners, Mormons, or moderates, or all three, in Los Angeles. Hayes also had a personal stake in the trial. Whatever his background geopolitically, he was an ardent defender of the law and a devout Catholic, institutions that bound him to protect others and to treat them fairly and with regard, although his religious beliefs had not apparently prevented him from owning slaves.

In view of Smith's ambiguous relationships to these women and their children, his rebellion against the Mormon Church, and the conflicting concerns that could influence the judge's verdict, the habeas corpus trial was destined to become a sensational public event of its time. Moreover, the social and political implications of the case extended far beyond the state of California. In 1857, the United States

Supreme Court would make its famous and controversial ruling concerning Dred Scott, a slave who had moved with his owner, John Emerson, from Missouri, a slave state, to Illinois and later to Wisconsin—where slavery was prohibited by the Missouri Compromise—before returning to Missouri. After Emerson's death, Scott sued his widow for his own freedom, contending that his former residence in a free state and a free territory made him a free man. The Supreme Court was deeply divided in its deliberations, but the court's southern members constituted a majority and ruled that the Missouri Compromise was unconstitutional and that Scott, as a Negro "whose ancestors were . . . sold as slaves," had no standing in court.

It is unknown whether Judge Hayes was aware of the *Dred Scott* case, which at the time of the Smith habeas corpus trial would have been making its way through the federal court to the Supreme Court. If he did know of it, he certainly would have recognized that the two cases paralleled one another in significant ways, and would have appreciated the importance of the decision he would make concerning the fate of the two women of color. If he permitted them to be transported to Texas, their status in the eyes of the law would be as compromised as was Scott's.

Beyond the controversy and publicity concerning the trial over which Hayes presided, however, was a painful and poignant human drama. Fundamentally, relationships were on trial, and neither the judge nor the many court spectators could know the hearts and minds of the people who confronted one another in a Los Angeles courtroom during three weeks of January 1856. However, nearly 150 years later, their story, once lost, has surfaced and speaks eloquently across the decades about the power and resilience of our ties to one another.

ACKNOWLEDGMENTS

I owe much to many people and can name only a few. If, as I believe, I was chosen to pursue this story and this book, then my gratitude goes first to Biddy Mason, and those she knew or loved who helped shape and enlarge us both: Hannah, Robert Mays Smith and Rebecca Smith, and Benjamin Hayes.

My deepest thanks go to those who gave me their time, energy, and enthusiasm during my travels to research this book. Bill Klemcke (Robert Smith's direct descendant) and Ethel Klemcke were unstinting in their personal kindness and generosity with family records and photographs. It is my greatest grief that I did not finish the book in time for Bill to read it. Bob Weed and other Smith relatives in Texas were hospitable and delightful company. I also wish to thank Norman Dorn, his mother, and his sister; the man I call Sam C.; Anne L. Brandt at the archives in San Bernardino who made me aware of Toby Ember's court case; Miriam Matthews who shared her unpublished bibliography; and Germaine Moon, A. W. Hebert III, Charles Beal, and Larry Surtees.

I am deeply appreciative of the patience and generosity extended to me by librarians and archivists in Edgefield, South Carolina; Jackson, Mississippi; San Bernardino, San Diego, and Los Angeles, California; and with the Church of Jesus Christ of Latter-day Saints in Seattle and Salt Lake City. The staffs at the University of Washington and the Bancroft Library were especially responsive. William P. Frank, curator of Hispanic and Western Manuscripts at the Huntington, deserves special mention. I am grateful to the historians and writers who reviewed the manuscript of this book and were helpful in their comments, especially Kevin Starr. I also wish to thank my excellent copy editor, Annette Wenda.

My family, especially Catherine and Sebastien, loves and supports me in whatever I do. My friends, in the United States and Italy, are also steadfast and stimulating.

Finally, there is one person who brought this book into being, who made it possible, without whom it would have been a stillborn, lamented dream: my editor, Dawn Marano. Her intelligence, humor, and nurturing sustained me through long, dark nights.

THE *Force* OF A *Feather*

Coming to the Wall

I feel very strongly that I am under the influence of things or
questions which were left incomplete or unanswered by my
parents and grandparents and more distant ancestors. It often
seems as if there were an impersonal karma within a family, which
is passed on from parents to children. It has always seemed to me
that I had to answer questions which fate had posed to my
forefathers, and which had not yet been answered, or as if I had to
complete, or perhaps continue, things which previous ages had left
unfinished.

—Carl Jung, *Memories, Dreams, Reflections*

FOR MUCH OF THE LAST TEN YEARS, my life has seemed a footnote to
a story that, having found me, would not let me rest. It is a story
owing its truth and significance to people who lived and died more
than a century before I was born, people whose circumstances and
legacy, whose race and religious beliefs, had little obvious relevance to

me and my life, but whose personal history, nevertheless, became entwined with mine. This is their story, but because their story became meaningful and urgent to me in ways I could not have predicted, it is a story I have come to believe we somehow share.

I first heard of the woman named Biddy Mason when I decided to write a newspaper column dealing with the genealogy of the many minorities in the United States. From various regions of the country, I selected prominent people of color—Cherokee Indians, Chinese immigrants, refugees from Cambodia, and representatives from Central and South America—and my intention was to research the families of these individuals, illustrating the often overlooked richness of our American heritage.

To represent African Americans, I wanted a woman of the West who had achieved prominence and riches in her time. I cannot remember the original impetus for the project or why I contrived these particular parameters. Perhaps I wanted to offer inspiring stories— although the fact that I considered wealth a measurement of success embarrasses me now. I might have thought her affluence would make her ancestry easier to trace. Already I dreaded the deadlines demanded by weekly columns.

I considered several candidates for the piece, then read about Biddy Mason, a slave who, on her way west, drove sheep behind her master's covered wagon and after her emancipation in California had become wealthy. My early research turned up several references about her philanthropy and church work. She was mentioned in books about pioneers; these books frequently noted that Biddy had an almost masculine strength, a description introduced probably innocently by one writer and unfortunately adopted by subsequent writers. In my mind I saw Biddy, tall, dark, strong in her own *womanly* right, walking in the dust behind a distant wagon. Before her rise the Rocky Mountains. The summer heat enveloping her on this interminable trail makes those snowcapped peaks seem an impossible vision. Behind her lay the spreading cotton fields of Georgia. She is Janus-faced in this moment, gazing back at the country where she had been born and forward toward a land she does not yet know, where she will one day die. She is fearful both of forgetting and of remembering.

There was no question Biddy Mason intrigued me, and I thought that the arc of her life from slavery to wealthy property owner would interest others as well. At the least, I was willing to commit a couple of weeks to researching her story.

My request to the Los Angeles Hall of Records for a death certificate for Biddy Mason was returned. The clerk searched, could not find a death certificate, and cashed my check. My interest waned. The minority genealogy project was abandoned. I went on to other writing projects, and Biddy Mason became a name barely remembered, like a once fragrant flower pressed between pages of a book that has been returned to its slot on a shelf.

Then one day I was sitting in a corner coffee shop where I often had lunch near my office on Seattle's First Hill. In the booth behind me, two women—African American, I assumed by their voices—were talking. Perhaps one was reading a magazine. I heard the rustle of pages.

"Bet you don't know who was the first black woman millionaire?" one of the women asked.

I cocked my ears. A face, a name, an image hovered on the edge of recollection. The other woman grunted inquisitively.

"Here she is."

"What did she do to get all that money?" the second one asked.

"She owned a string of hair salons. She invented the stuff that straightens your hair."

"I thought that was just sulfur."

And they were off into a discussion of hair products.

Biddy Mason! That was the name, and I saw her; rather, I saw her again in my reverie of her walking west, the Rocky Mountains before her, the cotton fields behind. But eavesdropping on the two women I learned that they were talking about Madam C. J. Walker, the hair-care magnate. Her rise from poverty to millionairess was indeed an inspiring saga, but I found myself wishing I could set the record straight, wishing I were able to tell the women that they were wrong, that before Madam Walker there had been another inspiring woman, a slave named Biddy. I did not know what to say. I had no background to present to these strangers, and I suspected that they would rightly resent my inept intrusion. It was then, I think, that I became committed to Biddy, to rescuing her from obscurity and ensuring that her accomplishments were recognized and acclaimed. I was suddenly no longer thinking in terms of a column, but about a book. Still, I knew I would be working from a sense of duty, seeing Biddy's resurrection as a worthwhile endeavor, basically as a way of being fair. What I did not know was whether Biddy and her story would sustain the commitment necessary for a project as ambitious as the one I was now considering.

In the summer of 1992, after giving the project snatched hours of unfocused attention, I decided it was time to fish or cut bait, as anglers say. I allotted myself a week to fly down to Los Angeles from Seattle to research this woman who had captured my interest, but not as yet my heart. I knew I needed a sense of Biddy as a human being. I wanted to find records of her family, both her descendants and her ancestors. Los Angeles seemed the right place to start: this was where Biddy had spent most of her life. If, after a week, I had not found enough to make a book-size commitment to Biddy Mason, I would let go and move on to other subjects.

I stood on the corner of a street in downtown Los Angeles. From an article in a magazine I had learned that Biddy Mason's original homestead had been chosen as a site to be commemorated by a project called "The Power of Place." The mission of the project was to locate places in Los Angeles possessing historical and social importance and to use a multicultural approach in celebrating and preserving them. The arts commission had provided me with a packet containing a map to artworks honoring Biddy Mason's life and home.[1] This was the folder I had in hand as I faced the blank wall of the block around which I had already walked twice.

I felt frustrated but also amused. In my head was the image of a slave woman driving sheep; in my hand was a packet of slick illustrations showing the degree of celebrity Biddy eventually achieved. Accompanying this mental incongruity was a physical predicament. I was near but somehow far from the monuments to this woman. It was as if I were outside a maze or labyrinth, unable to find my way in. I felt I was encircling a secret garden, and behind this drab wall awaited a world of riches and magic, with answers to my inchoate questions.

Finally I found a way into an arcade. I had expected a yellow brick road into a place as resplendent as the Emerald City, but here was simply a vestibule between buildings opening onto a concrete-paved courtyard. These were no benevolent fairy godmothers in sight, only the usual urban inhabitants: business people, a young man with blond hair waxed into spikes, a security guard watching a TV monitor. At a shoe-shine stand a Hispanic man vigorously sprayed a pair of loafers.

"Preserving them?" I asked. He laughed.

I looked around and saw that in the alcove by an elevator was a work of art in two parts: a photomural on the wall to the left, facing the elevator, and a reconstruction of a window on the wall opposite the elevator doors. The plaque on the wall read: "House of the Open Hand by Betye Saar, part of the Power of Place, 1989." People came in and out of the elevator without looking at the artwork. They carried newspapers or bags of food. The elevator doors opened and closed. I waited until there was a respite in the traffic to study the walls.

My first impression was that this was a minimal attempt to decorate bare walls. On my left, facing the elevator, was an enlarged photograph in sepia tones showing African American women standing on the steps and porch of a house with a picket fence. The age of the original photograph and the grain of enlargement cast the whole porch in shadows. Was the woman in the doorway Biddy Mason? I measured the woman's stature ("almost masculine"—how that description irked me), but, yes, that was probably Biddy. Who were the others? It had not occurred to me that other women were involved. Were these fellow slaves, relatives, daughters, sisters, or neighbors? I searched the shadows, trying to extract from the poor image some features or distinguishing qualities of age or expression. I could not. The shadows, like raw rock, refused to release the women.

The reconstructed window also seemed a modest work, but, as I looked closer, I saw that the details were fine and carefully chosen. The artist had selected her materials to echo the photomural: cream-colored wooden siding, a window with brown shutters, and a picket fence in cream and brown. Inside the window, fantasy began.

At the top of the reconstructed window was a brown velvet drape, on the left side a cream lace curtain, beneath the curtain a pair of wire spectacles, and on the right of the window a remnant of a brown quilt with worn patches. On the quilt were a spool of white thread and a folded fan. Between the spectacles and the folded fan was an apothecary's bottle, perhaps for chloroform, a midwife's medicine, but

Biddy Mason: Time & Place, commemorative wall by Sheila Levrant de Bretteville. Courtesy of Community Redevelopment Agency, Los Angeles.

holding now a spray of purple flowers. Wildflowers, I thought, or, more likely, herbs of which I was ignorant.

The focus of the window was an oval-framed photograph of Biddy Mason, the one often published in the history books I had scoured. Over the photograph was a netlike veil, such as women once wore to church.

Across the window, over the lace curtain, beside Biddy's picture, drifted velvet leaves, cream-colored, tinged with red and brown. The leaves were somehow satisfying. Filmmakers once indicated the passage of time by inserting shots of falling leaves.

To the right of the elevator, the vestibule became an open outdoor area with trees and metal tables where workers from nearby offices sat and ate. Their lunches were in takeout boxes or spread out on yellow wrappers. Two young black women sat at a table talking. Beyond the tables and trees was a passage leading to the opposite street, and in the passageway was a small fountain. Sunlight glinted in its spray.

On one side of the open area was a tall brown wall. The noonday sun was behind the wall, casting it in shadow. I had to raise my hand

and shift my position to see that this was not only a wall, but also a work of art. I thought of the monument to the Vietnam veterans in Washington, D.C., but this was a wall of history, not untimely death.

Biddy Mason: Time & Place, by Sheila Levrant de Bretteville, was an eighty-foot-long poured-concrete wall divided in panels corresponding to the decades in the life of a person. The wall was a combination of inscriptions and embedded objects. The early history of Los Angeles was also delineated in this tribute to Biddy Mason. An inscription read: "Forty-four settlers from Mexico establish the pueblo of Los Angeles—twenty-six have African ancestors, 1781." Implanted in the wall was a copy of the first map of Los Angeles, made in 1810. Another inscription told of the dedication of the Plaza Church in 1821.

Meanwhile, Biddy's life had begun. "Born a slave . . ." I came nearer, reading the words and removing my glasses to peer at the objects or their imprints. The people who were eating lunch had noticed my scrutiny, and one or two had arisen from their metal chairs to come see what I was doing. How many years had they lunched here, I wondered, without looking at this wall?

I did a preliminary scan of the display, trying to see it in its entirety, to take in its overall theme. Instead, I found myself focusing on a silhouette of a shape, a kind of *X.* I studied it and came up with several identifications or explanations. An axle? The *X* with which Biddy signed the deed to her first home? At my shoulder I felt the presence of another person and saw that a man was standing beside me, his glasses also perched upon his forehead, his eyebrows knit as he squinted at the wall. He was black, middle-aged, graying, his face unwrinkled, but showing the weathering of age. He held his glasses up by the rim; his were hands that had known manual work.

I touched the mysterious *X* on the wall. "What do you think that is?" I asked.

I thought of archaeologists on an excavation site, gathering shards and bits of bone. What was this? Where does it belong? Where does it fit in? Was this the artifact that would solve the puzzle and allow me to see the features of a face or the outline of a landscape?

The man stared at the *X* for a moment more, then shook his head. "Don't rightly know," he said.

We stood shoulder to shoulder for a few minutes, then moved away in opposite directions, as if agreeing we might be more successful in interpretation on our own, or perhaps there were simply other inscriptions to be read.

I returned to following the decades of Biddy's life. The first inscription concerned her origins as a slave. The second said: "Eighteen year old Biddy and her sister Hannah become the property of Robert Smith, a plantation owner, in Logtown, Mississippi, 1836." I read this casually, as one does an item of slight interest in a newspaper. I thought of the women in shadows on the porch. One of the women might be Hannah, Biddy's sister. An image of two small girls running through rows of cotton flashed in my mind. I conjured another image, another porch, and on it stood a white man: the owner of the plantation, the slave master, Robert Smith. How strange that I had accepted *slavery* in conjunction with Biddy, but had not yet associated that condition with the reality of *an owner.* But in that moment, Robert Smith stepped into my awareness and, although I did not yet know it, would become a major character in the story that would unfold before me in the years to come.

I reread the second inscription: "Eighteen year old Biddy and her sister Hannah . . ." I raised my hand and placed my palm against the letters, then ran my fingers over the words. The gesture was reflexive, unpremeditated. It was as if I expected to understand something more clearly through touch. Perhaps this is why visitors to the Vietnam War Memorial run their fingers across the names and make rubbings — in remembrance of the dead and also in an attempt, in some way, to call them forth.

But these ruminations occurred to me later. At the time, I simply stroked the wall instinctively, responding to some deep need for contact. And it happened. A jolt, a bolt from the blue, not an electric shock, but a sudden seizure of certainty. *That's not true!* said a voice within me, a familiar voice, my own. I was startled. Confused. *That's not true. That's not how it happened.* I actually jumped back, turned around, and held out my open hand as if to show a scar or expose a wound.

I have no way to explain that jolt at the wall. What I came to believe was that an exchange was made between me and the past, that an invitation was extended. Perhaps the past addresses each of us from time to time, and we respond in the language we know. For writers and historians, that language is expressed in research, in thought, and eventually in the written word. And so it was with me.

From that day at the wall onward, I was a traveler walking backward through time, working my way eastward, following an often elusive and barely discernible trail of historical records, in a sense retracing the journey that Biddy and Hannah had made westward. My research over the course of ten years took me again and again to California, then Utah, Mississippi, South Carolina, and Texas. Biddy, as I soon discovered, was the herald for a host of others long dead, and for a story much larger than her own biography. Biddy introduced me to Hannah, to her children and Hannah's children; to their owners, Robert Mays Smith and Rebecca Smith; and to Benjamin Ignatius Hayes, an otherwise unknown district judge who would sit at the vortex of a social and political storm, rendering a decision about a case that would profoundly change his own life and the lives of the people who confronted each other in his courtroom.

In another sense, thanks to Biddy, I was also sent that day at the wall on a journey into my own past and introduced to parts of myself and my history that I had almost forgotten.

ONE

The Dream

IN THE ACCOUNTS OF HISTORY, the cross-country journey of Robert Mays Smith would be portrayed as a reckless adventure, a wild, self-centered wandering without regard for the women and children with him, like a comet streaking across the sky, entrapping smaller bodies in its wake. The real impetus for Robert's travels began, as it does for many a young man, when he realized how eclipsed were both his present prospects and his future hopes.

He was a poor boy from Edgefield District, South Carolina, from a family without land or social status. His Mormon baptismal record states that his father, John Smith, was from Virginia and his mother, Sarah, from South Carolina, where Robert was born in Edgefield in 1804. There were Smiths and Mays in the cabins beside many creeks and rivers draining Edgefield District, and all struggled to survive. In fifty years, from 1780 to 1830, once pristine forestland became overworked farms. In the progress of degradation of natural resources—common in human history—the woods were slashed for timber, topsoil was depleted, and game had become rare. For those with land and financial resources, Edgefield was still a place of beauty and bounty. For the landless and the poor, however, it was an economic prison from which to escape.

A will, written in Edgefield on July 12, 1829, and "proved by oath" on September 13 of the following year, says: "I, William Dean, feeling the infirmities of age, make this my last will and testament." Among its provisions is this statement: "I give to my grandson Robert M. Smith $150."[1] It was a bequest, apparently, that became the grubstake for Robert's planned move west. To people living in Georgia and the Carolinas, the West was the newly opened Indian lands east of the Mississippi River where the earth was deep and rich, the trees thick and tall, and cotton bolls swelled like clouds in a summer sky. It was to Mississippi that Robert Mays Smith, inheritance in hand, planned to travel, as soon as he could buy supplies and secure passage.

The adult life of Rebecca Dorn, like that of many of the women of her time, was largely shaped by her family's and then her husband's situations and ambitions. In Rebecca's case, the life she left behind to follow the dreams of the man she would marry—Robert Smith—was one of wealth, social prominence, and privilege.

Rebecca's ancestors were German Palatine immigrants who came to Charles Towne, South Carolina, on a vessel named the *Dragon,* and traveled inland to establish a colony. On December 24, 1764, George Dorn was granted two hundred acres on Sleepy Creek in what was to become Edgefield District, South Carolina, establishing the family homestead passed on to successive generations of Dorns. Rebecca's mother, Sarah Burkhalter Dorn, was descended from Swiss emigrants who came to Georgia and the Carolinas. By the time Rebecca Ruth was born on April 7, 1810, the Dorn homestead on Sleepy Creek was a prosperous plantation of sixteen hundred acres.

There were ten Dorn children, eight boys and two girls, Rebecca and her sister, Mary, called "Polly." Two of Rebecca's brothers, Densley and Benjamin, were described as "deranged."[2] Rebecca was especially fond of Densley, five years her junior, and often took care of him. In her later years, Rebecca suffered an unspecified sort of ill health, but those infirm years were far in the future. During their childhood, Rebecca, her sister, and her brothers enjoyed an idyllic existence at the homestead on Sleepy Creek.

The Dorns were both educated and cultured. Rebecca's brother Solomon would later start the Manual Labor School, offering classes in "spelling, reading, writing, arithmetic, English, grammar, geography, natural philosophy, Latin, and Greek."[3] Another brother, William, would spend much of his life hunting for gold and, to the astonishment and scorn of his Edgefield neighbors, eventually find it and become immensely rich.

The Dorn boys were at liberty to pursue such endeavors because the work on the plantation was performed by several dozen slaves. Slaves also worked in the Dorn house. Rebecca and her sister, like many children of the affluent, probably had personal slaves who took care of their young mistresses' needs, and were companions or playmates as well. Rebecca's own slave was apparently a light-skinned girl named Hannah, twelve years her junior.

Rebecca Dorn, living in a handsome house in a serene setting, surrounded by loving relatives and friends and attended by slaves, may well have imagined that, after marriage, her life would continue the same way. Instead, one day, perhaps at a wedding, she met a blue-eyed stranger named Robert Mays Smith.

Robert Mays Smith and Rebecca Dorn married in 1829 or 1830 and apparently lived in Edgefield for a short time. The 1830 census for Edgefield District, South Carolina, lists as head of household a Robert Smith, with a wife of Rebecca's age, and a young man who was of an age to be her brother Densley. Also living in the Smith household was a young girl who was probably Rebecca's slave, Hannah. Many poor men might have welcomed or profited from being married to a rich man's daughter, but if Robert was living off his in-laws, then the subsidized lifestyle came to an early end. Robert Mays Smith's obituary states that he and his wife left South Carolina for Mississippi in 1830. At that time, Densley and Hannah returned to the Dorn homestead. Rebecca's leaving without her personal slave might be attributed to her father's refusal to let the young girl go, to a falling out with her family—who might have been distressed at Rebecca's mismatched marriage—or to Robert's insistence that they make their own way, without help of any kind. In 1830, Rebecca accompanied Robert to Mississippi and apparently never saw Edgefield or her family again.

A decade in southwestern Mississippi had given Robert a passel of children, but little else. According to the reported birthplace of one child, the Smiths were living in Copiah County in 1836. The 1840 census for Franklin County, Mississippi, shows Robert M. Smith with a wife and four children. The 1841 Franklin County Tax Records show Robert to be a poor farmer whose only possession worth inventorying was a grandfather clock, probably given to Rebecca as a wedding present. At night, in a two-room cabin, with his children sleeping two to a bed and his exhausted wife beside him, Robert could likely hear two things: the wind in the trees in the piney woods and the clucking of the incongruous clock.

The Mississippi land boom of the 1830s was strangling on its own success. Thousands of settlers such as Robert had poured into the new state, and those with money bought the best land and planted cotton. Small farmers, cattle ranchers, and loggers competed for the remaining land—and did so in humid heat accompanied by swarms of insects. The place they had struggled to reach was no better for most than the land they had left.

Despite the notoriety it would soon achieve and its perceived singularity, the Church of Jesus Christ of Latter-day Saints, or LDS Church, more commonly known as the Mormon Church, had its roots in the nineteenth-century religious revivals from which sprang numerous Protestant sects and denominations. The Great Awakening, the early period of these religious manifestations, was based on a dynamic evangelism that had at its core the experience of conversion. The conversions, emotional experiences often transforming the believers' lives, occurred during religious revivals—camp meetings—or protracted meetings during which penitents were prayed over. The Second Great Awakening, coming in the latter part of the century, added a new dimension in which the converts saw themselves as participants in a heroic history, a time of preparation for Christ's Second Coming, necessitating the reformation of U.S. society and the establishment of a new social order. In *The Year of Decision, 1846,* Bernard DeVoto would term Mormonism "a great catch basin of evangelical doctrine," meaning it incorporated all the trends and tendencies of a religious century.[4]

Although the religious ferment of the times was the fertile soil from which the new faith sprang, "the combination of millennialism and the westward movement assured its growth."[5] The prophet and founder of the church was Joseph Smith, who had visions and visitations and in time claimed to have been shown sacred Scriptures that he translated into *The Book of Mormon.* On April 6, 1830, in Fayette, New York, Joseph Smith formally established the Church of Christ, which later became the Church of Jesus Christ of Latter-day Saints. In less than a year, Smith decided to move his church from New York to Ohio and at the same time began a missionary system to recruit converts to the new religion.

The Mormon missionaries who took the church's message south during the 1840s were probably zealous but humble and dedicated men. They rode on horseback between far-flung farms, sleeping in open fields or unlocked barns, eating fruit from trees or whatever farmers cared to share, having in their saddlebags only essentials besides the central doctrinal document of their faith, *The Book of Mormon.* The strongest appeal of the church was to the dispossessed, offering them both hope and, after 1846, the prospect of a homeland, a New Jerusalem. To those like Robert Smith whose dreams had turned out to be chimeras, the new religion offered consolation and a way to become part of a close community.

The result of the LDS Church's southern initiative was impressive. Two of the missionaries riding throughout Mississippi during these years were Benjamin Clapp and John Brown. In less than one year, between August 1843 and June 1844, these two alone baptized almost two hundred converts. Two new branches of the church were organized, and one of them, the Little Bear Creek branch, was in Franklin County, Mississippi.

One day, when Robert returned to the cabin from a day in the fields or woods, he may have found an unfamiliar horse tied in front of his house, or perhaps Robert and his family were gathered around the dinner table when a knock came at the cabin door. In either case, Robert's convictions concerning the new doctrine were cemented within a few short hours, because the missionaries' diaries show that by the next day they had moved on. For the price of a tithe, the missionaries seemed to offer much to a man such as Robert: a belief that was absolute, a rationale for his sufferings, and hope for the future. In his increasingly desperate situation, he would have welcomed the idea of a

Rebecca Ruth Dorn
Smith. Courtesy of
Ethel Klemcke.

community interested in his welfare, would have welcomed hearing
himself addressed for the first time as "Brother Smith."

As Rebecca moved about the cabin, removing dishes and putting
the children to bed, perhaps she listened to the missionaries' words
and saw the beginning of a transformation in her husband's face. No
doubt she had been as distressed by their misfortunes as Robert. Rebecca was presumably a Baptist, as that was the church affiliation of
her parents, although the records of Little Steven's Creek Baptist
Church in Edgefield District, South Carolina, do not report her attendance as a child. Perhaps Rebecca was as captivated by the promise of
this new faith as her husband or swept along by his emotions. Perhaps

she calculated that she had to follow Robert into Mormonism or risk losing him as a provider altogether. Her childhood home on Sleepy Creek, her family, her friends, Hannah, and the sights and sounds she had known and loved were gone as surely as leaves in a stream. Robert and her children were now all she had in the world.

Sometime in the evening, Rebecca may have joined her husband and the missionaries in prayer, feeling the furtive stirrings of hope for their future as a family. What is certain is that on February 11, 1844, according to Mormon Temple records, Robert M. Smith and his wife, Rebecca, were baptized into the LDS Church.

During the next four years, the lives of Robert Mays Smith and his family changed dramatically. Sometime between 1844 and the spring of 1848, the Smiths became the owners of three slaves: a woman named Biddy and her two small daughters.

Not much is known about Biddy's early life: she was born on October 15, 1818, and was originally a slave on a cotton plantation in Hancock County, Georgia. One story maintains that Biddy ran north, sought asylum with the Cherokee Nation, and married one of their chiefs. Because the majority of Cherokees living in Georgia by the late 1820s were farmers and slave owners themselves, with laws in place forbidding interracial marriage, this story is likely apocryphal.[6]

It was not uncommon for slaves to assume the last names of their first owners. And, indeed, among the cotton planters residing in Hancock in 1820 were Thomas Mason Sr. and Thomas Mason Jr., evidently father and son, both of whom owned female slaves whose ages correspond with Biddy's at that time. The 1830 census lists both Thomas Masons, but by 1840 both were gone from Hancock County.

How Biddy got from Georgia to Mississippi where she became the Smiths' slave is also unknown. However, if either of the Masons did own her, their abrupt departure from Hancock County is a clue that yields a plausible conjecture.

By 1830, it was already evident that cotton crops took a tremendous toll on the landscape by depleting the soil. As a planter from Alabama put it, cotton was more destructive than earthquakes or volcanoes. "Witness the red hills of Georgia and South Carolina, which produced cotton till the last dying gasp of the soil forbade any further attempt at cultivation." In 1841, the grand jury of Hancock County presented a list of grievances to the Georgia Superior Court, complaining, "The making of cotton to purchase everything else necessarily causes us to be great consumers of the products of other states, consequently exchange must be against us. Under this unwise policy our lands have become exhausted, our citizens involved in debt, and relief is called for from every quarter."[7] The truth of these contentions is obvious in the migration of hundreds of farmers, plantation owners, and their slaves from Georgia's cotton belt to more fertile soil in Alabama, Mississippi, and Texas. The Masons and Biddy may have been among them.

—

The 1840 census for Franklin County, Mississippi, shows that Robert M. Smith did not own slaves, as does an 1841 tax list for the same county. Biddy's acquisition by the Smith family at this juncture remains a curious and unexplained occurrence. During these years, Smith could barely support his wife and children, let alone purchase a slave or take on three more dependents. But although the historical record does not document Biddy's arrival among the Smiths, it does offer a few possible explanations for it.

By the fall of 1844, Robert and his wife, Rebecca, were practicing members of the Mormon Church. The LDS Church in Mississippi at this time comprised a number of branches scattered across the state, and it is possible that a wealthy member of their branch or of the larger community of believers—perhaps a wealthy plantation owner—decided to assist a family in need with the gift of Biddy. Another benefactor might have been Rebecca's older brother Robert Dorn, who had lived in Mississippi since 1834. He resided with his family on a sizable plantation in Tallahatchie County, in northwestern Mississippi, and owned several dozen slaves.

But why would the Smiths welcome a female slave, burdened with children, in lieu of a male to assist Robert with the farming? In the spring of 1845, Rebecca was pregnant again. A female slave could take the workload from her shoulders and, if necessary, serve as a midwife. That Biddy had children was also an advantage: dependents made it difficult for a mother to run away.

When Biddy joined the Smith household, she had with her Ellen, her daughter born in Hinds County, Mississippi, in 1838, and another daughter, Ann, who was between two and three years of age. Before leaving Mississippi with the Smiths, Biddy would give birth to a third child.

The paternity of Biddy's children has been a source of speculation among several writers. Some have attributed all of her children to Robert Mays Smith; another claims he fathered her two youngest.[8] Clearly, the former assertion is incorrect and the latter, at best, flawed. The identity of the father of Ellen, who was born well before Biddy arrived in the Smith household, is unknown. Biddy's second child, Ann, was born in Mississippi in 1842 or 1843, before Biddy had become a Smith slave, and her paternity is also unknown. Only Biddy's third child, Harriet, born in 1847, could possibly have been sired by Robert Mays Smith. Again, however, there is no proof extant concerning this claim.

The Smiths may have still been adjusting to Biddy and her children's incorporation into their lives when another event further unsettled them all. On May 30, 1846, Rebecca's father, John Dorn, died in South Carolina. One can only imagine the turbulent sea of emotions in the Smith family at the time: Rebecca's worries and grief, Robert's barely concealed elation over the prospects of her inheritance, and the perhaps heated discussion that ensued when Rebecca made it clear she intended to add another member to the household—her childhood slave, Hannah.

By 1846, Hannah, twenty-five years old, was by some indications a favored slave on the Dorn plantation. She attended church with the Dorn family, as did several of the slaves of other families. As an adult she would be described as "almost white,"[9] and it might be speculated that she or her mother (or both) was a blood relative of one of the Dorns. If Hannah did live briefly with the Smiths before they moved to Mississippi as the 1830 census suggests, one wonders whether it was John Dorn who forbade his daughter from taking Hannah with her and why.

It may have been that Hannah herself did not want to accompany Rebecca and Robert. On the Dorn plantation, there were thirty to forty slaves, and Hannah was probably related to many of them. Some of her children would bear the names of several of the adult Dorn slaves: Mary, Jane, Nelson, and Martha. When Hannah was sixteen years old, she married or formed a significant union with a slave named Frank. Slave marriages in Edgefield District ranged from ceremonies performed by white ministers or slave preachers, followed by a "nice supper," to the traditional stepping over the broom together. Orville Vernon Burton, in his chapter "Slave Marriages" in his book *In My Father's House Are Many Mansions,* his comprehensive study of black and white families in Edgefield, South Carolina, said: "The marriage ceremony may have varied, but it was always a meaningful event shared with others in the community."[10]

In 1838, Hannah and Frank had their first child, a daughter, Ann. Their next two children, born in 1843 and 1845, were boys, Lawrence and Nelson, sometimes called Nathaniel. On September 9, 1843, when she was pregnant with Lawrence, Hannah was baptized into Little Steven's Creek Baptist Church. The church record refers to her as "John Dorn Senr' Hannah."[11]

This was Hannah's life: living in the quarters on Sleepy Creek amid family and friends, raising her children, and attending Little Steven's Creek Baptist Church. In a matter of months, every trace of that familiar setting would be erased.

On June 10, 1846, the *Edgefield Advertiser* carried a notice: "Died, at his residence near Sleepy Creek, on May 30, 1846, John Dorn, Sr., in the 79th year of his age after a painful and protracted illness. He had been an orderly and pious member of the Baptist Church for about 25 years. He was always cheerful; and amid the most trying scenes and misfortunes in life, seemed to possess the most perfect equanimity."[12]

The demise of their master, John Dorn Sr., would have cast a pall over the people in the slave quarters. Some might have grieved the man who had been their owner for so many years, but all faced uncertainty about their futures. Their worries were hardly unfounded. Ultimately, not only would the Dorn homestead be auctioned and sold—the house and the land under it, the wagons and the livestock—but so would every man, woman, and child in the slave quarters.

The terms of John Dorn's will were explicit as to the disposition of his slaves: "It is my desire, that immediately after my Death, my Executors cause all my Slaves to be loted [sic] out into Nine parcels as nearly Equal as possible."[13] For inheritance purposes, then, the Dorn slaves were to be valued and grouped to form equal lots, without any obvious regard to marriage and kinship. As John Dorn expected and as was customary in the South, these groupings would be recorded on slips of paper that would then be drawn from a hat, thus awarding a particular heir his or her share of the "human" portion of the estate.

What occurred instead was a dispute between the heirs involving Densley and Benjamin, the mentally incompetent Dorn children.[14] Some of the heirs contended that these brothers certainly could not participate in the division of slaves, and, moreover, provision for their long-term care had to be considered. The agreement, after arbitration, was that everything relating to the estate, including slaves, would be sold at auction to the highest bidder, and all monies received would be divided equally among the heirs, with allowances made for the care of Densley and Benjamin.

The ad for the auction appeared in the *Edgefield Advertiser* on October 7, 1846:

Will be sold, to the highest bidder, by the next, on a credit of twelve months, at the late residence of John Dorn, Senr., Dec'd, all his real and personal estate, consisting of Sixteen hundred and some acres of land, recently surveyed by Andrew H. Coleman, and divided in four tracts.

The first known as the Home Tract, containing 594 acres, with a large and comfortable Dwelling House, with good improvements.

The second is known as Quarter Tract, 530 acres, with a good Dwelling House and improvements.

The third is known as the Fork Tract, 216 acres adjoining said quarter.

The fourth is known as the Culcalzier Tract, 280 acres.

The above named land joins James L. Still, Wilson Kemp, and others.

Also

THIRTY-TWO NEGROES
About
2500 BUSHELS OF CORN

and Fodder, 10 Horses, 2 Good Road Wagons, 200 carts and Oxen, 50 or 60 head of cattle, 70 head of Hogs, Household and Kitchen Furniture. Terms made known on day of sale.

All persons having any demands against the estate, are requested to come forward, duly attested, and all persons indebted
to the estate are requested to come forward and make payment, as
a final settlement will be made as soon as the law directs.

ROBERT DORN

SOLOMON DORN

Executors[15]

The auction took place on October 26, 1846, on the grounds of the
Dorn homestead near the head of Sleepy Creek. Only a sensitive ob-
server might have been aware of the tumultuous emotions undergird-
ing an otherwise commonplace estate sale. However lovely the backdrop of golden autumn light through loblolly and sighing yellow
pines, it could not mitigate the terrible human drama about to be
played out. The buyers moving in and around the house—inspecting
furniture and kitchenware in the rooms of the house and on the porch;
wagons, carts, and equipment in the barns; and animals in corrals and
pens—would have looked no differently upon these goods than upon
the slaves waiting in their quarters or lined up against the house, completely powerless to affect the transactions about to be made.

Among items put up for bid were livestock, including a yoke of
oxen, thirty-nine head of cattle, and thirty-five hogs; farm equipment,
including a wagon, an ox cart, and a set of blacksmith tools; furniture,
including a sideboard, a cupboard, and two pine tables; then household items and crops such as corn, wheat, and shucks.[16] The slaves may
have been sold intermittently, or at a specified time, depending on the
will of the bidders. Because the headline in the ad had been "THIRTY-
TWO NEGROES," the auctioneers may have kept them until last to ensure buyers stayed for the earlier bidding. Thirty-two slaves had been
advertised for sale, but only thirty-one were actually sold. (Old Mary,
who may have been Hannah's grandmother, had been valued at $1.50,
then was listed as "Lost." She had in fact escaped the auction block—
but by dying, not by running away.)[17] Their names, preserved in the
record of sale, read like a haunting litany: Robin, John, Jon, Nournime
and child, Alonz, Harry, Caroline, Jane, Mandy, Bill, Bill Jr., Joe,
Howel, Sarah, Bob, Penny, Martha, George, Grow, Grow Jr., Tom,
Nelson, Frank, Sam, Joicy, Bart, Hannah, child Nelson, Ann, and Lau-
rens (Lawrence).

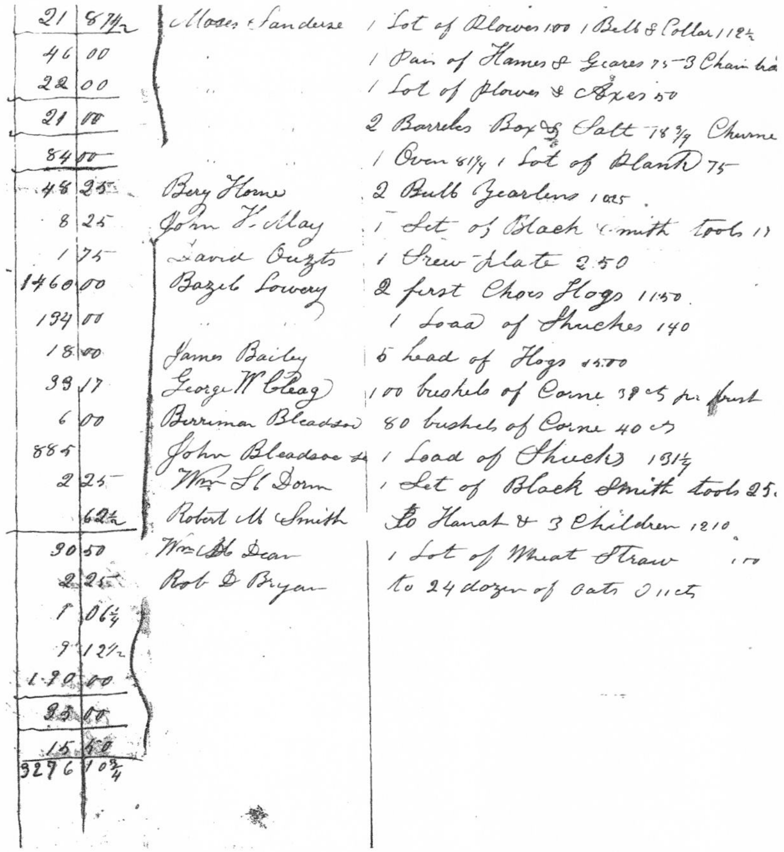

21	87½	Moses Sanderse	1 Lot of Plows 100 1 Bell & Collar 112½
46	00		1 Pair of Hames & Geares 75 3 Chain ha
22	00		1 Lot of plows & Axes 50
21	00		2 Barrels Box & Salt 18¾ Churne
84	00		1 Oven 81¼ 1 Lot of Plank 75
48	25	Bery Horne	2 Bull Yearlins 1025
8	25	John F. May	1 Set of Black Smith tools 11
1	75	David Ouzts	1 Screw plate 2.50
1460	00	Bazel Lowery	2 first Choice Hogs 1150
134	00		1 Load of Shucks 140
18	00	James Bailey	5 head of Hogs 15.00
38	17	George W Cleag	100 bushels of Corne 38 cts per bush
6	00	Berriman Bleadsoe	80 bushels of Corne 40 cts
885		John Bleadsoe	1 Load of Shucks 131¼
2	25	Wm S L Dorn	1 Set of Black Smith tools 25
	62½	Robert M Smith	To Hanah & 3 Children 1210
90	50	Wm H Dean	1 Lot of Wheat Straw 100
2	25	Rob D Bryan	to 24 dozen of Oats @ 11 cts
1	06¼		
9	12½		
1.90	00		
35	00		
15	40		
3276	10¾		

Detail from the ledger showing the accounting of the auction of John Dorn's estate. Note that Robert Mays Smith purchased "Hanah" and her children but not Frank.

The buyer bidding highest for Hannah and her three children was Robert Dorn, Rebecca's brother. He also bought Frank, the father of Hannah's children; Nelson, who may have been her brother; and seven other slaves. The remainder was dispersed among other Dorn children, their relatives, and neighbors.

Within a few hours, the disposition of all the assets of the John Dorn Sr. estate would have been decided, and the relative calm of the auction obliterated by an ensuring chaos: wagons being loaded; other wagons already laden with bedsteads, stacked chairs, and butter churns or bushels of corn and baled fodder lumbering down the road; men riding horses and leading milk cows; and slaves being taken away by their new owners or returned temporarily to their quarters—none of them untouched by excruciating losses to their community of friends and family.

A comparison of names listed on the original nine lots that had been drawn up with the names on the record of sales drives home the magnitude of their tragedy: family members who might, under the plan described in John Dorn's will, have been kept together were instead scattered among many buyers.

At the bottom of a page in the sales book, for example, between the notations concerning William Dorn's purchase of blacksmith tools for $25.25 and William Dean's purchase of $1.00's worth of wheat straw, is the entry: "Robert M. Smith Hanah & 3 Children 1210."[18] Despite the fact that his name appears, Robert Mays Smith was not in Edgefield for the auction. The probate distribution shows that Robert Dorn was "Lawful Attorney" for Robert M. Smith and was signing on his behalf. Hannah and her children would be going to Tishomingo County, Mississippi, where Smith was still living as a tenant farmer. But Frank—who had been listed with Hannah on the original lot slips, ostensibly acknowledging their relationship—would not be accompanying her or their children. In the account of sales, Frank was shown as the property of Robert Dorn; he was bound for Robert Dorn's cotton plantation in Tallahatchie County, Mississippi.[19]

In John Dorn's will, Robert M. Smith had been appointed guardian of Rebecca's "deranged" brother Densley Dorn and, in compensation for his care, was to have Densley's share of John Dorn's estate. When the will was later arbitrated, the amounts given to the heirs were adjusted, but the final award of arbitration still shows: "Robt. M. Smith Guard. of Densley Dorn $3,171.26 the Amt of his Legacy the 26th October, 1847."[20] However—probably because of the Smiths' plan to move west—Densley wound up on Robert Dorn's plantation in Mississippi, and presumably the money for his care went to Robert Dorn.

Hannah and her children were, in fact, the only purchases that Robert Smith made the day of the auction for a cost of $1,210—more than a third of Rebecca's $3,171.26 total inheritance. Considering that the Smiths already owned Biddy and her daughters, the purchase of Hannah and her children was extravagant and unnecessary. Money that could have gone toward land or stock or even a male slave to help with working their farm was spent instead on what amounted to a liability: more mouths to feed. The logical conclusion concerning this transaction, then, is that Rebecca desperately wanted Hannah, and was willing to pay any price to get her, including the additional cost for Hannah's children.

It is impossible to know what Rebecca felt about separating Hannah and Frank. Perhaps, having been able to exercise any control over the decisions made by her brother and her husband, she counted herself lucky and went to bed as relieved and grateful as the realities of her situation would permit: at least Hannah was back in her life. For Hannah, however, sleep that night in October might well have been impossible.

After sixteen years of separation, Hannah and Rebecca were reunited in Mississippi sometime in the fall of 1846 or '47. Hannah and the other slaves that Robert Dorn had purchased either left Edgefield within weeks of the auction or may have remained in South Carolina as long as another year, until October 26, 1847, when the probate of John Dorn's will was finalized.

It is unlikely, considering the financial situation of the Smiths and her obligation to her own family, that Rebecca managed a visit home. Rebecca was likely, therefore, meeting Hannah's three children for the first time: Ann, nine; Lawrence, three; and the baby, Nelson. To her mistress, Hannah may have represented much that had been lost: her childhood on Sleepy Creek, a time when she had been cared for and safe. Much had changed since then. Rebecca, now thirty-six years old, had lived almost half of her life as a poor farmer's wife. Hannah, who was ten years old when she last saw Rebecca, was now a grown woman and the wife of a man from whom she had just been separated. The question undoubtedly hanging between both women was why Rebecca had bought Hannah and her children, but not Frank. If they spoke of it, what explanations might Rebecca have offered? If she had spent more of her inheritance to buy Frank, the family would not be able to go west; she had had to choose between buying Hannah's children or her husband—and Rebecca's brother Robert Dorn needed him so much more. It is just as likely, however, with so many years and uncertainty between them, that Hannah masked her feelings and returned Rebecca's welcoming embrace.

In Mississippi, Hannah learned she was again pregnant. The key to the child's paternity may be whether Hannah left Edgefield in the fall of 1846 or 1847. The baby would be born in early April 1848, meaning conception had occurred in August or September 1847. If Hannah had come to Mississippi in the fall of 1846, then she became pregnant while living with the Smith family; if it was a year later, then the child was conceived while she was still in South Carolina, or at the Robert Dorn plantation in Tallahatchie County en route to Tishomingo County. Mary Boykin Chesnut's Civil War diary comments wryly upon the relationship of slave masters and the women they held in bondage and the inevitable offspring: "Like the patriarchs of old, our men live all in one house with their wives and their concubines; and the mulattos one sees in every family partly resemble the white children. Any lady is ready to tell you who is the father of all the mulatto children in everybody's household but her own. These, she seems to think, drop from the clouds."[21] If Hannah was pregnant when she came, Rebecca would have assumed the child had been conceived by the slave who was Hannah's husband. If she became pregnant after living with the Smiths, who were isolated from either black or white men who could have fathered the child, then Rebecca may have speculated with good reason that her husband was responsible. What may have been most painful for Hannah in those months in Tishomingo County was the uncertainty about whose child she was carrying.

On her arrival in Mississippi, Hannah and her children would have met Biddy and her children for the first time. Both had daughters who were nine years old, as well as younger children who were comparable in age. The six Smith children, most of whom were boys, ranged in age from thirteen years to newborn. Four adults and twelve children were now under one roof: the house on the farm in Tishomingo County would have been crowded, to say the least.

In spite of the hectic and congested household, it is not hard to imagine a friendship developing between Hannah and Biddy over time, and the two of them exchanging the kind of confidences that women will. Both would have been aware, however, of the difference in their relationships to the Smiths, especially to Rebecca. However congruent her situation was to Biddy's in other respects, Hannah had known her mistress as a girl; they had lived on the same land and knew the same people. Hannah and Biddy were both slaves, but, to Rebecca, Hannah was a companion, a friend, and, if not strictly family, certainly part of her family.

During these years of tremendous upheaval in the Smith family—beginning with the death of Rebecca's father and culminating in the arrival of Hannah—the fledgling LDS Church to which they belonged had similarly lurched from crisis to disaster toward seeming disarray.

Mormon prophet Joseph Smith and a number of his followers had arrived in Kirtland, Ohio, in 1831, establishing their new church there. Mormon colonies were also settled near Independence, in Jackson County, Missouri, and on the Big Blue River. On November 4, 1833, both sites had been attacked by mobs, and the entire Mormon population had been expelled from Jackson County. In time, Smith and the Mormons were also driven out of Ohio, and, though seeking refuge in Far West, a Mormon center in Clay County, Missouri, they found more strife and condemnation. On October 30, 1838, a mob murdered a number of Mormons at Haun's Mill. Joseph Smith and other Mormon leaders surrendered to law authorities in Missouri, were put in jail, but managed to escape to Illinois. For a short time, the Mormons seemed to have found a sanctuary in Nauvoo, Illinois. The Illinois legislature granted the city a charter favorable to Mormons, and plans to erect a massive temple were initiated.

But all-too-familiar antagonisms against the church soon reasserted themselves. The Mormons were anti-American, voting as a bloc in elections, and might be anti-Christian as well, engaging in strange beliefs and practices and declaring another text, along with the Bible, as holy writ.

The next four years were filled with a series of misfortunes and disasters: Joseph Smith was briefly kidnapped, his bodyguard was charged with killing a former governor, and Joseph's counselor was excommunicated on a morals charge. On May 17, 1844, Joseph Smith, "as a way of publicizing the Mormon plight," announced that he was a candidate for president of the United States. His opponents were infuriated. Diatribes against the church's growing economic and political power and the revelations about its secret polygamist practices became increasingly common. On June 7, 1844, a newspaper, the *Nauvoo Expositor,* published its first and only edition, containing "inflammatory allegations about Mormon plural marriage practices and policies."[22] On Joseph's order, the paper and press were destroyed. Smith and other leaders were charged with inciting a riot, and Governor Ford of Illinois ruled that the Mormons must submit to the local law. Smith and several of his apostles were arrested and held in jail in Carthage, Illinois. On the evening of June 27, 1844, a mob with blackened faces broke into the jail; killed Joseph Smith and his brother Hyrum; and wounded apostle John Taylor.

News of the assassination took several days to reach Mississippi. John Brown, making his missionary rounds, wrote on July 1, 1844: "I had heard of the martyrdom of the Prophet and Patriarch but could not believe it." He was in Noxubee County, Mississippi, when he heard. He says that when he became satisfied that it was true, "I had no desire to preach to the world. I filled the appointments I had, quit the field and returned home."[23] Home was Monroe County, and probably John Brown's arrival first brought the grievous news to the main group of Mississippi Mormons.

Back in Nauvoo, the Mormon congregation was in shock and the church in crisis. Within days of the prophet's death, Brigham Young, as president of the Quorum of the Twelve Apostles, assumed leadership of the Mormon Church. In January 1845, the Illinois legislature revoked the charter for Nauvoo. Still, the Mormons stayed. "For more than a year and a half after Joseph's death, his people hung on, preparing for their inevitable eviction from the city." What kept the Mormons in Nauvoo were "two crash programs—the temple and the preparation for migration."[24] Young and the twelve apostles knew they would have to leave Illinois, and while the temple was being completed they considered places they might go. First, the choice was narrowed to "Oregon and California country"; then, after reading reports of the areas and talking with travelers who had been there, they considered "two contiguous unsettled areas, both of which they might occupy: the valley of the Great Salt Lake . . . and Utah Valley, the Valley north of Utah Lake and southeast of Salt Lake Valley. . . . By mid-1845 Brigham and the Twelve had definitely settled on the Salt Lake Valley as the most suitable site for a settlement." By fall of that year, Young

Brigham Young, 1855 or 1856. Courtesy of the Historical Department–Archives Division, Church of Jesus Christ of Latter-day Saints.

announced the Mormons would leave Illinois "as soon as grass grows and water runs." At the same time, "the president also sent John Brown to Mississippi to organize a migration of southern Mormons to the Salt Lake Valley in the spring of 1846."[25]

John Brown had been recalled to Nauvoo in 1845. "In the snow and storms of January 1846, John left for Mississippi; he directed the hasty preparations and led forty-three persons in nineteen wagons out on 8 April 1846. He planned to return in the fall of 1846 for the rest."[26] This advance party, instead of pushing on to Salt Lake Valley, was forced to detour and spend the winter in Pueblo, Colorado. John

Brown led a small party back to Mississippi for the rest of the Mormon families, arriving in Winter Quarters in October, then continuing on to Mississippi in January 1847. His intention was to prepare the remainder of the Mississippi Mormons for departure that spring, but Brigham Young sent instructions for him to return to Winter Quarters with a few able-bodied men and leave the main body of Mormons in Mississippi for another year. Brown obeyed; he and the men with him joined the wagon train leaving Winter Quarters on April 17, 1847, and arrived in Salt Lake Valley on July 21, 1847.

The main group of Mississippi Mormons had spent the years 1846 and 1847 preparing for the momentous move. But, characteristic of what may have been his need to go his own way, Robert did not begin preparing for a trip to the valley of the Great Salt Lake. He had decided to use the balance of Rebecca's inheritance to finance their move to Texas. Although a Mormon colony had been established in that state by one Lyman Wight, Robert's son William would later write of a less particular motivation for his father's decision: "People there [in Mississippi] had the Texas fever bad. My father was one of them and he commenced making preparations to move to Texas. The war came on between the United States and Mexico and checked the movements of those who were preparing to move to Texas. However, as soon as they were convinced that the United States troops were victorious, they renewed their preparations to move to Texas." William said his father started for Texas in the spring of 1847 and intended crossing the Mississippi River at Memphis, Tennessee. When they arrived at Memphis, however, "the river was impassable as the levee had gave way and the river bottoms were overflowed."[27]

Contemplating the flooded Mississippi River, Robert probably thought fate had dealt him another blow. First, there had been his failure to prosper in the piney woods; then came the delay in reaching his promised land, Texas. Disillusioned, Robert turned his wagons around and went to Tishomingo County. There he rented a farm and planted a crop to feed his family and slaves until, as William reported, he could start again for Texas the following spring. During the winter months that followed, Robert and Rebecca had another child, a boy, whom they named Joseph. Their chosen namesake, the martyred Mormon prophet, indicates that they still considered themselves among the faithful of the LDS Church.

During the layover in Tishomingo, visitors came to the Smiths' farm "to buy corn for their animals and other supplies." In one account, William identified these visitors as "volunteers of the United States returning from California," but, in another, as members of the Frémont expedition. According to William, these guests spent the night with the Smiths, and it was they who reported the discovery of gold in California. William wrote: "When father talked to these men and learned that they were on their way home to get their families and take them to California, he made up his mind to accompany them to the Golden State, and all agreed to meet at Council Bluffs, on the Missouri River, the following March."[28]

What attracted Robert to California may well have been the travelers' tales, but not necessarily reports of gold. Images of abundant land and endless sunshine may have been enough to lure him. For several generations, the concept of the West had been a moving mirage, enticing the disgruntled and the dreamers to abandon the known for fantasy. Initially, the West was the Indian lands just west of the original colonies, then it became a band of territories and states clustered along the Mississippi River, and finally the West was the name given to the plains and mountains of what we now call the Midwest. Eventually, the West came to be the unsettled land along the immeasurable Pacific Ocean. For many Americans, perhaps because the limits of frontier had been reached, California became the ultimate vision of the West. For Robert Mays Smith, California may have been, as it would be for Okies and Arkies during the Great Depression, an almost mythical Pacific paradise. In any case, the visitors' stories of gold or available land were sufficiently compelling to make Robert immediately revise his plans for the family's next move.

On March 17, 1848, the Smiths left the farm in Mississippi, and they and their wagons started rolling for California via Salt Lake Valley. For Robert, the commencement of a journey so long delayed was undoubtedly welcomed; for Rebecca, Biddy, and Hannah, more likely the trip seemed the resumption of one long bad dream characterized by upheaval, misery, and worry.

With each mile, Hannah left Frank farther and forever behind. Her baby was born the first week in April 1848, when the Smith wagons passed between Illinois and Missouri. According to a later description, the little girl could not "easily be distinguished from the white race."[29] Hannah named her baby Jane.

In his diary, John Brown, who had returned from Salt Lake Valley to guide the Mississippi Mormons, reported on their departure from Monroe County in 1848: "All things being ready, we started on the 10th of March in wet muddy weather. We had eleven wagons in the company, there being some six families with a number of black people." Their passage caused a commotion. "Our company of 11 wagons attracted the attention of people as much as a menagerie of wild animals would. Every man, woman, and child, both white and black, turned out to see us as we passed."[30]

Robert's son said his family started from Tishomingo County, and this fact is confirmed by John Brown's report giving the date each family arrived in Winter Quarters, the gathering place of the Mormons in what is now Omaha, Nebraska. Brown said the three wagons of Robert M. Smith and family arrived on May 17, at the same time as John Lockhart's. Considering their simultaneous arrival at Winter Quarters, it is probable that Smith's three wagons traveled with the single wagon of John Lockhart. The rest of the Mississippi company's twenty-two wagons came into camp on May 23.

In his enumeration of the Mississippi company, on May 27, 1848, John Brown said Robert M. Smith's party consisted of nine white and ten colored persons. (Robert is shown as having three wagons, one horse, two oxen, eight mules, and seven "milch cows.")[31] The former would have been Robert, Rebecca, their six children, and John Cook, a young man from Mississippi, not a Mormon, who drove one of Robert's three wagons. The latter included Biddy with her three daughters and Hannah with her four children, including a baby born en route to Winter Quarters. The one person of color unaccounted for was perhaps a twin of the newborn baby who later died, or a male slave borrowed from one of the Mississippi Mormons to drive the third wagon.

The Smith party, though, traveling apart from the main Mississippi company, probably took the same route to Winter Quarters. John Brown's diary describes crossing Tennessee, Kentucky, and winding up at Metropolis on the Ohio River. There the Mormons hired a steamboat to take them up the Mississippi. "The boat was small and we filled it with eleven wagons, thirty white persons, twenty-four colored persons, one yoke of oxen, and twenty-four mules."[32] Brown and party traveled up the Mississippi, disembarked near St. Louis, then crossed Missouri on land, following roughly the route of the Missouri River. They arrived near Council Bluffs and waited to cross the Missouri River to Winter Quarters.

The difficulties encountered, as Brown enumerates them, were many: bad weather, muddy roads, sloughs too deep for wagons to ford, mules and horses completely mired in mud, flooded creeks, and ice. In describing the trip, John Brown four times uses this phrase, "It was one of the most disagreeable times I ever saw."[33] Yet his summation is positive:

This Mississippi Company has now performed a journey of 917 miles by land, excepting about 200 miles which a part of the company traveled by water. There have been no deaths on the way. There was one birth. We had very little sickness. There was no loss of property of any consequence excepting one ox belonging to Brother McKowan, which got his neck broke. . . . The company are all well, excepting one case of the chills and fever, and all appear to be in fine spirits.[34]

While waiting to cross to Winter Quarters, John Brown reports a visit by the Mormon elders. "We were camped with Brothers Lockhart and Smith of Mississippi. The Powell brothers . . . were camped nearby, so the Mississippi Company was quite an admiration."[35]

On June 2, 1848, while his family remained in the camp near Winter Quarters, Robert Mays Smith rode away on an errand. John Brown's diary describes the events of that night:

This evening at 10 o'clock there happened one of the most distressing accidents I ever witnessed. I had laid down to rest, and scarcely fallen asleep when I was roused by the sudden report of a gun, followed by low, death-like groans. I sprang up and ran to the spot where the gun was fired and here I beheld a young man by the name of John Cook lying partly on the ground and partly on Brother Crosby's lap. He was bleeding. He had just breathed his last. He had a belt pistol loose in his bosom loaded with shot and cap. A horse that was tied to a feed box fast to a wagon pulled the feed box down and Mr. Cook looked after the horse. He stooped down to untie the rope when the pistol slipped out of his bosom and the butt struck on the ground with the muzzle pointing upwards. It fired, and he, being in a stooping position, received the whole load in his neck. He raised up and ran some ten paces to the fire. When in the act of falling, some of the brethren caught him. He exclaimed, "Oh, Lord!" once or twice. Besides this he said nothing more than to groan. He was dead in less than three minutes. His groans appeared to be the effects of surprise rather than pain. He died easily. The whole camp was roused up with the shock, and all appeared to mourn the loss of Mr. Cook. He had no relatives in camp. He had come from Mississippi with Brother Robert M. Smith. He had driven a team and was calculating to go to the valley with Brother Smith. . . . Brother Smith was in Missouri at the time.[36]

Robert had gone to find the men returning to California, intending to join his wagons to theirs, and was either unsuccessful or perhaps learned they had left without him. He had promised to meet them in March, and it was now the first week in June. Riding back to camp, Robert heard John Cook's death groans or arrived to find a deserted camp with everyone gone for Cook's burial on a bluff overlooking the Missouri River. Robert surely understood his predicament: a family traveling alone had little chance of hooking up with another wagon train, especially with no one to drive the third wagon. California as a destination was no longer viable, and if Robert wanted to take his family west, he would need the help and protection of the Mormons.

⁓

The encampment of the Mormons at Winter Quarters was an immense, chaotic settlement composed of makeshift structures and camps spread out on lands of the Potawatomi Indians. The trek of 1847 had brought the first Mormons into the valley of the Great Salt Lake. "The migration of 1848 had as its nearly exclusive purpose the evacuation of Winter Quarters."[37]

For the trip, the people were divided into units of tens, fifties, and hundreds. The first two companies were to be led by Brigham Young and Heber C. Kimball, with Willard Richards and Amasa Lyman jointly leading the third. John Brown was appointed captain of the fourth ten in this third company. Among the men in Brown's unit was Robert M. Smith.[38]

The 1848 expedition totaled 926 wagons carrying 2,417 people. Brigham Young's company consisted of 397 wagons, 1,229 people, 74 horses, 1,275 oxen, 699 cows, 184 loose cattle, 411 sheep, 141 pigs, 605 chickens, 37 cats, 82 dogs, 3 goats, 10 geese, 2 beehives, 8 doves, and 1 crow. Kimball's company had 226 wagons; 662 people; 1,253 horses, mules, and cattle; plus sheep, pigs, chickens, cats, goats, doves, a squirrel, and beehives. The Richards-Lyman company, including Robert Mays Smith, his family and slaves, had 300 wagons, 526 people, and a similar veritable Noah's Ark of animals.[39]

On Friday, July 7, 1848, Brown's unit set out from the Elkhorn River. The journey to the Utah settlement would cover 1,031 miles and last 130 days. From the Elkhorn, the Mormon Trail followed the broad Platte River through Pawnee land, passed Grand Island, and took the northern branch of the Platte River past well-known landmarks—Ash Hollow, Ancient Ruins Bluff, Chimney Rock, and Scott's Bluff—to Fort Laramie. There the trail crossed the Platte, continued on the southern side past Laramie Peak, and, at what is now Casper, Wyoming, recrossed the Platte, using the Mormon ferry built by the earlier company of pioneers. After passing Independence Rock and Devil's Gate, the trail left the Platte, following Sweet River to the valley of South Pass, the gateway to the Rocky Mountains.

The most common hardship was the unremitting difficulty of travel. Mormon diaries have countless entries about muddy roads, flooded rivers, and hills that were almost impassable. Other obstacles included weather that ranged from scalding sun to bitter cold, the daily quest for campgrounds and water and grass for the animals, and the wear and tear on wagons. Common accidents were falling from a wagon or being run over by one. Deaths occurred from illness or premature birth. The losses were made worse because there was no time to grieve. Loved ones were left in hastily dug graves by the side of the trail, and the wagons rolled on.

But some aspects of the journey were thrilling. The travelers saw prairie dogs, antelope, thundering herds of buffalo like "black clouds on the prairie," and Sioux Indians, most of whom were friendly. The days were hard, but in the evenings there were songfests, comical readings, and occasional dances. Tempers sometimes erupted, hence the watchman's cry: "Eleven o'clock and all's well and Gates is quarreling with his wife like hell." Brigham Young, although he bossed, lectured, and scolded his flock, generally applauded their behavior: "Never has there been a people of the same number since the days of Enoch that has journeyed under the same circumstances with less murmuring than this people has."[40]

The last part of the journey was arduous. Although the distance from Fort Bridger, a trading post in the Rocky Mountains, to Zion, as the Mormons called the valley of the Great Salt Lake, was only a hundred miles, the pioneers had to contend with rugged terrain, mountain fever, and, on the morning of September 14, 1848, snow. Their oxen were failing at an alarming rate. Wandering meanders meant that creeks had to be crossed many times. There were more mountains to ascend and less grass for the cattle. Finally, atop Big Mountain, pioneers caught their first glimpse of the basin of the Great Salt Lake. Although "many hills and bad roads intervened," they were homeward bound.[41] On September 20, Brigham Young and the Council of Twelve led the first company in. Kimball's company came on September 23. The Richards-Lyman company brought up the rear, but all units were safely in by October 19.

Hosea Stout, reflecting on the trip, spoke for the pioneers' relief and exhaustion: "Thus ends this long & tedious journey from the land of our enemies & I feel free and happy that I have escaped their midst. But there is many a desolate & sandy plain to cross. Many a rugged sage brush to break through. Many a hill and hollow to tug over & Many a Mountain & Cañon to pass, and many frosty nights to endure in mid summer."[42]

Robert and Rebecca's stay in Utah lasted two and a half years, from October 19, 1848, to March 24, 1851. When the 1848 emigrants arrived in Salt Lake, they found the settlement rudimentary and the conditions harsh. Pioneers from the previous expedition had set up a community within the boundaries of a fort, but the bleak terrain and cruel winter weather in this high desert surprised and disappointed many of the new arrivals. The southerners settled in Cottonwood, southeast of the main community.[43] Some of the families from Mississippi had sent slaves ahead with the pioneers of 1847 with instructions to build shelter and plant crops. These fortunate families had cabins and food waiting when they arrived. Everyone else scurried to cut logs from trees in the nearby canyons. Many of the families spent the first winter in their wagons. Robert Mays Smith had no male slaves to send ahead, so he was one of those racing against the weather to build shelter for his family. Perhaps the Smith family and their slaves spent the entire winter in the same three wagons, or, if Robert managed to jerry-build some kind of dwelling, the eighteen people lived there together, in one or two rooms, for the long winter months.

Elder Orson Hyde explained the attitude of the church toward the resident slaves in the *Millennial Star* of February 15, 1851:

> We feel it to be our duty to define our position in relation to the subject of slavery. There are several men in the Valley of the Salt Lake from the Southern States who have their slaves with them. There is no law in Utah to authorize slavery, neither any to prohibit it. If the slave is disposed to leave his master, no power exists there, either legal or moral, that will prevent him. But if the slave chooses to remain with his master, none are allowed to interfere between the master and the slave. All the slaves that are there appear to be perfectly contented and satisfied.[44]

The church's hands-off attitude toward slavery was undoubtedly designed to protect it from passions on both sides of the issue. In Missouri and Illinois, church authorities had learned the horrific consequences of involvement in local and national politics. Elder Hyde was explicit about the church's stance in this new land: "The Church, on this point, assumes not the responsibility to direct. The laws of the land recognize slavery, we do not wish to oppose the laws of the country. If there is sin in selling a slave, let the individual who sells him bear that sin, and not the Church. . . . It is for you to sell them, or to let them go free, *as your own conscience may direct you.*"[45]

BIDDY AND HANNAH and their children became part of the community of people of color living in the valley of the Great Salt Lake. Several of them were free people who had converted to Mormonism, made their way to Nauvoo or Winter Quarters, then joined the wagon trains going west. Notable among them were Jane Manning James and her brother, Isaac Manning, who were personal servants of Joseph Smith and, later, Brigham Young.[46] Most of the people of color, however, were slaves, and many belonged to the families of the Mississippi Mormons. Several slaves accompanied the advance party from Mississippi that wintered in Pueblo, Colorado, in 1846 and entered Salt Lake Valley on July 2, 1847. Green Flake, a slave, was in the first wagon through Emigration Canyon.[47] Whether the slaves residing in Salt Lake Valley, either in the fort or at Cottonwood, were as "perfectly contented and satisfied" as Elder Hyde claimed is doubtful, considering complaints against their slaves registered by several owners, but what is certain is the slaves found support and companionship in each other.

After some seven months on the trail, grappling with the needs of a newborn, Hannah may have been the most relieved of any in the Smith party to arrive in Salt Lake Valley in spite of the living conditions. And perhaps these circumstances were soon mitigated in her mind, for it was in this little enclave of homesick settlers that Hannah met the next man she could love.

Toby Embers and his brother, Grief, were originally slaves of an Embers family in Knox County, Indiana, where John and Elizabeth Crosby, patriarch and matriarch of the Crosby clan, lived in the early 1800s.[48] The Crosbys bought the two brothers along with other slaves and within a few years moved to Monroe County, Mississippi, where they were baptized into the Mormon Church. When a Crosby daughter, Ann, married Daniel Thomas, Toby Embers was given to Ann by her parents as a wedding present, and Toby became the property of her husband. Toby's birth date, between the years 1797 and 1802, meant in 1848 he was at least in his late forties, already an old man in those times and by the standards of those who sold slaves. He either was unmarried or had been separated from his family when sold by his former owner to Daniel Thomas, who had left Mississippi on April 8, 1846, with the first migration of Mormons to Salt Lake Valley.

Hannah was twenty-six years old and the mother of four children. We cannot know what attracted the young mother to the older man; perhaps it was Toby's knowledge of this new land, the kindness he may have extended, or his understanding of the forced separation from her husband that she had endured. Whatever the nature of their bond, the proof of it came in late 1849 when Hannah gave birth to a son, Charles Embers.

Spring came late and reluctantly. The summer of 1849 brought hordes of gold seekers en route to California. In his diary, Parley P. Pratt, Mormon pioneer and apostle, reported on the impact of the '49ers: "Emigrants now came pouring in from the States on their way to California to seek gold. Money and gold dust was plenty; and merchandise of almost every description came pouring into our city in great plenty." Some Mormons broke rank and joined those hurrying to the California gold fields. Brigham Young railed against these defectors: "We are gathered here, not to scatter around and go off to the mines, or any other place, but to build up the Kingdom of God." He thundered at those who insisted on going: "If you Elders of Israel want to go to the gold mines, go and be damned."[49] Robert Mays Smith was not among those who left. Perhaps he did not want to be counted among those who wintered with the Mormons, then deserted them as soon as the weather warmed. More probably, Robert stayed in Salt Lake Valley because his wife, Rebecca, who was thirty-nine years old, was pregnant and could not endure another long wagon trip. Robert Mark Smith, the last child Robert and Rebecca would have, was born on November 14, 1849. Nine days later, on November 23, 1849, Robert Mays Smith, along with a number of other Mississippi Mormons, was asked to volunteer for an expedition to explore the country to the far south of what would become Utah Territory.

Parley Pratt, who was on this expedition, later said, "We encountered severe weather, deep snows and many hardships and toils." The journey going and coming was eight hundred miles. "In much of this distance we made the first track; and even the portion which had been penetrated by wagons was so completely snowed under that we seldom found the trail." One morning, the camp was completely buried in snow. Pratt roared like a trumpet and commanded the men to arise, and "all at once there was a shaking among the snow piles, the graves were opened, and all came forth! We called this Resurrection Camp."[50] The explorers ate frozen black biscuits. Many had frostbitten limbs. Several were seriously ill. Yet, the men and their exhausted animals pushed on.

Robert M. Smith is mentioned twice in accounts of the expedition.[51]

He was among the men chosen to go by horseback to explore the Virgin River, and he was part of the group, mostly men with families, sent home by horseback in late January 1850, rather than staying behind with the wagons to wait for spring.

The survival of the women and children left behind in the winter months while their men explored the country to the south was mainly due to the remarkable stamina and fortitude of these pioneer women. Already they had endured the hardships and deprivations of the trek to Salt Lake. Their diaries testify to their full participation in the camp chores, and many drove wagons and herded animals as well—all the while bearing and burying babies and tending to the children they already had! Wallace Stegner praises the "frequent devotion and heroism" demonstrated by the Mormons: "Especially their women. Their women were incredible."[52]

In her diary, Eliza Marie Patridge Lyman, plural wife of Amasa Lyman, notes both the hardships she suffered in her husband's absence and the help given by church authorities and other women. On April 8, 1849, she wrote: "Baking the last of our flour today and have no prospect of getting any more til after harvest." On the twenty-first, she wrote: "Sister Emily brought us 15 lbs. of flour. Said Pres. Young heard we were out of bread and told her to bring that much although they have a scanty allowance for themselves." Three days later, she added: "Jane James, a colored woman, let me have about 2 lbs. of flour—it being about half she had."[53]

Presumably, during Robert's absence, Rebecca, Biddy, and Hannah demonstrated the strength and resilience of the Mormon women and survived with the help of neighbors and emergency provisions sent by the church. Unlike many of the women, Rebecca did not have the support and companionship of her husband's plural spouses. Rebecca's thoughts about Mormon polygamy are not known; there is no evidence that Robert Mays Smith took or even considered taking other wives. At the least, Biddy and Hannah provided Rebecca with help, support, and, most of all, company.

Weeks passed without word from Robert. Christmas and then Robert's birthday came and went, and Rebecca's fortieth birthday was approaching. Widowhood in a hostile land far from family and home was hardly a future she would have chosen. Then, finally, on February 1, 1850, after an absence of six weeks and having survived a return trip of incredible hardship, Robert Mays Smith entered the cabin in Cottonwood and embraced his wife and new son. Robert and Rebecca now had seven children: John Dorn, sixteen; William Densley, fourteen; Elijah Benjamin, twelve; James Sidney, eight; Sarah Flora, five; Joseph, three; and Robert Mark, who was two and a half months old when his father returned.

A census of Utah County, taken in 1850, included Robert and Rebecca and their seven children. On the last page of the census, the slave inhabitants were listed. Robert M. Smith was shown as the owner of Hannah, twenty-eight, yellow female; Biddy, twenty-five, black female; Ellen, eleven, mulatto female; Ann, seven, black female; Harriet, three, mulatto female; Ann, thirteen, yellow female; Lawrence, nine, yellow male; Nelson, seven, yellow male; Jane, three, yellow female; and Charlie, one, yellow male. Noted beside the names of the slaves were the words, "Going to California."[54]

In 1850, Mormon leaders began exploring the establishment of a Mormon colony to serve as an outpost of the church's central headquarters and as a way station for missionaries to other countries. By 1851, plans had been made to send two elders, Charles Rich and Amasa Lyman, to California, along with a sufficient number of settlers for a new community. Brigham Young asked for volunteers to accompany Rich and Lyman to California, expecting approximately 20 persons to respond. When President Young arrived at Peteetneet (now Payson) on May 24, 1851, to address those about to depart, he found 150 wagons, with 437 persons, Robert Mays Smith and his family and slaves among them. Young later wrote: "I was sick at the sight of so many Saints running to California, chiefly after the god of this world, and was unable to address them."[55]

No doubt some of the Mormons queued up to leave Utah Territory were interested in searching for gold, but many, including the majority of the Mississippi Mormons, most likely just wanted to live in a land less forbidding with a climate more similar to the one they had left behind. In 1850, when the announcement came concerning the establishment of a Mormon colony in California, Hannah and Toby must have feared the worst. Should either one of their masters decide to leave Salt Lake Valley, their child would lose his father and each of them another mate. However, in the spring of 1851, both Robert Mays Smith and Daniel Thomas were among those planning to move to California. Hannah and Toby would be together after all, in a land that was sunny, warm, and—most important—free.

—

On June 9, 1851, Robert and his party arrived in California, part of a wagon train rolling into a grove of sycamore trees near Cajun Pass. The crossing had been difficult, especially the final stretch through the Mojave Desert, with wagons mired in dust, oxen collapsing, and people of all ages walking without water, day and night.[56] The emigrants stayed in Sycamore Grove all summer while Rich and Lyman rode throughout southern California, seeking land to buy on which they would establish the colony. During their time at Cajun Pass, on July 5, 1851, the Mormons selected their first High Council, a trio of men who oversaw financial and judicial matters for the new colony. William Crosby was to be bishop of the new branch, with Robert Mays Smith as one of his two counselors.[57]

When Rich and Lyman returned from scouting for property, they brought mixed tidings. They had indeed succeeded in purchasing the Rancho del San Bernardino from three brothers, named Lugo, whose father had received the ranch as a Mexican land grant. The cost, however, was prohibitive—ultimately, $77,500—with payments due every six months at the ruinous interest rate of 30 percent per annum. Nevertheless, the Mormon leaders made a down payment of $7,000 and received permission to move onto the land.[58]

On November 23, news came that Indians had killed all whites on Warner's Ranch, sixty miles south of San Bernardino. The emigrants promptly changed their plans; instead of building individual residences, they began constructing a fort to enclose eight acres and their dwellings and wagons. Outside the fort, they posted a watch for Indians and, as Mormons were known for doing wherever they were, began surveying fields, plowing, and putting in crops.

Robert Mays Smith had not come to California to live within other men's walls. Even though he was a member of the High Council, he chose not to move his family within the fort and started scouting the surrounding country.[59] On rolling hills, known as Jumuba, along the Santa Ana River, he found the cattle ranch he had sought his entire life. The land was outside the acreage claimed by the Mormons and apparently open for homestead. The cattle that Robert had brought from Utah were soon replenished by fresh head from Los Angeles. The ruins of a Spanish homestead became the walls of the Smiths' new home. Within a few years, Robert had a thriving ranch with abundant grass for a growing herd and a comfortable house for his family and the women and children who had come to California with them. After twenty-one years of hardship, deprivation, and disappointment, it seemed Smith had finally realized the dream he had followed across a continent.

Meanwhile, the Mormon colony also prospered. After the Indian threat subsided, the settlers laid out their new city and began constructing roads, stores, shops, and church structures, including a great adobe bowery where the faithful worshiped. On September 4, 1852, a harvest feast and dance were held, and "[e]very person upon the place White Black & Red was fed or invited."[60]

But the high spirits soon dissipated. With stability and prosperity, suppressed tensions began to surface. A common complaint was that "the whole community assumed the obligation for paying the debt on the ranch, although ownership rested with the two apostles." Lyman and Rich had formed a private corporation from which plots of land were purchased. The settlers were responsible for paying off Lyman and Rich's mortgage on the ranch at the same time they were obligated to purchase land from Lyman and Rich for their own homes and farms. Lyman and Rich also founded several businesses, including grist- and sawmills, and the people paid for their goods and services. The elders saw their entrepreneurship and assumption of debt as acts of good stewardship. Some settlers, however, felt exploited and began to question and disagree with Mormon doctrine. Lyman and Rich complained: "The clouds of corruption are darkeley lowering around us and the lovers of corruption have but to ask and they can find sympathy and friendship in persons of some who call us br[other]s."[61] A number of settlers, including the Powell brothers and others from the Mississippi Mormons, broke with the church and became violently opposed to it. With each renunciation, the Sunday sermons, usually preached by Charles Rich, became more accusatory and repressive, engendering outright rebellion. Robert Mays Smith, however, because of his distance from the fray and his contentment with his ranch and family, refused to join the dissidents, many of whom had clustered in the hills nearby.

On March 1, 1853, Amasa Lyman and Charles Rich reported

reaching a milestone. "Having made total payments of $25,000 and having issued a note for the remaining $52,000 in two years, they received a deed for the property."[62] The deed for the Lugo brothers' ranch was based on the original land grant to their father, a complicated document written in Spanish with acreage calculated in leagues. When they sold the land to the Mormons, the Lugo brothers filed a petition with the United States Land Commission to clarify its boundaries. The Mormons learned, to their dismay, that the land grant was for eight leagues, or 35,000 acres, half the land they thought they had purchased. The land commission ruled that because the land the Mormons paid for was less than they expected to receive, they could select "any 35,000 acres" from the original spread belonging to Señor Lugo. All property outside the final boundaries was to become public land, subject to squatters' rights. No time limit was specified for the selection, and Rich and Lyman took several years to determine which land was the most productive. At first the land north of the settlement looked fertile, but after a few years of farming, alkaline showed in the soil. The Mormon elders then eyed land south of the settlement, including an area on the Santa Ana River called Jumuba.[63]

Perhaps Robert Mays Smith, whose term as counselor had ended in May 1853, learned about the decision at a church meeting on April 8, 1855, or on June 23, 1855, at a special three-day conference to transact branch business.[64] He was told that Rich and Lyman had set the final boundaries and that the place he had homesteaded would soon be taken. Robert's reaction can be judged by two entries of the colony clerk. On August 17, 1855, Richard Hopkins wrote:

> The spirit of dissension and apostasy is daily becoming more evident. Some men who have occupied responsible stations in the church here are very violent against the authorities[.] Among them is RM Smith one of the High Council who is going to leave and take his family. . . . [T]his spirit is growing more public than it has been and goes to verify the assertion of Bros. Lyman and Rich on our arrival in the Country that if we ever had trouble here, it would be started by those in our midst.[65]

An entry for the following day says: "Aug. 18, 1855, Saturday. The cattle was put in our Ranch . . . but none from the heard [*sic*] of R.M. Smith as he is moving off his stock."[66] In late summer of 1855, Robert Mays Smith separated his cattle from those of other church members and, for the fall months, ran his head on the rolling hills of Jumuba while he sought a way to stay on his beloved homestead or the means to purchase another ranch.

During these months, Robert tried gold mining. The Mormon clerk's journal entry for September 29, 1855, says, "There is some excitement in relation to a gold mine near Mt. San Bernardino. Old Man Weaver reports that we can make seven dollars a day to the hands."[67] Although Robert had originally started for California to find ranch land on which he could raise cattle, he now recalled the tales of gold brought back by Frémont's soldiers and returning miners. In Salt Lake, in the fabled year of 1849, he had watched hordes pass through Mormon Territory in quest of the riches waiting in California's rivers, streams, and hillsides. As long as he had the homestead on Jumuba and his herd of cattle, Robert was able to resist the siren call of gold, but, in the fall of 1855, he had become another desperate, landless man mucking in mud and wading in waist-high water, hoping for a few gold flecks in his pan.

Week after week of panning yielded nothing but sand. One can imagine how bitter Smith must have been knowing Rebecca's brother William Dorn, after years of being mocked for gold hunting, had finally struck a vein of mind-boggling breadth and, at sixty-one years of age, had married a sixteen year old, reputedly the prettiest girl in all of South Carolina.[68] For Smith, though, there would be no found fortune. His only asset—and his only means of making a living—was his cattle. But without land to graze them on or a house for his twenty-two dependents, the herd was worthless.

At this time of despair, Robert's dream of living in Texas, thwarted once by the swollen Mississippi River, returned. Perhaps he reviewed his past road with its many branches, and, in retrospect, cursed himself for having come to Utah and California. If he had waited one more year in Mississippi, the waters would have receded, the Mexican War would have been over, and Texas would have become a new state. He and his family would be settled there now, on a homestead of their own, with acres of free grass for his growing herd and nothing hanging over him but the cloudless sky. Above all, he and his family could have been spared a two thousand–mile trip to California and the heartbreak and hardship they had known ever since. In the throes of his personal turmoil, Smith likely decided that Texas was where his destiny had been all along. All he had to do now was tell his wife.

For a quarter of a century, Rebecca Dorn Smith had followed her husband, first to Mississippi, moving several times within the state; then to Winter Quarters; then across plains and mountains to Utah Territory, staying in a small cabin surrounded by snow as high as her chin; and then across the Mojave Desert to a ranch in California. The church she had joined, reluctantly perhaps, had over the years become a comfort and maybe even a conviction. She had lived among these people for a dozen years, and now Robert was asking her to disavow them, to put this land and these people behind her. She had traveled endless miles, in rough wagons over rutted and muddy roads. She had lived in places that made the modest slave quarters on the Dorn homestead seem like mansions. Rebecca was forty-five years old. She had bouts of bad health. Her children were almost grown. She had thought they had finally reached the end of their travels, but Robert was saying no. One more trip to Texas, to Texas where her brother was. Yes, it would be good to be close to family again. So few were still alive. But another trip? Through the desert again? Robert said they were going home. *Home.* The word conjured all the places she had lived the past twenty-five years, the cabins, wagons, tents, and houses, and all she had done to make each a home: curtains, quilts, swept floors, whitewash on the walls, a sprig of wildflowers in a bottle, and a book or two. All left behind. Gone. Now she was even leaving her church. Would anything be left? Rebecca would have had one of her calculating, self-searching moments. She still had Robert, her children, Biddy, Hannah, and their children too. Perhaps Robert was right. If they could just make it to Texas, they would all finally be home.

An entry in the Mormons' Tithing Ledger says, on November 15, 1855, that Robert M. Smith paid his annual tithe, but this year, instead of bringing cheese, butter, or wheat as he had previously, Robert paid cash.[69] In early November, Robert had sold part of his herd in the cattle markets of Los Angeles and returned to Jumuba with wagons to prepare his family for departure. He was paying off the Mormons, calling it quits, and leaving California and the ranch on the Santa Ana in debt to no one. They were going to camp in the hills near Los Angeles while he laid in provisions and hired trail hands for the long trip ahead.

Once again, Hannah was faced with a forced separation, this time from Toby. The planned departure undoubtedly seemed a looming disaster that threatened to bring to a head the difficulties between them. Although they had crossed the trail from Salt Lake Valley together in the same wagon train, upon arriving in California, Toby Embers had resided in the home of his master in the fort that became San Bernardino, and Hannah on the ranch Robert had homesteaded on the Santa Ana River. Over the years, they would have seen each other infrequently, during trips to town or perhaps on rare days when Toby could ride out to the Smith ranch.

But Toby might have seen their arrangement as temporary, until he could get money together to buy, or find time enough to build, a place of their own. This presumes, of course, that Toby Embers knew he was a free man in California and that he saw the possibility for a different future if he could somehow get money together to begin it. His later acquisition of real estate supports both his awareness of his free status and the importance he attached to stashing away money so he could avail himself of opportunities when they came.

The issue of Hannah's children and her fidelity to him, however, may have become an irreconcilable difference between them. On the trip to California, Hannah had again been pregnant. A son, Marion, was born in 1851. A year later, Hannah had had a little girl named Martha. Toby claimed Charlie and Martha, but not Marion.[70]

In the fall of 1855, when Robert Mays Smith made his decision to leave California for Texas, Hannah was pregnant yet again and faced the prospect of carrying yet another child on a long journey, this time while in her eighth or ninth month. Toby may have tried to convince her to stay, arguing that she was free now and that it was only a matter of time before the two of them could be a couple in a home of their own. Apparently, however, Hannah's choice was to remain with the Smiths, and as the day of their departure approached, Toby took the only action he could think of, perhaps hoping to compel Hannah to remain: he apparently took their first child, Charlie, to San Bernardino and refused to return him.

Hannah, heavy with her pregnancy and most likely torn by conflicting allegiances and longings, climbed into a wagon once more and prepared to leave a home, Jumuba, and the relationships she had forged there. Neither Hannah nor Toby could have anticipated the firestorm that would soon engulf her.

—

On Christmas Day 1855, while camped in a canyon in the hills of Santa Monica, Robert Mays Smith had his fifty-first birthday. The family's campfire would have been kept well stoked to fend against the weather: as the LDS Church clerk in San Bernardino noted in his journal, "Dec. 25, 1855 Last night was the coldest we have ever experienced in this country. . . . [T]he mercury sank as low as 33 degrees above zero."[71]

A birthday cake? An exchange of gifts? Or perhaps Robert's somber mood precluded any celebrating that night. Perhaps the family simply tiptoed around the blue-eyed man staring into the wind-whipped flames, looking once again for a future.

TWO

White Woman Running

FROM THE AIR, the coast of southern California was a pale scallop cupping the Pacific, looking too fragile to be the edge of a continent, too insubstantial to service the collective adolescent fantasies of a nation.[1] The hills, blanketed with chaparral, gave way to the dense grid of suburbs and the glint of distant skyscrapers—then a red-brown haze obscured everything. I leaned my head against the window and thought of the incongruous circumstances in which I had come to Los Angeles before: once as a teenager, hitchhiking in, then much later as a screenwriter, meeting a limousine driver sent by the studio who waited for me at the airport gate. But maybe there was no conventional way or reason for arriving in this city, just millions of odd stories of hope or desperation, all of them washing up here sooner or later. The plane shook, cutting its speed, then dropped softly into the smudgy cloud.

MY PEOPLE WERE what is known as ridge runners, emigrants from England, Scotland, and Wales who came into America through Virginia, eventually settling in North Carolina, South Carolina, Georgia, Mississippi, Tennessee, and the Ozarks of Missouri and Arkansas. Living as they did on the top of mountains, they tended to be independent and solitary people, traits that I share. They loved music and storytelling, and their religious affiliations ranged from Pentecostal Christianity to a kind of pantheistic worship of the land and its features and elements: trees, rivers, rocks, wind, and rain. Several of my relatives married Native American women of the Delaware, Cherokee, and Osage Tribes. None, to the best of my knowledge and research, ever owned slaves, although this may have been due more to poverty than principle or because they lived far from the lowlands where cotton was grown. Some, I know, considered slavery a sin. In the Civil War, a few of my ancestors fought for the Confederate states and about the same number for the Union, but most, I think, would have preferred to stay on their mountaintops, letting the war on the far side of the horizon come to its own conclusion.

Despite divided loyalties, they and their descendants were all fiercely Southern. My grandmother boasted that we were related to John Randolph, the outspoken Virginian who opposed the Missouri Compromise in 1820, and she often hissed about Yankee carpetbaggers. When I was five years old, we visited Granny and Granddad on the Home Place, as everyone called the two thousand–acre family homestead. I remember sitting on the front steps outside in the dark, my face hidden in my folded arms, crying. I no longer remember what was said in my grandmother's parlor, but it had to do with race, and I protested, knowing it was wrong, and received a sharp remark or, more likely, a snicker that sent me squalling into the dark.

My father came to sit on the step beside me and stroked my blonde hair. "Honey, you just don't understand how things are down here."

I lifted my face, hot and tear-streaked, and bellowed, "And I never want to, either!"

But I did register the distinction he made in trying to comfort me: *Down here*, he had said—*that* I understood and was grateful. We were *from* the South—my father, mother, brothers, and me—but we did not live there. My father's work as a construction engineer took us all over the country, from the shipyards of Norfolk, Virginia; and Joliet, Illinois; to dams in Montana and Washington. He worked on the Hanford Project, the nuclear reactors by the Columbia River, and on the radar stations of the DEW (Distance Early Warning System) line on the Yukon River in Alaska. Some construction workers left their families behind, but my mother was resolute in her decision to live wherever my father found his next job, and so she spent much of their married life packing up five children and the parts of a household that could be put in boxes.

Despite my confusion (why did I think differently about race than many of my relatives?) and conflict (how could people I love say or feel such things?), I still loved the South. For years, it existed for me as a romantic abstraction. It was the pastoral backdrop to my parents' stories where people worshiped in brush arbors, ate dinner on the ground, were baptized in shining rivers, rode horses and mules, hunted with baying hounds, and knew where in the boundless woods they could find ginseng and stretch berries to put in homemade bubble gum. It was a place where people stayed put—no small attraction to me, growing up, moving from town to town, always the new girl in class, the shy one with the speech impediment. My glowing impressions of the South received an infusion of vitality every time we visited, or "went home" as everyone said, but as my father's jobs took us farther north, the trips to the Home Place became infrequent and finally stopped. The South became a distant, almost mythical place, and eventually I came to believe I had lost any sense of identification I once had with it, whether positive or negative.

It was not difficult to deceive myself about this. People of color were not part of my family's migratory life. They existed outside our experience, which, considering the many places we lived, now seems a suspicious perception. Surely, in Virginia, Alabama, Arkansas, North Carolina, Texas, Illinois, Montana, Oregon, and Alaska, we would have encountered a few persons with black or brown skins. I remember none, except the Eskimo and Athabascan natives of Alaska. Like our ancestors, I suppose, we stayed on our hilltops and kept ourselves out of the fray.

Then came the school play in Walla Walla, Washington—a drama from a slim, yellow Samuel French book. I was fourteen years old, and thanks to several speech therapists over the years, I could at last stand on a stage and deliver lines that people actually understood. My part was not the lead, but it was the showiest role in the play, with much movement, eye-catching reactions, and all the best jokes. I was the black maid. Backstage, I applied dark-brown makeup to my face, stuffed my dark-blonde hair beneath a curly black wig, and dressed myself in a traditional servant's black uniform with white apron, collar, and cap.

There were two performances scheduled on consecutive evenings. The first night, I smeared dark makeup on my legs and strutted onto the stage. The second night, knowing I would not have time to scrub off makeup before the cast party after the show, I borrowed black stockings and, for garters, used rubber bands—which snapped during the last act. To keep the stockings from falling, I played the rest of the scene knock-kneed, and was rewarded for my resourcefulness with squeals of laughter and enthusiastic applause. I hobbled out for a curtain call, then, back in the wings, shed my stockings.

Standing there, exultant, with the smelly black socks balled in my hand, I looked out at the departing audience. I saw—and it was a moment when your vision falls upon a scene with such intensity that everything around it is seared away—a black family making its way out of a row of seats: a father, a mother, a boy, one of the few black students in the junior high school, and another child, his brother. The boy had brought his parents and little brother to see his school play. In a flash, I felt it all: the family putting on their coats and leaving the house, riding in the car to the school, happy, excited, expectant, finding their places in the auditorium, saying "Excuse me" to all those knees, then settling down to watch the play. I felt their faces watching my performance. Now, behind the curtain, I watched them leave. I heard the quiet in their car on the long ride home.

Two years later: I am sixteen, a high school dropout living in Little Rock, Arkansas, where I attend business school because, as I have been told, I must do something with my life. What I do instead of attending typing classes is spend afternoons in the public library teaching myself Italian: *io sono, tu sei, noi siamo.* I carry a dime-store notebook in which I practice conjugating verbs of a language blissfully foreign to everything I know. Usually, I lunch on cheese and apples from home; today I am eating at the Woolworth's in Little Rock.

These are the days of Gov. Orval Faubus, and in order to attend high school, a young woman not much older than I am, along with eight of her fellow students, had to be escorted by a phalanx of state troopers to class. To show my solidarity with her and her people and my disgust with my own, I have seated myself at the lunch counter on the other side of the store between two black men. When the black waitress comes, I order a tuna fish sandwich. Her mouth opens, closes, then she shrugs.

I eat my sandwich, the pickle, the potato chips. I can hear myself chewing. I keep my eyes on my plate, except once, when I look up into the mirror in back of the pie case. My gaze pans across a row of black faces. In the mirror, each pair of eyes meets mine with an expression as opaque as onyx. *Feel better? Think you done something fine? Get out of my face. Got no time for silly little white girls who want to feel good without putting anything on the line.*

The next day, I am standing by a highway, hitching the first of a series of rides that will eventually deposit me and two suitcases, one containing a set of encyclopedias, in Los Angeles, California. The encyclopedias had been left to me for safekeeping by my family before they moved to Alaska, so, in one sense, by hauling them west with me, I am fulfilling a trust. I am also amused—even at sixteen—to be toting the world's accumulated wisdom to Hollywood. Like thousands of other teenage girls, I may be starstruck, but I know I am different: I have a brain—and I am sitting on proof of it as I waggle my thumb at the approaching car.

I am leaving the South behind—forever, I think. What I do not know is that for decades I will be haunted by these two aspects of myself: the girl on the stage who realizes the effects of her own ignorance and the one on the revolving stool at the lunch counter in Woolworth's who wants to do something, but is afraid gestures and questions may be misunderstood, futile, or too small to make a difference.

⚬

As the plane descended into the haze blanketing the city, I thought of that cocky runaway with no plans for finishing high school, lugging fifty pounds of reference books. That was more than thirty years ago. Now I am middle-aged, college-educated, and this time I am back in Los Angeles on a dubious mission: to find out everything I can about a former slave named Biddy Mason and the woman I am convinced was not her sister: Hannah.

MY HOTEL IN DOWNTOWN LOS ANGELES, chosen for its proximity to the county courthouse and the nearby county law library, was a warren of empty hallways with doors rescued from anonymity only by their ascending numbers. Flanking the walls were machines that dispensed beverages in cans and snacks in sacks, laundry carts heaped to overflowing, and fluorescent-green exit signs. The rooms were barely more than cubicles, with hardly enough space to walk between twin beds, an air conditioner with seemingly only one setting (frigid), a minirefrigerator, and a closet-size bathroom. Attached to the hotel was a restaurant named Epicenter. An earthquake had recently shaken California, and I was housed in an insubstantial structure above a widening crack, and was not amused, although I referred to the restaurant in a flippant way on postcards to my daughter and friends. At night, in the tiny room where the air was cold as a tomb, I lay on the bed and waited for the shudder of colliding tectonic plates.

One morning, I was looking for the downtown Los Angeles Public Library, was turned around, and could not find it. The trunks of the trees along the street were covered with graffiti. Standing on the corner was a slender, young African American man dressed in custom-tailored clothes, sunglasses, and gold jewelry. In his hand was a cell phone. He looked up and down the block, past me, through me. I decided, based on his appearance, that he was a drug dealer and this was his corner, or he was a lookout for someone else selling drugs. "Excuse me," I said. His head turned toward me, and his eyes behind the reflective glass presumably focused on me, but I saw only my own distorted face. "Do you know where the library is?" I asked. He stared at me — I felt the stare — and I was aware of the absurdity of my question. Did I suppose he had a library card, that he went in and hunted among card catalogs or on computers for a book — by whom, on what — that libraries were his scene at all? I pictured him in a store, pointing to a rack of clothes — did he buy off the rack? — and peeling a bill of a large denomination off a roll of bills. He would pay in cash, not with credit cards. Credit cards and library cards belonged to another world, I thought—my world. Then why, if I did not think he knew, had I asked him where the library was? I realized with a pang that I was curious about him, wondered if the scenario I had built about him was true or a myth of my own making. But I did not know how to ask. The young man jerked his head, and I looked beyond him to a lumber-encased building and recognized that it was the Los Angeles library. "Thank you," I said.

The interior of the library was a mess. Renovations were under way following a recent fire. Security gates and guards were posted at the entrance for both entering and exiting patrons. Inside, a reference librarian found what I was seeking on her computer—*Home/Stead*, by Susan Elizabeth King, published in 1989—and sent me to Special Collections where I sat at a counter, waiting for what turned out to be a bundle instead of a book. I realized it was a packet that I had to open by untying and lifting cross-folding flaps. What did it remind me of? Unwrapping a treasure or, perhaps, raising layers of torn skin to reveal a wound. The book itself—handmade with delicate stitched binding and thick, soft hand-rolled paper—lay within its nondescript protective binder, a pearl disguised, concealed by its container. The first page was a rubbing from a tombstone: BIDDY MASON. The rest of the pages came in several hues, one a muted lavender, another almost auburn. I carefully turned the soft, fragile pages. The writings were selections dealing with Biddy's life, racial awareness, the strength of women, self-discovery, and physical and spiritual pilgrimages. Dolores Hayden, the director of the Power of Place public art project, wrote about Biddy Mason: "Her homestead was a place to unite her family and nurture her extended family." Linda Spikes Cox, a direct descendant of Biddy, wrote: "Our family thinks of her as a strong woman who was unusually determined to complete all ideas successfully." I understood that Biddy's influence was still felt among women, especially artists and writers, in Los Angeles.

I longed to take the book with me to read at my leisure, but, of course, this was a rare edition that would never leave the protection of the library. And just as well, I thought. The world outside this building was fraught and unpredictable—all those shifting faults, graffiti-defaced trees, and a history of riots in the streets. Only a few blocks from here, a black man named O. J. Simpson was on trial for brutally murdering his white ex-wife and her acquaintance, and an atmosphere of tension and suspicion pervaded, mixing uneasily with L.A.'s penchant for titillation.

When I looked at my watch, I was astonished to see that it was almost closing time. I returned *Home/Stead* to the librarian reluctantly, but before I did I copied one last quotation from it into my notebook: "One is not always aware how close a relationship exists between research and a subjective emotional need."[2] The sentence resonated with the truth of prophecy, although at the time I could not have said what my research was, exactly, or what emotional need it might eventually satisfy. It would be years before I understood.

On the third day of my research trip, I climbed aboard a Greyhound bus bound for San Bernardino, a town situated in a valley to the east of L.A. where Biddy and Hannah had lived with the Smiths. Everyone was brown or black, except me and a young college student. He sat beside an old man and tried out his Spanish.

"Moon . . . luna."

"Si," said the old man.

I could not tell whether he thought the boy a fool, or appreciated his effort.

"Sky . . . cielo. Earth . . . tierra."

I stared out at a desolate landscape: the freeway, cars, housing developments, then bare brown hills. The lapping sounds of the bus tires seemed to carom between the boy, the old man, the landscape, and me.

The boy said, "Sun . . . sol. The sun in the sky, not the son of a father."

"Si," said the old man.

An hour later, we disembarked at the station in San Bernardino, and, after checking my map, I began walking to my destination there. I noticed a woman coming toward me on the sidewalk—an old woman, black, slender, still beautiful. She wore her graying hair in a roll around her head. Her print dress fell in clean straight lines almost to her ankles. I wondered what Hannah might have looked like in old age. The woman smiled and said good morning.

I wanted to ask her about the African American community in San Bernardino or whether by some slim chance she had heard of the

Robert Mays Smith family, or of descendants of the two women Smith had owned who might still be in the area. Absurd to think that the first person I would meet might help me, but the day at the wall—that shock I had felt touching the exhibit about Biddy—had made me feel lucky, perhaps even, in some inexplicable way, chosen. But my shyness won out. The woman walked on by. I turned and watched ruefully until she was out of sight.

The public library in San Bernardino was small but modern. Once inside, I found myself again feeling disoriented and somewhat assaulted by the conspicuous security precautions. California historical materials were kept upstairs, in the Heritage Room; downstairs, a uniformed, armed guard sat by the front door—unless he was escorting someone to the rest room where he waited outside until the person emerged. The security here, like in Los Angeles, was a reminder of the recent riots. At the library, I found only a few articles relating to the Mormon colony in San Bernardino, but the librarian referred me to the San Bernardino County Archives, about ten blocks away.

It was there, in a vault of a room that felt more like a morgue than a repository of archives, that I met Anne L. Brandt, who was not the head of the archives but worked there as an assistant. She was a young woman, in her thirties, quiet and efficient. I asked her about Biddy, Hannah, and early black settlers, and she was able to direct me to some documents on the Mormon colony and the people who remained behind, but she had little information on the women themselves. When I mentioned Toby Embers, the father of two of Hannah's children, her eyes lit up. She went into the file room and retrieved a folder containing the transcript of Toby Embers's trial. Her excitement was evident. Finally, someone who could appreciate what she had discovered among the papers! Then we looked for Toby Embers's will. It showed that Toby had left his house to Hannah, and she, in turn, had transferred it to their children. (Sadly, the house would eventually be sold for delinquent taxes.) I was eager to see the house, and Ann gave me a copy of an 1862 map showing its location, but said a Bank of San Bernardino was now on its site.

BEFORE I HEADED BACK to Los Angeles for the evening, I decided to visit the bank. When leaving the city that morning, I had slipped a hundred-dollar bill in my purse in lieu of a wad of traveler's checks and now wanted to change it so I could take a taxi back to the Greyhound station. The teller sent me to the officious-looking bank manager who listened, without expression, to my request and then said no, they could not help me. Look, I said, I have credit cards. I have identification. No matter, he said, and refused to discuss the situation further.

I sat dumbfounded in the armchair in front of his desk. I could not help but imagine what might have once been here: Toby and Hannah, happy and hopeful, dancing together at the housewarming party for Toby's house, which had been replaced by this airless, impersonal place.

At ten that night, I was back in downtown Los Angeles at the Greyhound depot and frustrated yet again. The taxi drivers would not take me from the depot to my hotel, saying a short trip was not worth their while. I did not relish walking in the dark through what I could see was a bad neighborhood.

One evening, returning from the law library, I had gotten turned around and had not been able to find my way back to the hotel. I walked into an inner-city ghetto, but it could have been Dresden after the Allied bombing: a surrealistic place of half walls, broken windows, twisted metal frames, and alleys with heaped garbage cans — had the city stopped picking up garbage? — and along the dark walls leaned what I thought were empty cardboard boxes. I have no idea why I reached out to touch one, but I did — and jumped back with a shriek. A woman had been sleeping inside it; the whites of her eyes flashed awake in her dark face. She glared at me like a corpse disturbed in its coffin.

Did I say, "Excuse me"? I know I meant to. I saw in the shadows, then, other dark figures, moving among the crumpled cardboard boxes. I saw the bottoms of feet, bare and crusted. This is Hell, I thought. I have finally come to Hell. And I turned and ran, not knowing or caring where, just away, any direction that might get me back to the other world, to the right side of the tracks, to ignorance.

A lot of good that retreat had done me. Here I was again, feeling that same shameful panic rising in my chest. I wondered if I would end up spending the night slumped in a plastic chair at the Greyhound station. "What am I supposed to do now?" I asked the taxi drivers. They shrugged, pointed toward a nearby municipal bus stop, and rolled up their windows.

I walked quickly, purposefully, eyes forward, as the books tell you to. On the way, I passed a cluster of Hispanic men. "You want a taxi?"

one called. I turned and saw a short, stocky man with a slack face in his forties or fifties. "Sure," I said, overriding in an instant everything I had ever learned about getting in cars with strange men.

We crossed the street to his "taxi," a twenty-year-old sand-colored Chevrolet, crumpled fore and aft by repeated collisions. He hurried to open the door; I sat in the front seat beside him. His English was on a par with my Spanish, but we talked anyway. He had been doing this all day and wanted to go home. He had a wife and four daughters. He had been born in Los Angeles.

I told him I was writing a book about Los Angeles, how it had been in 1850, when it had become a state. He knew nothing of California history, not even how recently his ancestors had owned all of it, and he was too tired for a history lesson—I could see it in his eyes. How presumptuous of me anyway, to think that anything I knew could change his life, or anyone else's or my own, for that matter.

In no time we were at my hotel. I gave him a couple dollars for the ride, then thought again. I reached back into my purse and tipped him the hundred-dollar bill.

MY FINAL DESTINATION on this visit was the Los Angeles County Courthouse. Like Americans all over the country, I had been seeing the courthouse on television every day for more than a year. I was familiar with the faces of the accused and the victims, as well as participants in the trial: the jurors, the judge, the lawyers, the spectators, and the witnesses. The throes of the trial of Orenthal J. Simpson had fueled a frantic media frenzy. Every morning on the courthouse steps, there was a milling crowd. Some people had been there since dawn to register for the lottery for the few seats open to the public inside the courtroom. Many stayed after the tickets were distributed. There were dozens of reporters, a contingent of police, and hundreds of tourists, vendors, and evangelists.

Somewhere in the complex, I knew, was the Records Division of Los Angeles County where I might find the transcript of the habeus corpus trial. Inside the courthouse, I received directions to the repository of records. Out of the glare of the morning, I took a dark elevator and followed a sterile corridor to a suite of offices with RECORDS stenciled on the door, behind which were walls lined with files and books, and a counter where one filled out a form requesting records of closed law cases.

I stood there for several minutes, wondering what to write. A young woman behind the counter obligingly listened to my tale about the 1856 trial and brought out an index book listing the early habeas corpus cases in Los Angeles County. The entries on parchment pages were written in penmanship so elegant the names seemed inscribed. I could not find Robert Smith, or Biddy Mason, or Hannah, and did not know what other names to look for. The woman suggested I speak to her supervisor who had been there for years and knew everything, and disappeared into an inner office to fetch him.

The tall, graying man who approached the counter moved stiffly, as though standing and leaving his desk were arduous tasks rarely undertaken. He listened without expression behind his wire-rim glasses as I told him about my trip from Seattle, my research for a book, and the particular documents I was seeking about the Biddy Mason trial.

Yes, he had heard of Biddy Mason. Yes, records from those early trials should be here in the archives. He imparted the information icily, staring at me over his eyeglasses. He said he was also writing a book, but that his specialty was military history. "Not," he said disdainfully, "social history."

"Social history is military history," I objected. Was he trying to tell me that what was important about the Civil War were the opposing generals who sketched battles on pieces of paper? *That* would have been news to the thousands of soldiers on both sides who had been willing to die for what they believed, not to mention the millions of black people whose fates depended upon the outcome of their fight. Where in the hell did he think wars came from if not from the conflicts and clashes of social history?

"Don't be absurd," the man said and walked away.

I tried to convey an apology through the young woman at the counter, but her supervisor would not see me again.

I have been trying hard to understand why I cannot remember that walk through the crowd on the steps of the Los Angeles County Courthouse. I absolutely cannot remember it—not in the sense of being there, having feelings, or being aware of the people around me. Those memories are held away from me, walled off from my consciousness. I know what I had to have been seeing: how the sky was its usual bleached California color, how the edges of white buildings, their roofs, advertising signs, and shabby yellow-brown palm trees stood against it. But that is only me looking at me, trying to reconstruct the morning. I remember someone asking as I tried to wend my way through the throng there for the Simpson trial, "Is she somebody?" but the rest of the scene is eerily silent.

What I know—can taste—is how truly afraid I was, just terrified, and this is what shames me, how frightened I was of the black people around me, how afraid I was they were going to hurt me. I kept seeing that dead white woman in her driveway drenched in blood, the pool of it around her, and the smashed eyeglasses not far from her fingers, and I thought, *These people all around me approve that woman's fate. Yes, I thought, they knew and approved. Yes, of course, the L.A. police were racist and, yes, black people have been continually repressed and sent to jail for crimes they did not commit, but this was a murder, and to them it was all right and I was a white woman and they could as easily kill me and justify that.*

And so I remember only backs of people, the fabrics of their shirts, pants, dresses, even belt buckles and shoes, but not their faces, except for the face of one woman who let me pass, and I remember worrying about my glasses, like in basketball or volleyball games when I was a child, worried that they would be knocked off and then I would be truly powerless, blind, groping on the ground, unable to find any way out of this crush of people, and I was so happy the police were nearby, that they would protect me—even as corrupt and evil as they might be—that they would believe and protect me because I was a white woman.

Everything was upside down, inside out, wrong! How had it gotten to this? How could things have become this crazy? At that moment, on those steps, I doubted that we would ever find a way to live together. And this is why I keep all those memories so far away from me, safely away, behind that dense, impregnable wall of almost oblivion.

The last night in my cramped hotel room, I packed my suitcase for an early departure the next morning. I stacked my notebooks and papers, folded the inverted maps, bundled together the many brochures I had collected, and fitted them into the bottom of the suitcase. Next came the shoes heel-to-toe in the corners and my clothes, all but the sweater I wore over my nightgown against the air conditioning and what I would wear on the plane. These were spread on the opposite twin bed like a desiccated scarecrow; they made me feel lonely.

The television was on, but the sound was muted. Images flickered silently, like hand shadows on a child's wall: O. J., Johnny Cochran, Nicole's sister, Ron Goldman's father. Outside my door, people passed in the corridor, and from their muffled conversation I caught two words: "The trial." The Simpson trial, Biddy and Hannah's trial—both held a few blocks from where I now stood. I felt that I was at the center of a great network of faults not only spreading throughout this city and state, but also pervading the entire country. The epicenter *is* here, I thought, and the issue is still race. Somehow, of course, the issue is always still race.

I turned off the TV, and it was as if I had snuffed out a candle in the darkness. I sat on the bed beside my morning costume. I had not found the verdict at the courthouse, and the transcript of the trial was guarded by a man who studied wars but not the societies that waged them. I had no idea where to look next. Worse, for the first time, I had become aware of the real dangers of this project I had undertaken, not only the possibility that physically I might come to harm, but also the realization that emotionally I was at risk. Already I had become hypersensitive to the presence of people of color, saw them when I would have overlooked them before, sought them out when I would have avoided them, wanting from them and from myself some interface or resolution. Whatever my intentions—that I would excavate an aspect of African American history that had been overlooked or lost—an inward journey of introspection and assessment had begun. And now that I was on the verge of it—or had already, without suspecting, embarked upon it—I was afraid.

In the mirror over the dresser, the woman looked back at me. *Is she somebody?* Yes, but who? And what is she running from or toward?

THREE

The Writ

IN THE WEEK BETWEEN Christmas and New Year's Day 1855, Benjamin Ignatius Hayes, just returned from presiding over a week's session of the district court in San Diego, prepared to move his wife and son to a new house in Los Angeles. A few miles to the east, in the hills of Santa Monica, Robert Mays Smith, his family, his slaves, and the trail hands Robert had hired to accompany them on the long trip ahead were camped, making plans for their departure for Texas.[1] Smith expected to be on the trail by New Year's Day. But fateful circumstances and personal choices were about to change those travel plans and bring a California judge, born in the South, and a disaffected southern Mormon into a confrontation that would change both of their lives.

Ten months after Robert Mays Smith and his family had arrived in Salt Lake Valley in 1848, thirty-four-year-old Benjamin Hayes had begun his own journey to the West. Unlike Smith, however, who seemed ever at the mercy of unfortunate circumstances, Hayes was a man with an inner sense of direction and a secure means of livelihood. This is not to say that life for Benjamin had always been easy and full of promise. In fact, the Hayes family's fortunes had constantly risen and fallen, tracking the changing occupations of Benjamin's father. John Hayes was a painter, tavern keeper, and city sheriff of Baltimore, Maryland. On December 3, 1830, when Benjamin was fifteen, his mother, Mary, died, leaving behind seven small children.[2] John Hayes managed, with the help of relatives, to keep his family together and insisted on their attending school.

Both of Benjamin's parents were of Irish descent and passed their Roman Catholicism on to their firstborn son. At one time, in adolescence, Benjamin considered becoming a priest. His faith, respect for tradition, and bookishness might have made Benjamin a good priest, but these same traits led him to a different profession. Instead of entering a seminary, Benjamin Hayes attended St. Mary's College in Baltimore and, in time, was admitted to the Maryland bar. He was twenty-four and had studied diligently for three years. He wrote in his diary: "[W]ith what joy I paid my fee of $3 to the Clerk, and hastened to the hall to settle with the old apple-woman, from time immemorial entitled to her perquisite of a couple of dollars! Still I remember her warm wishes for my success, as the money dropped jingling into her side pocket. Dear old apple-woman!"[3]

With a law degree in hand, Benjamin had to decide whether to set up practice in Baltimore or move to places with more possibilities. His father's struggles to survive in the East may have convinced him to move west, or, like many young men, he may have simply wanted to strike out on his own.

In Liberty, Missouri, in the early 1840s, Benjamin practiced law with several associates. During these years, he and two friends founded a temperance journal. Benjamin's new abstinence—he had inherited his father's weakness for liquor—and the founding of the temperance journal coincided with his courtship of Emily Chauncey.

Emily Chauncey had also been born in Maryland, in Harford County, adjacent to the county of Baltimore. Benjamin thought it ironic and wonderful that, missing each other in Maryland, they would end up in the same small town in Missouri. "Providence seems to have so directed my steps," he would write, "that she should be the source of all the happiness I have enjoyed, or expect to enjoy, upon earth."[4]

Emily Chauncey was a petite, pretty woman with black hair and shadows beneath her eyes that hinted of delicate health. She could not walk far and often coughed into the dainty handkerchiefs tucked in her waistband. She had received a plain education at Lindenwood and read "useful things."[5] She met the intense young lawyer from Maryland in Liberty, Missouri, and they were married in St. Francis Xavier Church, the Catholic cathedral in St. Louis, Missouri, on November 15, 1848.[6] He was thirty-three years old, she twenty-seven; older than most who entered into marriage, both had high standards and had chosen to wait.

They were people with simple tastes and sensibilities, preferring to stay at home rather than engage in a more social life. During the first months of their marriage, their evenings were spent with Benjamin reading to his bride from one of his many books, or the two of them talking. "Her conversational powers were good," Benjamin wrote, "and she could give a lively and interesting account of any thing she witnessed."[7]

As a consequence of his marriage, Benjamin became a slave owner. When his wife's father, John Chauncey, died, the family slaves were distributed to his heirs, including at least two to his daughter Emily. As Emily's husband, Benjamin became their owner, in the same manner that Robert Mays Smith owned slaves because his wife inherited them or used her inheritance to purchase them.

On September 10, 1849, less than ten months after their wedding, Benjamin left for California with plans for Emily to follow. The separation was excruciating. Benjamin's letter of September 20, 1848, ends: "Last night, as I lay wrapped in my blanket, I dreamt of home and of my dear wife. Do not ask if I ever cease to think of you. Never. How much I desire success, for your sake. You must always pray for me, dearest. Take care of your health this winter. Look lightly, if possible upon my absence. . . . Farewell, my dear wife, for a little while."[8] Benjamin and Emily would not see one another again for two years and six months.

"I started from Independence on September 10th," Benjamin writes in his journal. "Lewis, a slave belonging to the family, accompanied me six miles, to aid in getting a fair start for the mules. He led the pack mule. I then said goodbye to Lewis, who seemed affected."[9] It is noteworthy that Hayes was careful to record the names of the men who traveled west with him, but the long lists always ended with "and one

Benjamin Hayes, circa
1848. Courtesy of the
Security Pacific
Collection, History
Department, Los
Angeles Public Library,
Los Angeles.

colored man" or "and two colored men." That is to say, after Lewis, men of color, slave or free, did not warrant a recording of their names.

The account of Hayes's journey west in 1849 portrays a man joyfully, almost gleefully, setting out into a world ripe for description. Even misadventures seemed welcomed because they contained a story. Shortly after beginning his journey, Benjamin, trying to restrain a stampeding mule, suffered a bad rope burn to his hand and stopped at a house along the road where, for five dollars, he was allowed to spend the night. In the morning, his avaricious host accompanied him to a turnoff, observing darkly: "How easy I could kill you now, and nobody would even know it!"[10] Benjamin shuddered, but remembered the words and later shaped the encounter into a memorable anecdote.

His confidence in the role of Providence, which would prevail throughout his life, was, in his travels, quite evident:

> I was in a gay assemblage one night about seven days after my arrival at Soccoro when J. Cruise brought the startling news of the massacre of Mr. White's party. . . . For me the event had perhaps a deeper interest than for any who were listening to the narrative. When I was on the eve of my departure from Independence, I was introduced to Mr. White. . . . I was recommended to accompany him. That I did not, but persevered in overtaking the others, was it not Providential? Another evidence of the kindness with which the Almighty has watched over, protected, and blessed me through my whole life. I do so consider it.[11]

He wrote his wife: "It has been a great consolation to me, my dear wife, that I went to confession before I left; it keeps me cheerful and composed, patient, and ready, I trust, to meet any difficulty that may present itself. I put my prayer-book in my pocket to-day, to read at my leisure moments." His faith and inner resolve also helped Benjamin maintain his abstinence from alcohol. In a diary entry of November 20, 1849, he reported declining an offered drink, saying, "I had drank nothing of that kind for nearly two years."[12]

At first, Benjamin traveled alone, but he later joined a party crossing to California on the Santa Fe route. Like all westward travelers, Benjamin marveled at the sight of buffalo, antelope, and Indians. He remarked on the weather, rivers, the quality of grass, and the condition of horses and cattle, and recorded the names of people and places, dates of lives and events, measurements of distances and landmarks, costs of ferry passages, and how and when buildings were constructed. Some of his diary entries were jotted notes: "Old friends . . . returning emigrants . . . anxious night . . . merriment." Often he would add "origin of the name." This was a reminder to himself to add the background or history of a site or landmark.

The seasoned lawyer was obsessive about preserving documents. He saved a list of the items in his travel outfit, detailing everything from two pairs of warm mittens, which cost $1.00; to a buffalo robe, which had been a present; to eleven yards of red flannel to trade with Indians, which cost $6.60; to a canteen, which cost 45 cents, attached by a strap worth 20 cents; to ink powder worth 15 cents.[13] He would later footnote this list, noting how he had used the various items and what he wished he had brought.

On December 13, 1849, Benjamin's party made camp near the village of St. Xavier del Bac near what is now Tucson, Arizona. Benjamin was "struck with the strange appearance of Indian wigwams . . . adobes . . . and a splendid church of solid structure, whose dome and belfreys overlook the town and to a wide extent of mountains and plain." He stayed outside the church until ten o'clock. "A glimpse of the beauty of the inside through a high window, exciting our curiosity to the highest." After bribing the custodians, he was allowed inside. He noted innumerable statues of saints, twelve "oil paintings by masters, sent no doubt from Europe," four old missals, the oldest printed in 1762, and parish records of births and deaths. He described how sunlight made the altar glitter like gold. He wanted to know the age of the church, and a Mexican told him it was built two hundred years earlier, but a Pima Indian said "mas."[14] Benjamin, standing in the filtered golden light, was a historian at work, in the urgency of his quest, in his attention to dates and details, and in his appreciation of the contrast of the grandiose past with primitive present conditions.

As Benjamin's party approached California, he grew eager to know this new land: "We linger on the confines of the reputed delicious climate, where, I am told, the trees are now loaded with oranges and olives, and the grape is still fresh on the vine." Finally, on February 6, 1850, Benjamin started out for Los Angeles. On a hill covered with grass and blooming flowers, he looked down upon the pueblo. "My design at present is merely to stop at Los Angeles until I can write up my Notes of Travel, to be sent to my wife for her amusement during my absence."[15]

Somewhat ironically, the first person to greet Benjamin was a former slave named Peter Biggs.

> I tied my mule to a pillar of the corridor in front of the Hotel (since known as the Bella Union). It was the dinner-hour. I went in and dined. In the crowd I recognized no person; but, presently, an old acquaintance introduced himself, in the shape of Peter

Biggs, formerly the slave of my friend, Mr. Reuben Middleton, of Liberty. "Pete" was delighted to see me; did not delay to communicate to me many useful items; in fact, rendered me services which I esteemed valuable.[16]

Biggs, in fact, provided Benjamin with his first client, a man of color who needed an attorney to draw up a bill of sale.[17]

As the days passed, Benjamin evidently abandoned his plans for a brief stay in Los Angeles. Still wearing his traveling clothes and a heavy soldier's coat, he began attending court proceedings—somewhat rudimentary occasions that were held in the homes of prominent Los Angeles citizens. He borrowed law books in Spanish from Abel Stearns, one of the pueblo's richest and most influential residents. Within weeks, Benjamin had found a law partner, Jonathan R. Scott, and the two young men went into business. A memorable early adventure occurred when a disgruntled stranger mistook Benjamin for an enemy, fired upon him, and left the young lawyer with a hole in his hat and the trace of a bullet's passage on his cheek.[18]

"Went to Mass" is a refrain in Benjamin's journal during this time. He delighted in the Spanish influences that permeated Los Angeles culture, combining the civility of southern life with Catholic ritual. One of his early letters to his wife describes his attendance at the Plaza Church: "Yesterday I attended a magnificent ceremony; it was the Octave of Corpus Christi. To-morrow there will be another grand procession, in commemoration of the Reina de los Angeles. You would delight in the religious festivals of the City."[19] He made friends with the local priests, especially Father Blas Raho, whose faded photograph would be found among Benjamin's papers and who was instrumental in bringing the Sisters of Charity to Los Angeles.

Benjamin Hayes quickly became prominent in the Los Angeles law community. He was one of the signers of a petition to the governor asking for the establishment of local political and legal offices. In 1850, Benjamin ran for the recently established office of county attorney and was elected. A salaried position thus secured, he could send for his wife.

On June 28, 1851, Benjamin wrote Emily, suggesting the best disposition for one of their slaves who apparently had a child of unusual size: "Tell Grace her child would be quite a curiosity here, a young lion (or lioness, I forget which). If you should not bring her, do not sell her,

The original Plaza Church, Los Angeles. From Benjamin Hayes, *Pioneer Notes.*

give her to one of your sisters, as they live in a slave state, or set her free, as you may judge proper. I really suppose, however, that her welfare would be best promoted by keeping her in the family."[20]

On December 27, 1851, Emily left St. Louis, without slaves, and began her long journey to California. Because of her frail health, she would not go overland, but instead traveled to New Orleans. There she took a boat to Havana, disembarked in Panama, rode sidesaddle on a mule across the Isthmus, boarded another boat to San Diego, and arrived in San Francisco on February 14, 1852, Benjamin's thirty-seventh birthday.[21]

The Hayeses' first residence in Los Angeles was a boardinghouse for miners and travelers where Emily had one of her first lessons in the relaxed decorum of the West. The landlady told her: "You want anything, Mrs. Hayes, you got to sing out!"[22] Within a few weeks, Benjamin was able to provide them with a house. "[It] is at the foot of a high hill, from which we can see all the surrounding country. It is a mud house," Emily exclaimed, meaning adobe, "with a mud floor." She continued:

> The walls are whitewashed, but the ceiling looks like an old smoke-house, and leaks finely when it rains. There is a little

fireplace in one corner where I do my cooking. . . . On one side of the room we have a wash-stand on which I am now writing and where I keep the few books I have, and over this hangs the Madonna which the priest gave Mr. Hayes for me. . . . Opposite this is the bed, a thirty dollar bed with a single bed mattress on it, blankets for pillows. . . . Around the bed we have a calico curtain.[23]

The delights of a temperate climate likely impressed them both. As Emily writes, "[W]hen [Benjamin] is not reading he is in the garden pulling up weeds or transplanting flowers. We will have a great variety of flowers this summer, most of them wild flowers."[24]

"Gardening all of these days. The flowers transplanted last month all flourishing; seeds sown last month coming up, pink, poppy, lark-spur," Benjamin's diary notes. "An Indian girl who used to wash for us came in and sauntered through the garden. After looking round every-where, she seemed to think there was very little useful in it, asking me, `Why, Senor, do you not sow calabazas and zandias?' What a question for the heart of a florist! In self-defence I appealed to my *chiceros* (peas) but she replied, `There are so few of them!' I believe she was right; I must think more of the onions and potatoes."[25]

Emily described a visit to an orange orchard with "large trees hang-ing full of fruit, others just blooming and the air filled with the fra-grance of the bloom." Benjamin was thrilled with his wife's response to the climate and country. "Emily has very much improved; seldom has a cough, even in damp weather."[26]

Another attraction of California was its people. "I have received more calls than I ever did in my life, nearly all Spanish, of course. . . . The ladies of the country are very pleasant," Emily writes, whereas Benjamin notes, "[I]t is the chief pride of a native California lady to dress up to the height of the fashion. At church, all kneeling, blended together—not in pews—with their varicolored silks, showy, beautiful shawls or rebosas thrown easily and gracefully over the head, they make a gay appearance." He noted the reserve of his own wife's dress: "Emily dresses pretty much as at Liberty. She has not bought a new dress until today, and that of calico!" He remembered that once at a ball where all the women were dressed and decorated, Emily had worn in her black hair "simply a piece of sea-grass, white and delicate, a handsome thing."[27]

In 1852, Benjamin was elected the first judge of the Southern District of California, for the counties of Los Angeles, San Bernardino, and San Diego. He was delighted by one Irish soldier's hail: "Ha, Judge, I want a bit of your advice, for ye're not one of these Johnny-come-latelys!"[28]

On January 1, 1853, Benjamin notes: "Exchange of kindnesses between friends on this happy New Year. Shall I see another? To the mercy of God I commit myself and mine." Later that same day, he took his oath of office, promising to uphold the constitutions of California and the United States.[29]

The first entry in Benjamin's diary about fatherhood occurs on April 27, 1853, when John Chauncey Hayes, bearing the name of Benjamin's father and Emily's maiden name, was born. The next entry says: "The journal of last year ended in April at the birth of the boy. Since, I have hardly written a line, although often I must have watched the heavens with an anxious eye. He is now well, and to quote his mother, `the sweetest thing in the world.'"[30]

The phrase "he is now well," the lack of seven months of entries in an obsessively kept diary, and Benjamin's beseeching heaven "with an anxious eye" prove that the early months of the baby's life were perilous. That Chauncey, as he was to be called, came through made him only more precious to his doting parents.

In the fall of 1854, Emily became pregnant again. She and Benjamin eagerly anticipated another baby, a companion to growing Chauncey, but the baby girl, Sarah Louisa, died the day she was born, April 22, 1855. Benjamin buried the baby himself. "My own hands bore it into the Church, my own hands laid it into holy ground." Emily's physical fragility might have played a role. The few friends attending the funeral service would no doubt have worried over her wraithlike appearance. They did not feel that the newborn's death meant as much to a father as would have the loss of an older child. Benjamin disagreed, confiding to his diary, "I felt so."[31]

Despite these vicissitudes, Benjamin's political ambitions continued to grow. He was a Democrat and interested in his party's progress, corresponding regularly with governors and state officials. His diaries are filled with discussions of local and state politics. Southern California politics were dominated by men born in the South or with southern sympathies. Because of the affinity between the plantation life of the

Emily Martha Hayes and son Chauncey, 1857. From Benjamin Hayes, *Pioneer Notes*.

South and the hacienda culture of southern California, most southern emigrants settled in that part of what would become the new state, with many of these southerners clustered in the pueblo of Los Angeles. These southerners formed an oligarchy, shaping the social and political life of the city. On September 12, 1851, a petition "with a view of effecting the speedy formation of a Territorial Government for the southern counties of California" had been circulated, and among its signers was Benjamin Hayes.[32] If southern California became a territory, with its own laws, it would almost certainly permit slavery, reflecting the desires of its southern-born oligarchy. The petition proved futile, but the emotions behind it continued to percolate, especially in Los Angeles.

When a federal position, U.S. district judge for the Southern District of California, was established, Benjamin's friends persuaded him to apply for the appointment. "Numerous recommendations were forwarded to Washington from this quarter."[33] President Franklin Pierce even received a petition for Benjamin's appointment. Yet, despite his formidable backing, the candidacy failed.

Benjamin wrote that he "was pretty well reconciled to the result" and remembered how he had cautioned himself against wanting any office too much. On February 14, 1854, his thirty-ninth birthday, he avers: "I must commence a new career—see if I can be better, with the grace of God."[34]

In the following months, Benjamin continued to edit his travel journal and began collecting local historical documents. "Today I requested the Padrecito to give me a list of the deaths in San Diego since January, 1850." The priest said he had charge of the parochial books, but Benjamin would have to write to the vicar for permission to use church materials. "You are going to write a history, are you not?" Benjamin refuted the charge. "No, Senor. I take much interest in everything that relates to the country I live in, and merely want to have correct information on some matters I deem important." Benjamin's denial was truthful. He did not yet consider himself a writer, but his friends were more perceptive. "Friend Rose appears to think I had some object, so he said, in talking with him about his rancho, [that he] suspects I am going to 'write a book.'"[35]

This book, a history of this new land, was in later years to inflame Benjamin's imagination and consume years of his life in its research and writing. In 1850, however, newly arrived in California, beginning a law practice, and, from 1853 through 1855, having become the first southern-district judge, he was still a man who saw his lifework to be unraveling the truth behind the conflicting stories told by the claimants appearing in his courtroom. There would be time later to add details to the records of those appearances and to ponder their meaning. Benjamin Hayes the historian was still obscured behind the mask of judge.

Maryland to Missouri to California: Hayes had come a long way, figuratively and literally, to find hope and opportunity, where a man could advance on his own merits in a society with laws and politics that were still in the making. Benjamin wanted to be involved in the creation of a new world. He had yet to discover how tenacious was the grip of the past and how rare and difficult it is for a man to emerge anew.

The knock on the door of Benjamin Hayes's home would have come early in the day: the raid on Robert Mays Smith's camp took place at night, and there had to be time before that for discussions and preparations. When Benjamin opened the door, he would have seen two men, David Alexander, sheriff of Los Angeles County, and Robert Clift, sheriff of San Bernardino County.[36] The matter being brought to Hayes's attention then involved two of the three counties—Los Angeles, San Bernardino, and San Diego—under the jurisdiction of the district court.

The lawmen were on a specific and urgent errand: they needed Judge Hayes to sign a writ of habeas corpus (from the Latin "You have the body"). It is a court order, usually conveyed by a sheriff, directed to a person detaining another or others, commanding him to bring the person or persons detained before a court or judge to determine their legal status. According to the sheriffs' preliminary investigation, one Robert Mays Smith was preparing to transport a number of women and children of color from California, where, according to law, they were free, to Texas, where they would once again be considered slaves. Confronted with the sworn charge and assured by the two sheriffs that necessary preparations had been made for the safe transport and housing of the women and children, Benjamin would have had little choice but to sign the requested order and return it to Sheriff Alexander.

Many people later claimed to have instigated the visit to Judge Hayes's home and the subsequent chain of events that led to the unprecedented trial concerning slavery and freedom.[37] Charles Owens, son of Robert Owens, a free black man who sold horses to the U.S.

government and local ranchers, would say that he and a friend, Manuel Pepper, were interested in Biddy's daughter Ellen and Hannah's daughter Ann. Dismayed at the prospect of the girls' departure, they went to Charles's father, told him Smith was camped in the Santa Monica hills en route to Texas, and Robert Owens alerted the sheriff of Los Angeles County. Another version is that Robert Owens visited the canyon camp, and Biddy told him of Smith's plans and her fears and asked him to get word to the sheriff that she wanted to sue for her freedom. Members of the First State Convention of the Colored Citizens of California, which had met in San Francisco the month before, would say they demanded that the sheriff of Los Angeles County intervene in Smith's planned departure.

Several people in San Bernardino could also have alerted Sheriff Clift about Smith's plans to move to Texas. Liz Rowan, a former slave who lived in the Mormon colony in San Bernardino, had known Biddy and Hannah since their days in Mississippi. She and other former slaves would have known about the imminent departure of their friends and the perils their destination, Texas, might represent. Toby Embers, also living in San Bernardino, certainly knew that Hannah was being taken away and that he might never see her or his children again.

Whoever the original informant might have been, Sheriff Clift went to Sheriff Alexander—Smith's party was now within his jurisdiction—told him of the charge, and agreed to accompany him and his men to the campsite, probably to identify Smith, whom he knew. The two lawmen then went to Judge Hayes to explain the situation and secure the writ they needed to protect the Smith slaves and their children.

Watching the men ride away, the judge would have been filled with foreboding for the physical harm that might come to the men entering the dark hills or to the many people, especially the women and children, in Smith's camp. He might also have entertained some concern for his own political future. He was a southerner and had owned slaves himself, and whatever his actions concerning this matter, he was certain to offend some of the people who had elected him to office. Perhaps he speculated that this was the real reason behind the request for the writ of habeas corpus. The nation was lurching toward a civil war; with this single document, Hayes's enemies could be intending to force him to declare his loyalties.

Later, during the quiet hours when Emily and Chauncey were both in bed and Hayes likely remained awake, waiting to hear the outcome of the raid, he may have reflected upon his past relationships with slaves and the issue of slavery.

One of his earliest boyhood memories was coming home from a swim in Spring Gardens in Baltimore. Caught by the rising dark as he passed "Potter's Field and the burying-ground of an African church," he ran, casting "uneasy looks at the high posts of the fences as they were reflected on the waving cattails of the adjacent swamp, looking for all the world like so many tall spectres in chase of me."[38] Perhaps he had thought that with this move to California he would leave behind those fearful memories, but now, waiting for word about the serving of the writ, the dark specters of his past once again seemed to be breathing down his neck.

In the camp in the hills of Santa Monica, there were approximately twenty-five people: Robert; his wife, Rebecca; their seven children; Biddy, Hannah, and their ten children; and the five or six trail hands Robert had hired. As the sun slid behind the hills and sank into the Pacific Ocean, the campfire would have been lighted, and within the dark walls of the canyon, it would have seemed a single glowing coal. The horses, unsaddled and fed, would have been turned into a makeshift corral. The trail hands on horseback, guarding the cattle, might have appeared to be stone sentries at the mountain pass.

Moving within the circle of the campfire, the women would have prepared the evening meal while the men and boys checked equipment, made necessary repairs, and repacked supplies for the trip. They would eat in shifts, and then it would be time for cleanup and putting the children to bed in the wagons. The women slept in the wagons also, but many of the men unrolled bedrolls and stretched out beneath the star-peppered sky. As the campfire died, the silence of the night would have seemed more impenetrable, broken only by the rising wail of distant coyotes.

Then came a sound that made those standing guard reach for their holsters: the approach of horses or the rattling of wagon wheels. If, as one account has it, the raiders came "swooping down . . . in the middle of the night," then the tactic was risky: Smith and his men would immediately think that rustlers had come for the cattle.[39] The recognition of Sheriff Clift was all, probably, that kept the men in camp from opening fire.

Clift would have explained to Smith the reason for the raid, and Sheriff Alexander would have presented him with the writ that permitted the lawmen to take his slaves and their children into protective custody, pending a hearing in town. Smith would have conceded: to resist would have meant a gunfight with his wife and family caught in the middle. One can imagine Smith's wife, Rebecca, and her children watching in fear and disbelief as the deputies went among Smith's wagons, rousing Hannah and Biddy and their children. Then the crowded freight wagons would have disappeared into the black hills, the retreating torches becoming a line of light.

When Biddy, Hannah, and the children clambered down in the dark from the wagons that had carried them from the Smith encampment, they would have been directed toward the county jail on Spring and Franklin Streets behind the Los Angeles courthouse. What a strange and sad scene it must have been, twelve exhausted and bewildered people, arriving they knew not where in the cold predawn hours: two lone women shepherding ten children, ranging in age from two to seventeen.

The decision to send Hannah, Biddy, and their tender offspring to the county jail, pending the outcome of their case, was apparently painful to Benjamin Hayes. As he noted in an article written about the case:

> They had been kept a day or more from intercourse with any who could influence them—an arrangement calculated to be more prejudicial to them than to [Robert Mays Smith], for it left them isolated from even the kindly glance of sympathy. And their confinement (necessarily) in the public jail—as they could not comprehend the reason—might well have inspired them with distrust for their application, and drawn from their fears an answer favorable to [Smith's] objects.[40]

The parenthetical word *necessarily* indicates the judge's ambivalence. But Hayes's rationale concerning their accommodations had a practical component: the "necessity" being served was affording the former slaves a safe place to stay. Robert Mays Smith was accused of trying to take the women and children from California by force, after all. If they had been dispersed among homes in Los Angeles, each of those houses would have had to be guarded, an investment of men and money that neither the district court of southern California nor the sheriff's office of Los Angeles could afford.

The Sisters of Charity, newly arrived in Los Angeles—perhaps at Hayes's invitation from his home state of Maryland—were in the process of starting an institute and orphan asylum, but, at the time Smith's people were taken into custody, its doors had not opened.[41] Moreover, even when that facility was ready, Benjamin expressed fears about the effect on the nuns and other children of being surrounded by armed law officers.

Beyond the practical logistics of housing those in custody, Hayes's comment indicates a psychological justification for sequestering Hannah and Biddy and their children in jail. Uncomfortable as the conditions were there, he reasoned, their resolve to leave Smith would be tested. In other words, if they considered being in jail preferable to being with Robert Mays Smith, the judge would have important information about the nature of their relationship with him.

True, the building where Hannah and Biddy and their children were placed was only two years old. Los Angeles's first county jail had been a truly barbaric place: a single shed with massive beams to which prisoners were attached by chains. But the new facility, though adorned with a costly brick facade one might expect to find on a hotel, *was* still a jail, reportedly "the safest between San Francisco and the City of Mexico, and people came many miles to gaze in awe and wonder upon its impressive walls."[42]

The interior of the building, dimly lit by candles or lanterns, was divided into a series of cells separated by adobe walls with barred doors and windows. The jailor, who was nicknamed Turnkey, probably went about his job in a perfunctory way, without much sympathy for those he put behind bars, but he may have been adverse to keeping women and children locked up—though this might well have been necessary sometimes to ensure their protection.[43] The number of jail cells is not known, but, considering the number of cowboys and miners arrested and thrown in the hoosegow each week, six or eight cells would have been required.

Inside the cells would have been bunk beds, or cots, and chamber pots—sparse furnishings, but not shocking to people who had traveled in covered wagons and lived in tents. But all the cells, save those occupied by Hannah, Biddy, and the children, were empty, their previous occupants released or removed. Most would have simply been let go, handed their boots and gun belts, and told to get out of town. There may have been a cell or two in the sheriff's office where the worst inmates or those who had to be kept in custody, pending trial, were held. However, during the time that the former slaves were housed in the county jail, the miners, cowboys, and farmers who poured into Los Angeles on the weekends to get drunk, perhaps find a willing woman, and shoot up the town had a welcome reprieve from incarceration.

The logistics of caring for the daily needs of two women and ten children would have been considered somewhat daunting. Access to exercise or recreation was probably unfeasible, but they would have had to be fed, presumably three meals a day; given clothing, assuming they had come only with what they wore; and provided with means of personal hygiene, including soap, water, and a place to bathe.

Whatever assurances they were offered concerning their accommodations the night of their arrival, though, Biddy, Hannah, and the children would have been justifiably frightened and indignant. "[T]hey could not comprehend the reason," Judge Hayes reports in his article.[44] Indeed, how could anyone explain why they were to be imprisoned while the man accused of wanting to harm them was allowed to go free? And when would they be released? Would days overlap one another, one week flowing into the next, while they sat on cots behind barred doors and windows?

We might well imagine, too, the consternation and inner turmoil of Benjamin Hayes when he learned that one of his new charges in the county jail was within days of delivering her eighth child.

The preliminary hearing for the case against Robert Mays Smith was probably held in Judge Hayes's chambers.[45] It was New Year's Day; a larger room would not have been necessary because those in attendance would have been few: the judge, Sheriff David Alexander, Robert Mays Smith, and perhaps his wife, Rebecca. At the hearing, Smith would have been called upon to respond under oath to the charges in the petition for the writ of habeas corpus, permitting the court to determine whether a cause of action existed and merited a trial. If Smith had agreed with the charges in the petition or had indicated he did not mean to contest them, he would have been free to go on his way—without, of course, Biddy, Hannah, or their children. Smith's deposition, however, clearly refuted the allegations against him and asserted he meant to contest them.

Hayes would later report that Smith's return to the writ alleged that in Mississippi he had owned Hannah, Biddy, and their children as slaves, that "they left Mississippi with their own consent, rather than remain there," that subsequent children were born to the two mothers, and that "he has supported them ever since, subjecting them to no greater control than his own children, and not holding them as slaves; it is his intention to remove to Texas and take them with him; Hannah and her children are well disposed to remain with him and the petition was filed without their knowledge and consent."[46]

Having received Smith's response, Judge Hayes set a date for the trial and perhaps advised Smith to retain an attorney. One other critical matter was apparently brought to the judge's attention before adjournment that morning: Hannah's condition. As the purpose of the hearing was to ascertain the response of the accused, Biddy, Hannah, and their children would have remained in protective custody in the county jail. Likely as not, Judge Hayes had not visited them. As a judge, he would not have risked prejudicing himself by interviewing them outside of court before any legal proceedings had commenced. It is probable, then, that he first learned of Hannah's condition from Robert Mays Smith or Rebecca, but he might also have heard from Dr. A. H. Cooper, a local physician who would testify later in the trial and may have visited the women and children in jail. At any rate, Hayes's response was immediate: he ordered her release. However, given Hayes's characteristic circumspection, Hannah would have first been brought from the county jail, across an alley from the courthouse. Hayes could have stepped across that same alley himself to see how close she was to delivering, but would have wanted to witness her response to being reunited with the Smiths.

Apparently, Judge Hayes was reassured enough by what he saw, and also released into Smith's custody Hannah's twelve-year-old son, Lawrence, presumably to be of assistance to his mother.[47] However, because one of Hannah's older daughters would have been of greater help during childbirth, we might well read into Hayes's choice more evidence of his astute forethought: if the Smiths tried to leave California with Hannah and her newborn child, Lawrence was someone who could *run for help*.

On New Year's Day, while the pueblo of Los Angeles was recuperating from the celebrations of the night before, a pregnant woman and a boy climbed into a waiting wagon with a middle-aged man and woman. The wagon rambled down the dusty road. Robert Mays Smith apparently took Hannah, his wife, and the younger children back to the ranch on Jumuba. Hannah gave birth to her eighth child, a son named Henry, four days later. That afternoon of the hearing, Benjamin Hayes walked home to the new house filled with boxes and trunks where he, Emily, and Chauncey had moved that morning. Biddy, in a jail cell with nine bewildered children in adjoining cells, waited for the trial to begin.

A baker, a white man who had a shop near the home of Robert and Winnie Owens, a free black family residing in Los Angeles, recalled that due to the pressing circumstances of the habeas corpus case, Judge Hayes convened court on New Year's Day and that people of all colors and classes flocked to the courthouse.[48] Court documents prove that the trial actually began two weeks later, on January 14, 1856. The baker was obviously confusing the start of the trial with the initial hearing. What might also be deemed obvious from the baker's account is the notoriety the Smith case had attracted in the two weeks since Hannah, Biddy, and their children had first been brought under protective custody. Even the distant *New York Times* would carry an account of the trial. After the trial, Judge Hayes would note how he felt the pressure of "public opinion," indicating that the case was widely discussed and probably eagerly attended.[49]

Clearly, word had gotten out, and on this otherwise undistinguished Monday morning, the courtroom gallery would have been packed as the trial was called to order and the complaint against Robert Mays Smith was read. The tension in the courtroom would have been palpable between Smith and his attorney, Alonzo Thomas, seated on Judge Hayes's right and the individuals to his left: Biddy and the attorney for her and the indisposed Hannah and their children, along with the affiant who had originally sworn the petition for the writ of habeas corpus against Smith.

In his account of the trial for the *Los Angeles Star,* published a few weeks after the trial, Hayes quotes directly from the reading of the complaint that morning: "In this case the benefit of the write of habeas corpus is sought for fourteen persons of color, namely—HANNAH (aged 34 years) and BIDDY (38), and their children, to wit:—Ann (17), Lawrence (12), Nathaniel (10), Jane (8), Charles (6), Marion (4), Martha (2), an infant boy (2 weeks)—all children of Hannah; Mary (2 years), child of said Ann; Ellen (17), Ann (12), Harriet (8)—children of Biddy."[50]

> The petition states that they are free, having been brought into the State of California in the year 1851 (in the Fall, it seems,) by Robert Smith, who has resided here with them ever since, and now holds them in servitude, and is about to remove to the State of Texas, carrying them with him into slavery. The defendant's return to the writ alleges that in Mississippi he owned, as slaves, Hannah, Ann, Lawrence and Nathaniel, and Biddy and her three children above named; he left that State for Utah Territory; Jane born in Missouri (Illinois?), Charles in Utah Territory, and the other four in California; they left Mississippi with their own consent, rather than remain there, and he has supported them ever since, subjecting them to no greater control than his own children, and not holding them as slaves; it is his intention to remove to Texas and take them with him; Hannah and her children are well disposed to remain with him and the petition was filed without their knowledge and consent; It is understood between Smith and said persons that they will return to said State of Texas with him voluntarily, as a portion of his family.

However succinctly these facts might have been stated for the record, it was already evident to Judge Hayes, only two weeks after the preliminary hearing with Smith, that this case was anything but clear-cut. Hayes's own biases concerning the matter had been in play from the start, and he admitted as much in his article in the *Los Angeles Star* and later in the *Sacramento Daily Democratic State Journal:*

> Born and educated in one Slave State and having always resided in another, until I came to California, I ought to appreciate the kindly attachment that grows up between master and slave, which is often warmer and more durable with the master than with the slave. Give [Smith] credit for this, meanwhile where is SELF INTEREST? Without an over share of the world's goods (it seems, some five hundred dollars and an outfit) and his own white family to maintain, is not there a stronger impulse, beneath his "Patriarchal" complacency, to incur the cost and toil of taking this number of negroes through a wilderness of two thousand miles? Still, it is not so important to distinguish the predominant motive, as to see THE INEVITABLE RESULT OF HIS CONDUCT ON THEIR RIGHTS. Even without a bad intention, a man is not to be permitted to do a positive injury to others, when it can be prevented.

Regardless of Smith's motives or his relationship to Hannah, Biddy, and the children, Hayes concludes, the result of Smith's move to Texas would be an intolerable reinstatement of slave status upon them. That point having been resolved in his mind, Judge Hayes suggests he was then able to direct more scrutiny toward the character of Robert Mays Smith himself, exclusive of any affinity for Smith's regional identity.

In his response under oath to the charges in the petition of habeas corpus, Smith had alleged that the petition was filed without the knowledge, permission, or consent of Hannah or Biddy. In other words, neither of the women, he maintained, had seen cause to bring this action themselves—a fact that should speak volumes about a willing, even welcomed, relationship to Smith and his family.

Judge Hayes reports what his rebuttal to Smith's contention had been; that if this were true, it was up to Smith to prove it "affirmatively" by calling upon Hannah and Biddy in court or by bringing in other witnesses. "If other proof existed—that they had ever once intimated to one human being their dissent from the petition, or even their willingness for a moment to go with [Smith]—such proof he ought to have offered, and, if it existed, no doubt would have produced it. Where were the numerous members of his family, or his neighbors?" Hayes asks, writing of the trial in retrospect.

That Smith would not be able to produce such testimony might, in and of itself, have weighed heavily in Judge Hayes's verdict. However, as Hayes writes, "subsequent events indicate[d] it would have been exceedingly dangerous to have attempted the proof by such witnesses, with an exercise of the right of cross examination that belongs to the vilest criminal." As Hayes insinuates, certain occurrences during the trial and following his verdict heightened his suspicions that, despite Smith's protests and disavowals, his actions and intentions were not purely innocent or altruistic. And as day two of the trial dawned, the dark underbelly of the case was about to come into full view.

One obvious indication of the unusual and incendiary nature of the suit against Robert Mays Smith is indicated by the names *missing* from the trial record and the larger historical record as well. Although the alarm concerning Smith's departure from California was likely raised by a person of color, the identity of that informant has never been confirmed. The law against Negro testimony in California at this time was confusing and contradictory. A person of color could swear out a complaint against a white person, but could not testify in open court against a white person, in either a criminal or a civil case.[51] Therefore, in order for a complaint to have any meaning, it had to be supported, if not brought, by a white person. A third party—that is, a white member of the community—would have had to agree to sign the petition for the writ of habeas corpus on behalf of the petitioners, Hannah, Biddy, and the children. Unfortunately, the name of that individual, the affiant to the writ, as well as the name of the person or persons who subsidized payment of the petitioners' attorney, if different, are unknown. Those identities and that of the attorney have been deliberately withheld from the trial records.

The reason for this becomes obvious in light of the events of January 15, 1855. On that Tuesday morning, the second day of the trial, Judge Hayes entered the courtroom, took his place on the bench, and was confronted with a disturbing anomaly. Biddy, who the previous day had been seated between the affiant to the writ and her attorney, now sat alone at the plaintiffs' table, the chairs on either side of her empty.

Alonzo Thomas, Smith's attorney, introduced an immediate motion for dismissal, informing Judge Hayes that the petitioners' attorney had been discharged. Everything was explained in a note passed to him that morning: "I, as attorney on the opposite side, being no longer authorized to prosecute the writ, and being discharged by the same the parties who are responsible to me, decline further to prosecute the matter." Both the motion and the note—first read in court then carried to the judge's bench for examination—flabbergasted Hayes. He asked Biddy if she had discharged her attorney. No. He asked her if her attorney had spoken to her before he quit. No. Clearly, she did not understand what had transpired.

We can imagine Judge Hayes's anger. Did the petitioners' lawyer truly think he could just quit the case, without explanation or even informing his clients? Regardless, whatever the attorney *thought* was proper was not going to go unchallenged. Benjamin promptly denied Thomas's motion to dismiss the case, adjourned court, and issued subpoenas for both of the missing men. That afternoon, Sheriff Alexander and his deputies would have scoured the streets and back alleys of Los Angeles. On Wednesday, perhaps aided by informants, they located the recalcitrant attorney.

On Thursday morning, he was delivered to Judge Hayes. He had quit at the request of the affiant, he said, who had been threatened with physical harm by some unnamed person. According to the attorney, the affiant had offered him one hundred dollars to drop the suit, which was in addition to the one hundred already paid for his services. The lawyer had not advised his clients or consulted with them concerning their wishes; he had not thought it necessary.

There is no evidence that the affiant to the petition was ever found or testified about the threat directed at him. By Thursday, he was probably as far away from Los Angeles as a whipped horse could travel, and perhaps Judge Hayes elected not to waste resources trying to find him. The affiant was not, it was true, actually a party to the suit, despite his signature on the petition for the writ and the legal fees he had paid or channeled for another benefactor to the cause. The trial could proceed without him—but not without a lawyer for the petitioners, Hannah and Biddy and their children.

"Any citizen can understand how disastrous it might be to his rights and interests, in our Courts, if such a precedent in an attorney were approved and practised on," Benjamin noted concerning the situation.

> No attorney can desert his clients at his own pleasure, without good reason therefore and fair notice to them. The Payment of a fee by a third person does not constitute him a party to the suit. However charitably inclined to aid the real parties in this proceeding, the affiant was not one of the parties, and had no more to do with it than any other stranger, particularly after the writ had been executed, the parties all before the Court, and the cause in progress of trial.

Having questioned the petitioners' attorney—and informing him that he was obligated to continue on the case—Judge Hayes turned his attention to Robert Mays Smith. Had he had been involved in threatening the affiant of the petition? Smith's lawyer, on behalf of his client, strenuously denied any involvement. Nevertheless, Judge Hayes was skeptical. "It is possible—yet strange, if possible—that the defendant had nothing to do with (to say the least) an ill-advised stratagem to frustrate the writ of HABEAS CORPUS." Hayes later wrote that Smith's attorney denied that his client had anterior knowledge of it. "He had the benefit of the denial, in one view that it might have been taken of it. In itself—if [Smith] were believed to have been privy to it—the act would have been incompatible with an innocent intention. It has too much the air of force. It gives room for a painful suspicion."

One of the oddest aspects of the trial is where Judge Hayes did and did not apparently direct his suspicions about behind-the-scenes machinations. Robert Mays Smith's affiliation with the LDS Church is never mentioned—not in the legal records or in newspaper accounts of the trial—and in fact, it seems to have been strenuously avoided. This seems curious, particularly in view of the mystery surrounding the affiant to the petition for the writ of habeas corpus and the means by which funds were secured to retain the petitioners' attorney.

Many of the Mormon leaders in California were outraged about Smith's break with the LDS Church and even saw to it, a few weeks after the habeas corpus trial, that Smith was excommunicated. The Smiths and their slaves had traveled with a Mormon company across the breadth of the country, lived among them for more than a decade, and, in California, the Mormon men had elected Smith to the church's High Council. The affiliation—and its dissolution—had been significant. And just as there were possibly members of the Mormon community interested in protecting Hannah, Biddy, and their children, there were perhaps others more intent on striking a blow in retaliation for Smith's defection from their ranks. They may have helped alert the sheriff, provided the money to fund the lawyer, and found an affiant to put forth the original petition.

It is unlikely that a man as astute as Benjamin Hayes would overlook such possibilities or think Smith's past relationship to the Mormon Church was not germane to the case. And it is nearly unthinkable that he did not know Robert Mays Smith had been a Mormon. The logical conclusion would seem to be that Hayes was diligent in protecting the church from any association with the trial—and the complicated local politics and allegiances would have been part, at least, of the reason for doing so. He had been elected district judge for the counties of Los Angeles, San Diego, and San Bernardino, and the Mormons of San Bernardino constituted a formidable voting bloc.

As far as the progress and outcome of the trial was concerned, Hayes might have been in a double bind. The twin specters of bribery and intimidation had manifested, but he was powerless to exorcise them. The peril they posed would have been frighteningly apparent to a man of Judge Hayes's sensibilities and ambitions. Best, perhaps, to simply pretend they did not exist; best to focus on matters he could do something about—such as this matter of Hannah and Biddy and their children before him.

FOUR

Meeting Mississippi

IN THE UNIVERSITY DISTRICT IN SEATTLE, not far from my home, was a small branch of the Family History Library of the Church of Jesus Christ of Latter-day Saints. The first time I visited it, a few months after the disturbing trip to Los Angeles, I was relieved to continue my research in a building where I was not greeted by a security guard. Still, I approached the library worried. Like most people, I had a headful of preconceptions about Mormons—most of them casually acquired and unexamined—and clouding my focus on this day at least were my concerns about the church's controversial relationship with people of the African American race.

Until 1978, when the LDS Church announced a "revelation on priesthood," black males had not been eligible to hold the priesthood, a lay-clerical role crucial to all devout Mormon men. The proscription was not to be found in the church's central doctrinal text, *The Book of Mormon;* in fact, 2 Nephi 26:33 states, "And he inviteth them all to come unto him and partake of his goodness; and he denieth none that come unto him, black and white, bond and free, male and female; and he remembereth the heathen, and all are alike unto God." The scriptural justification was based, rather, on abstruse interpretations of references in the Bible to the mark of Cain and the curse of Ham. According to the church, during the war in Heaven between Jehovah and Lucifer, some preexisting spirits had been "less valiant" than others. God had decided, therefore, that certain of his children, presumably the "less valiant," those destined to have darker skin, should not be eligible to hold the priesthood during their mortal lives.[1]

The issue of blacks and the priesthood seems not to have been directly addressed during the founding of the church, although the early leaders apparently shared prejudices against black people with other Americans of the period. The subject came to the forefront after the fledgling church's move from New England to Missouri, a battleground between slave owners and abolitionists.

In 1833, the Mormon press in Missouri published an article about the immigration of free Negroes to Missouri that was misconstrued as an invitation for free Negroes to become Mormons. This led to anti-Mormon activity that church leaders sought to quell, saying they had no desire for Negroes to become members of the Mormon Church. This position, inadvertently reached or stated, solidified during subsequent debates about slavery.

In 1852, after the Mormons had established themselves in the territory of Utah, President Brigham Young spoke plainly: "[A]ny man having one drop of the seed of [Cain] in him cannot hold the priesthood and if no other Prophet ever spake it before I will say it now in the name of Jesus Christ I know it is true and others know it."[2]

The black people residing within what came to be Utah Territory in 1850 were unaffected by Lincoln's Emancipation Proclamation, issued on January 1, 1863, which declared free all slaves in territories in rebellion against the Federal government, but the subsequent Thirteenth Amendment, ratified on December 6, 1865, extending freedom to slaves throughout the entire United States, removed any doubt as to their status, if confusion still lingered. This change or clarification of legal status did not alter the Mormon Church's position regarding blacks and the priesthood, which Mormons claimed to be a matter of spiritual, not human, law.

Subsequent leadership upheld Brigham Young's pronouncement,

but as the church intensified its missionary work nationally and globally during the twentieth century, membership among peoples of color increased exponentially. It was not until the 1960s during the Civil Rights movement, however, that intense public censure was brought to bear on the Mormon Church.

According to Armand L. Mauss, in *Neither White nor Black: Mormon Scholars Confront the Race Issue in a Universal Church,* "At the national convention of the NAACP July 1965, a strongly worded resolution condemning the Mormon 'doctrine of non-white inferiority' was introduced by the Salt Lake and Ogden Chapters and passed by the entire convention."[3]

By 1969, the scrutiny was causing church leadership to publicly address its traditional relationship to people of color. On December 15, President Hugh B. Brown summarized the LDS Church's position relating to the exclusion of blacks from the priesthood: "[Founder of the church] Joseph Smith and all succeeding presidents of the Church have taught that Negroes, while spirit children of a common Father, and the progeny of our earthly parents Adam and Eve, were not yet prepared to receive the priesthood, for reasons which we believe are known to God, but which He has not made fully known to man." But, quoting previous president David O. McKay, Brown offered this assurance: "Sometime in God's eternal plan, the Negro will be given the right to hold the priesthood."[4]

Many LDS scholars and innumerable thoughtful members continued to agonize over what they perceived as an indefensible aspect of their faith, but remained steadfast to the church, hoping for the promised divine reconciliation. Nearly ten years later, on June 8, 1978, Brown's successor, President Spencer W. Kimball, announced that God had at last sent the long-awaited word: "He has heard our prayers, and by revelation has confirmed that the long-promised day has come. All worthy male members of the Church may be ordained to the priesthood without regard for race or color."[5]

As I entered the LDS Family History library, I was recalling that fewer than twenty years had passed since the revelation abolishing the church's exclusionary practices toward blacks; it was not enough time, I reasoned, to expect much more than a chilly reception to my questions about a Mormon slave owner named Robert Mays Smith and the records the church might hold concerning him, his family, and their life in Mississippi.

I was wrong. The volunteer librarian, a woman in her thirties with thick glasses, was kind, competent, and amusing. She apologized for her slowness in finding books and citations, explaining she was going blind. Nothing could be done, she said; she had to learn to live with it. I asked timorously about records, such as bills of sale, relating to slavery, and we worked together, looking for leads for a while before the librarian asked what I was researching.

At first, I was evasive, mentioning Robert Smith's conversion to Mormonism in Mississippi and his trek across the country. I watched her I spoke. She listened intently, without a trace of defensiveness, and soon I found myself elaborating, telling her about Hannah and Biddy and the events that led to a declaration of their freedom in California. Her face followed my voice like a plant seeking light.

"They were free?" she asked, then spoke the word again as though rejoicing at the end to an interminable night: "Free!"

From the plane window, the valley of the Great Salt Lake was a wide white bowl surrounded by snowcapped peaks. The airport was filled with exuberant, brightly clothed travelers who wrestled luggage and skis from carrels and then climbed onto shuttles, also brightly colored, that would take them to resorts. I hoisted my single, well-worn navy satchel onto my shoulder and climbed onto a waiting bus. Inside were middle-aged women and men whose suitcases, like mine, were filled with tablets and books. I was an interloper of sorts on this tour of genealogists from Seattle, taking advantage of a cheap airfare and low hotel rates; my interest was not genealogy, per se, but in the vast holdings at the LDS Church's main Family History Library and its history department esteemed by researchers around the world.

The church's interest in preserving genealogical and other pertinent historical records stems from its doctrine that the dead as well as the living may receive the gospel of Jesus Christ. Accordingly, church members are encouraged to identify their ancestors who may then be brought into the fold by the proxy performance of the ordinance of baptism in one of the LDS Church's temples. Nonbelievers, however, are welcome to use the resources amassed for their own purposes. The benefit has been immense for historians and many others worldwide.

In early 2001, after eleven years of work, the church released a CD-ROM holding cross-indexed names of and personal information about seventy-two thousand depositors to the Freedman's Savings and Trust Company, an institution established in 1865 to protect the savings of newly freed slaves.

When I visited Salt Lake, work on this project was just beginning, and it would be several years before I learned of it—or owned a computer with a CD port, for that matter. I had come prepared to do research the old, painstaking way. I hoped to find books or microfilmed original records relating to the acquisition of Biddy and Hannah by the Smiths, resources not available in the tiny Seattle branch of the LDS library.

When I signed up for the tour, I was told I would have a roommate, and my only requirement had been that she not talk too much. Now, in the hotel room, with its twin beds, end tables, lamps, and dresser with mirror, I learned that my roommate was a woman in her late sixties—nice, orderly, and pleasant—who was almost deaf. When she wore her hearing aids, in both her ears, she had minimal hearing, but most of the time the devices remained on the dresser and no sound could reach her.

The first night we talked a little, her eyes following my lips, and learned names, where we lived, and what we were each up to on this trip to Utah. Genealogy was her passion, and coming to Salt Lake was the apogee of a lifetime of research. I tried to make conversation, until she told me she was perfectly happy sharing a room in silence, if that was all right with me. Chastened (ironically enough by a rooming preference I myself had stipulated), I shut my mouth. After that, our communication consisted of smiles when we passed on our way to and from the twin beds. The deaf woman went to bed early, turning to face the wall. The contours of her body under the thin white blanket reminded me of a winter landscape.

Thus began a lonely time. The other tour members, who belonged to an association in Seattle, did their research in the Family History Center, while I went daily to the Church History Department in another building in Temple Square. The weather was bitterly cold. The sidewalks were snowpacked, and grime-laced piles of snow lined the streets. Sometimes the weather warmed a bit, but then a front would arrive, and with it a wind driving flakes that stung my cheeks. My days were spent scouring books and staring at microfilm; at night, I would lie on my twin bed in the dim and silent room, feeling as though I were caught in a child's glass globe, sealed off from color and sound, surrounded by a relentless, swirling snowstorm.

And so it was, spending hour upon hour alone in my own company, in a place where I might have expected to claim some moral superiority with regard to issues of race, I began to question my own attitudes and behaviors. I began to confront my memories of a trip south the previous summer. I began thinking about Mississippi.

The Mississippi State Archives are located in a cluster of buildings, part of a municipal complex in downtown Jackson that serves various needs of the state's citizenry. At the top of a steep flight of stairs, I found a large room dominated by bookshelves and study tables that, although it was still early in the morning, were already occupied by several dozen people: a handful of older men, most of the rest middle-aged women.

At a table against a back wall was a young black woman. She sat with both elbows on the table, as if she was hunkered over a plate of food. On each side of her, taking up most of the table, were books neatly stacked, not toppling as mine would soon be. Maybe, I thought, she was searching through slave records—which was what I intended to do. I joined her at her table, pulled back a chair, deposited my books and papers as neatly as I could, and sat down. She did not look up. She was tall and thin, but large-boned, with square hands and broad wrists. Her shoulder-length hair was straight and pinned to one side with a barrette. Several times she stood to retrieve or return a book, and always she ignored me.

Must be from up north, I thought, then smiled, aware that I was condemning myself: my own southern-bred manners had long ago evaporated, and I knew that, like her, I broadcast my Yankee education with impatient gestures, rudely direct questions, and indifference to my effect upon others.

In the restroom of the archives, I washed my hands, then cleaned and dried my eyeglasses. Research was a dirty, sticky business. The door opened and my table mate entered. I ripped off a paper towel.

"How's it going?" I asked.

She stopped on her way to a stall. "How is what going?" she asked.

"Your research. What you're working on."

"Oh." She seemed to hunt for an answer. "I just started."

"Are you researching your family?" I asked.

I watched her face in the mirror as she turned. "Who else would I be researching?" she jabbed.

I rubbed paper over my dry hands. "It could be a job," I said. "Some people do it for other people."

She lowered her head and gave me a look. "I'm only interested in my own people." She entered a stall, shut the door, and locked it.

"Good luck," I said. I crumpled the paper towel and aimed it at the waste can. Two points—if anyone was keeping score.

On my way to the swimming pool one afternoon at my hotel in Jackson, I met a woman in the elevator.

"Oh, you can't be going to swim in that pool!" she said. "My husband's lawyer has an office in that building across the park, and he says at night all the black boys who work in the hotel go up there and swim and they do the most awful things. I wouldn't be caught dead submerging myself in that dirty water."

I told her she should tell the hotel management if she believed the pool was unclean. She said she had, and, of course, they denied it vehemently. I had shrugged and gone on up to the roof. One of the reasons I had chosen to stay in this ziggurat of a hotel—modern, many-storied, sterile—was to be able to swim.

Now I sat on my towel beside the pool, making small circles in the cool water with my hand. *Why don't you dive in? If that nasty woman had said some white boys peed in the pool, would you have believed that? But maybe the young black men had been mistreated by the hotel management or its guests, and this was their way of getting back at them. Oh, come on! Why would anyone pollute water in which they themselves swim? Maybe they don't care. Go ahead. Stand up. Resist. Be brave. Dive in.*

The ripples left my fingertips and moved one by one across the surface of the pool.

A half block from the state archives was a cafeteria that served wonderful, hearty southern cooking. Many of the researchers went there during the lunch hour when the archives were closed. I filled my tray with dishes and carried it to an empty table. The cafeteria was busy. Most of the tables were occupied, and the people eating were about equally divided between blacks and whites. I had begun my meal when I saw the young black woman from the archives come in. Her eyes swept past me, but I knew she had seen me. I looked around and saw that she and I seemed to be the only unpaired people in the place, except for an old white man sitting at a table by the cash register. He was directing a rambling monologue at the waitress behind the cash register. My table mate considered the old man, then looked back at my table without meeting my eyes, as though trying to decide which of us was the more distasteful prospect. I had expended my ambassadorial efforts in the rest room and was not about to be rebuffed again. I stared at her, letting her know I saw her dilemma and was not about to solve it by sending out waves of welcome. Apparently, she took my stare as a challenge because she came to my table with her tray.

An elaborate pantomime in our strange and intricate little war followed in which she asked, with a raised eyebrow and a tilt of her head, if the seat across from me was occupied. I, in turn, told her with a twitch of shoulders—not quite a shrug—that as far as I knew it was free, but I was not eager for her to sit there.

She sat. "How is your research going?"

I looked up as she poured cream from a small tin pitcher into her coffee and stirred. *Oh, I'm easy! Smile at me and I'm grateful. Pat my head and I'll roll over and waggle my paws.* I smiled. "I'm digging dirt," I said. "Dry, sun-baked, rock-hard dirt."

The woman laughed. "Don't I know," she said.

And we were off. For almost an hour, we commiserated about the difficulties of research, how it is like shifting through tons of pitchblende for a pinch of radium.

Her name was Brenda. She was from Chicago. Her mother lived in Pascagoula down on the Gulf. Brenda was allowing herself three days on her way home from visiting her mother to look in the state archives for information about her family's roots. Her grandmother, also in

Pascagoula, was still alive and had spoken of aunts, uncles, and cousins.

"That's where you were raised?" I asked. "Pascagoula?"

Her eyes went flat. "No," she said. "I never lived there. Not as I can remember. My father divorced my mother when I was five and took me to Chicago with him. My grandmother, his mother, raised me."

"But you come to visit your mother," I said.

"Now I do," Brenda said.

I sat thinking about this maze of relationships.

"What about you?" Brenda asked. "Your folks from Mississippi?"

We were standing beside the table, shouldering the straps of our purses, getting ready to leave.

"No," I said reluctantly. "I'm a writer."

On our way back to the archives, I told her about the book I hoped to write.

"I wondered why you were rummaging around in black history. Didn't think you were looking for kin." Her voice had changed as subtly and surely as an autumn day, still warm as summer, but carrying within it the coming frost.

One morning, on another day in the archives, I took a break from the small print of books, the illegibility of microfilm, and the confinement of walls. Brenda and I had been keeping some distance, by unspoken agreement, since our lunch in the cafeteria. I stood on the front steps of the library and looked out upon the tree-lined streets and old buildings of Jackson. Behind me, I heard a step and turned. Brenda had followed me out. She stood behind and above me, looking out, like me, at the town.

"Taking a break from the book?" she asked.

I knew what was coming as certainly as if a weather vane had swung to indicate a storm. I said nothing, just waited.

Her eyes took on a furious glint. "You have no right," she said. "It isn't your history to write. There are hundreds of books you could research. Pick other people, white people, your own!"

"I can write about anyone and anything I want," I said. "That is my freedom as a writer."

"So you come over to our side of town and find yourself a pair of black women with a spicy story to make some money off of? You're still doing it—using, abusing, and tossing away. First it was our bodies. Now it's our stories."

"Brenda," I said. "I'm just researching a trial that happened a long time ago. Some of the people were white and some were black. I just want to find out what happened and why."

"Well," Brenda said. "Your troubles are ended. You can save yourself all the time and trouble. I can tell you why. I can tell you why right now."

I picked up the gauntlet. "Why?"

She hissed. "You're too damned dumb to talk to. There's no chance at all that you could ever comprehend anything at all about my people." She whipped around and was up the steps before I could respond.

Behind me, in the state archives named for her, hung a portrait of the famous Mississippi novelist Eudora Welty. Most every day I found myself, chin on my palm, staring at it. In *The Optimist's Daughter*, Welty's protagonist, Laurel, burns her parents' love letters after their deaths—a desecration that upset me, as both a historian and a writer, although I understand that respect is sometimes more appropriate than research, that there are things better left alone, times when one must admit an inability to comprehend or appreciate and walk away, withholding what cannot, or should not, be said.[6]

But, as I watched Brenda's retreating figure, I wanted to explain that sometimes respect is a matter of finding and making known what would otherwise be lost or remain hidden, that sometimes stories choose us and do not ask for credentials and references—only that we be willing to learn them by heart, to tell them as honestly as we can.

My last evening in Jackson. Towel over my arm, I stood in my swimming suit beside the hotel pool that, since my last trip to the roof earlier in the week, had been drained. A maintenance man in yellow overalls was standing in the bottom working.

"What happened?" I asked. "Are you cleaning it?"

"They're closing it for the season. People been complaining."

His voice, amplified by the empty concrete hole, seemed to carry the force of an accusation.

"Sorry," the man said. "Looks like you were all set for a swim."

"Yes," I said.

On my way back to the elevator, I took one last look at the rooftops and treetops of Mississippi.

—

I had spent the morning in the LDS History Department, reading diaries of the pioneers who had come to Utah in 1847 and 1848. Some were on microfilm, but others I was allowed to read in their original state, either as loose pages or within old bindings. As I read, I was amazed by the men and women who had taken time from the arduous work of traveling west to record their observations, hopes, and prayers. Jane Manning James, who had been a servant in New York State, escaped her lascivious master and literally walked to Nauvoo, most of the way on bare feet. A young man named Robert Campbell had been with Robert Mays Smith on the exploration trip to southern Utah. He kept a leather-bound journal—the leather discolored and brittle now—and on the journal's inner covers sketched petroglyphs he had seen along the way.[7] Wrapped in a blanket covered in snow, he wrote one entry holding the book above him so his writing would not get wet. Later pioneers had come to Salt Lake Valley pushing their piled belongings on handcarts.

The history department closed for lunch, and people left, most to go to the cafeteria in the building, but I headed out into the driving snow, protecting my legal pads and copies by shielding them inside my coat.

I knew from information received from a descendant of Robert Mays Smith that Robert and his wife, Rebecca, had been born in Edgefield, South Carolina, and that his wife's father was John Dorn. That afternoon, in the Family History Center, looking through the Miscellaneous Probate Records for Edgefield County, South Carolina, I found a microfilm of the contents of John Dorn Sr.'s probate file. First I read his will, saw that Rebecca Smith was listed as one of his heirs, and, on another page, saw that a bequest had been made to Robert M. Smith.[8] At that point, my heart started pounding. After John Dorn's death, an inventory was made of his worldly goods, including household items, farm equipment, and—I pushed the slow forward button, and the film creaked to another frame—slaves! I put my glasses atop my head—as I always do—and leaned forward to squint at the screen. Beneath thirty pounds of lard selling for 8 cents were listed Negroes: Joe, $700; Wade, $575; Jane, $600; Frank, $550; a name I could not read, $575; Robert, $600; and Hannah and child Nelson, $600.

I read the entry over several times before I believed what I saw. Hannah! It really was Hannah. I knew it because she was listed with Nelson, her baby, and the name below hers was Lawrence, her first-born son. I knew their names from Judge Hayes's verdict in the habeas corpus case. Oh, Hannah, after all these miles and months—was it years yet?—I found you!

I immediately knew two things: that Hannah and her children had belonged to the Dorn family before they came to live with the Smiths and—I scanned the names of the remaining slaves—that Biddy was not a Dorn slave and, therefore, was not Hannah's sister. The inscription on the wall was wrong and my intuition about it right. I might have gloated, but my curiosity was already compelling me on. How did it happen that Hannah left South Carolina to go to Mississippi to live with her dead master's daughter?

I scrolled past the probate pages until I came to a black screen with nine irregular white rectangles like pages torn from a tiny notebook fluttering over a dark canyon. At first, I did not know what I was looking at. The white rectangles had individual names upon them: Robert Dorn, Robert Smith, Alfred Turner, and other Dorns. The next frame again had nine white rectangles on a black background, and on each of these rectangles were written the names of several people and beside each name a price.

These, I realized, were the torn slips of paper put into a hat that the heirs to John Dorn's estate had drawn, slips of paper with the names and prices of slaves on the Dorn plantation, and—I touched the slow reverse button to pull up a former frame—on the back of each paper was written the name of the person who had drawn that slip. With a bit of going back and forth, I could, by matching the irregular edges of the rectangles, determine which person had drawn which slaves.

I was as delighted as if I had solved a great mystery. Then an uneasy feeling moved in. For some reason I was frightened—had the kind of dread when you feel something bad is about to happen, or has already happened and you have not yet turned the corner to confront it. Names in a hat. Heirs drawing slaves. I knew all that. Why was I

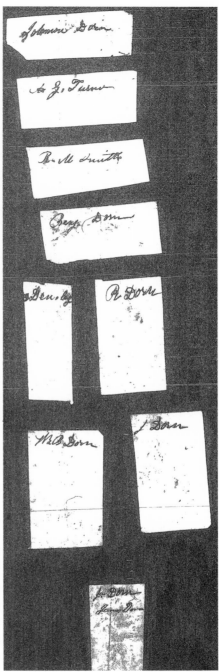

Lottery slips by which the slaves of John Dorn (listed with their assigned values on the front sides) were originally to be divided among Dorn's heirs "in equal lots," according to his will. The names of the heirs who drew the individual slips appear on the backs.

afraid? I rewound the film to the Bill of Allotment and looked at the listing for Hannah's family:

Frank	$650
Hannah	550
Child Nelson	
Lawrence	<u>175</u>
	1,375

The names and prices almost matched those on the slips that had been put into the hat. Then why was I so worried? It hit me. I realized I was missing Hannah's daughter, Ann. She was not listed with her mother, brothers, and Frank, her father. Where was Ann?

I scanned the other names on the Bill of Allotment and found her listed with Robin and John. She was valued at $325, the going rate it seemed (from a comparison of the other slips) for an older child. But why was she not listed with her mother, father, and brothers? I stared at the slips, trying to find a pattern. Most of them, judging by the prices attached to the names, seemed to have a grown male, a grown female, then one or two children, indicated by lesser costs. For an instant I thought, stupidly, "Seems like all slave families had one or two children!"; then I slowly read the totals for each of the slips: $1,375, $1,250, $1,500, $1,350, $1,550, $1,625, $1,600, $1,350, and $1,535. The difference between the highest total and the lowest was only $375—the value of an older child; you could not get much closer than that, not even if you tried.

Oh, dear. I felt it coming. Now I would have to face it. I rewound the film to John Dorn's will, and there it was: "It is my desire, that immediately after my Death, my Executors cause all my Slaves to be loted [sic] out into Nine parcels as nearly Equal as possible." I had read that, but it had not sunk in. I had read it as a provision in a will, a legal paragraph. I was looking at nine slips of papers showing equal lots of humanity—or as equal as manipulation could manage. I imagined two families being weighed on a pair of scales, and one scale sinking slightly lower—a family overloaded by a foot, an arm, a head: just lop it off and pile it on the other scale, and the scales can be in balance. A grotesque image, but wasn't that what I was seeing?

I could not imagine being owned—that sensation was too far from my experience to be real; freedom was as natural and necessary to me as breathing. How could I imagine what it was to live and not breathe? But I could imagine—because I am the mother of a child—how I would feel if she were taken from me, taken for the sole and ridiculous reason of making a column on a slip of paper match a column on another paper.

The bottom line, that was what this—slavery—was about: money! The people writing down and drawing the names were working with numbers—dollars and cents; Ann was not a child to them, not a child who had been a baby. And Hannah was not a woman who had given birth to that baby. They were both commodities and had no more right to claim relationship to each other than two bolls of cotton.

I then had two thoughts—one rueful. I knew I was upset because I could identify with Hannah. The fact that she was a mother with a daughter made it hit home. Always takes self-interest, doesn't it? The only pain we really feel is our own. Accompanying that was the realization that Hannah had not lost her daughter—thank God! Historical accounts show that she left South Carolina with three children—Nelson, Lawrence, and Ann—and when she went to the Smiths in Mississippi, she had all her children with her.

So how had that happened? I scrolled back and forth between images of documents in the probate file and saw the whole scenario: a will ordering slaves to be allotted equally, names drawn from a hat, a dispute between heirs, an arbitration, and, finally, the auction. Instead of having their names drawn out of a hat, the slaves were sold with the rest of the household, like merchandise or livestock.

Sitting there at the microfilm reader in the Family History Center, I tried to imagine the scene in Hannah's family on the auction day, but I could not do it. Images—memories—of my own family kept pushing Hannah's family away. I remembered my father—a sweet, inarticulate man who loved children—who every night would read in a monotone to us, sitting on his lap or draped over his shoulders: Mark Twain, Zane Grey, the Tarzan stories. My mother was a southern belle, pretty, flirty, always giggling; I fought fiercely with my brothers during the day, but at night we would sneak into one bed and swap secrets or tell stories. Had I been Hannah, had I been a slave on the Dorn plantation on auction day, I would have lost them all: my mother, my father, and all of my brothers.

But Hannah kept her daughter. That happened—would it have seemed a gift from God?—out of the blue, on auction day. My finger moving down the inventory of sale stopped at this listing: "Robt. M. Smith to Hanah & 3 children 1210." Robert Dorn, acting as attorney for Robert Mays Smith, had bought Hannah and all of her children. There it was. Proof. I almost relaxed. Ann was safe—still a slave, DeEtta!—but with her mother.

The ominous feeling returned. What was I seeing, or not seeing? Something was in front of my eyes. Hannah, her children—but no husband! The father of her children was not there. Where was Frank? My finger touched the screen of the microfilm reader as it moved up the list of items sold at auction. I came to the list of Robert Dorn's purchases: 5 gallons of peach brandy, a bed quilt, an old broom, the contents of a cupboard, a saddle, a pepper box, a barrel of flour, 198 pounds of fodder, a piece of meat, and nine slaves—human beings!—one of whom was Frank. He had been sold for $800, a good price when I compared it to the prices shown for the other grown men. He must have been young, strong, and healthy. Hannah, in 1846, was twenty-four years old. He would have been about the same age, or maybe a few years older. Hannah's lover, husband, the father of her children.

I sat in front of the microfilm reader and stared at the handwritten inventory of sale. If I was pulled between relief at Ann returning to her mother and horror at Hannah losing her husband, how torn apart Hannah must have been. I tried to imagine how Hannah felt watching her husband being sold away from her and her children. I could not. I tried several times to conjure an image of a man I loved—I could do that—but when it came to imagining me standing there watching buyers bidding for him, my fantasy failed me. There are places of pain I cannot enter. I close down. I have that luxury. Hannah did not. She watched. When Brenda had spoken to me on the steps to the archives in Jackson, Mississippi, I focused on what she said about my not having the right to write the story of the trial, but the last thing she said had passed me by: "There's no chance at all that you could ever comprehend anything at all about my people." Was she right? Did it have to happen to me or mine for me to understand?

In a jumble of despair and satisfaction, I leaned back in my chair and looked around the great room that is the core of the first floor of the Family History Library. Everyone was busily indifferent to my churning emotions. Aisles of bookshelves. Rows of computers. Files. Photocopy machines. A counter where you could request research materials to be brought from "the vault," the legendary indestructible storage chambers in the hills surrounding Salt Lake City.

It was ironic, of course, that I had found in the LDS library evidence that a crime had been committed against a young black woman and her family. Maybe the Mormons did not know what they had in those mountains! Then I realized—of course, they did. They had gone to Edgefield, South Carolina, looked at the court records, and photographed each and every one of them. Because they had done that and because they made their records available to anyone who asked, I could be a witness. I could tell what happened to Hannah's family.

Darkness comes early to Utah in January. By the time I made copies, returned the film, and left the library, it was night. As I ran across the alley that separated my hotel from the Family History Center, snow flurries covered my hair and coat. I was running not to get to light or warmth, but to a telephone. At that moment, I wanted more than anything in the world to hear my daughter's voice.

Almost a decade has passed since I met myself in Mississippi, standing on stairs overlooking Jackson after an argument, hesitating on the lip of a rooftop pool after a warning, but the subconscious, we are told, has no sense of time. Last night I dreamed of diving. I did. I climbed the ladder to the very top of the high dive and felt my way along the handrail. I could feel the panic in my chest. My lungs were heaving, but I could not seem to draw air. Then I felt the rubber of the diving board beneath my bare feet, and I knew I had to let go of the railing. I felt the board wobbling beneath me; I took tiny steps forward until I was a foot away from the end of it. Without my glasses, everything beneath me was blurred. All I knew was that the water was far below and awfully deep. I took another half step forward, so frightened I was sick. *But I cannot close my eyes because I cannot be up here in the dark. I must be somewhere.*

People were watching me. People were starting to jeer. "Jump! Jump!" My toes inched forward, at least I tried to push them forward, but my big toe was reluctant and curled into a knuckle. I willed it straight. *They don't care about me. All they want is action.*

Take one step into space, I told myself. That was the hard part after all, leaving the board. The rest is just falling. I had a flash of me dangling beneath the diving board, my legs wrapped around it, trying to climb back on. A step into nothing. I lifted my arms, turned my thumbs in, and stepped out. My head went down between my arms. I saw it then, rising beneath me, coming up at me like a great white sheet spread over the pool. *It is too late to stop. I have plunged into another page.*

FIVE

The Verdict

THE HABEAS CORPUS CASE, which had begun with a hasty but rou-
tine writ, had become in only two weeks' time a quagmire of peril
and confusion. Robert Mays Smith, to whom Benjamin Hayes had initially extended some benefit of the doubt, even deference, was now the
subject of the judge's suspicion: someone, perhaps Smith, had attempted to intimidate the affiant to the writ and to pay off the petitioners' lawyer. Now the affiant was nowhere to be found, and the
lawyer, who had been ordered to return to the case, was openly hostile to his clients' interests. Mormons, southerners, and people of every
political persuasion were reacting adversely to some aspect of the trial,
and, after only two days of testimony, the proceeding seemed likely to
stall.

According to Smith's return to the writ, Hannah and her children
wanted to remain with him. His response, though, begged the question
concerning Biddy. As Hayes later wrote: "It is remarkable, that the defendant does not pretend that BIDDY and her three children are 'well-

disposed' to remain with him. His own oath expressly excludes them from the (so-called) 'voluntary' arrangement. He could not safely swear as these four. He cannot, therefore, reasonably claim any control over them. If Hannah only is 'well-disposed,' Biddy must be averse and opposed to it, by his own showing."[1]

The most obvious means of determining Hannah's and Biddy's wishes would be to question them directly, but California state law made it illegal for blacks to testify against a white, in this case, a man accused of, in effect, forcing them back into slavery. Yet Hayes was charged with finding the truth and making a righteous ruling. How? On Thursday night, a solution occurred to the judge. Hayes sent messages to two close friends, received their answers, reviewed what he planned to do the next day, and finally got into bed.

The next morning, Hayes announced his intention of interviewing Biddy and the older girls for the purpose of testing their states of mind. These interviews would be held in the judge's chambers, away from open court and Robert Mays Smith—but "with the defendant's acquiescence," Benjamin said suavely. Moreover, he did not require that the plaintiffs' attorney be present, as he himself would be responsible for safeguarding the plaintiffs' rights. Finally, he had asked two "disinterested gentlemen," the Honorable Abel Stearns and Dr. J. B. Winston, to be present during the interviews.[2]

Hayes's maneuver was impressive and effective. Robert Smith had no choice but to consent to the interviews; to demur would have been tantamount to an admission of guilt. Hayes was not asking the plaintiffs to testify illegally; he was merely interviewing them informally. People of color were entitled to state their own feelings, even in California. Because Hannah and Biddy were not being called to testify against Smith, there was no need for them to speak in open court and be subject to cross-examination. By assuming responsibility for their legal rights, Benjamin removed the need for their lawyer's presence—and his influence on them, if his integrity about the outcome of the trial had indeed been compromised. Having two highly respected community leaders participate in the interviews provided Hayes with credible witnesses and some insulation from criticism. For the first time in the trial, and perhaps in their lives, Hannah and Biddy would be able to speak freely.

Biddy and the girls were interviewed separately. In his account of the discussions, Hayes provides the answers they gave, but does not report his questions. However, many of his queries can be inferred. Apparently, he was careful to make the questions pertain to what each knew, had been told, or felt. Not once did he solicit testimony against Smith, although it surfaced through their guarded responses. "Mr. Smith told me I would be just as free in Texas as here" was Biddy's statement, entirely permissible even in California, as she was merely declaring what she had been told. But, she admits, despite Smith's assurances, Biddy had forebodings; she "always feared this trip to Texas since I first heard of it."

Hannah's daughter Ann seeks clarification of this same point. "If I go back to Texas, will I be as free as here?" she asks. Benjamin tells her she might not be, which is careful wording. He knows she will become a slave in Texas, but he is unsure of what her status has been in California.

Biddy and the girls were also asked whether they wished to go to Texas with the Smiths and each told that the minor children would have to stay in California. Biddy's reaction was instantaneous and absolute: "I do not wish to be separated from my children, and do not in such a case wish to go." The sentiments of two of Biddy's daughters, seventeen-year-old Ellen and thirteen-year-old Ann, were in accord. Interviewed separately, Ellen said she wanted to go where her mother went; Ann wanted to stay where her mother stayed.

Hannah's daughter Ann had her own two-year-old daughter to consider. She did not wish to leave her child, but neither did she wish to lose her mother. "I want to stay where my mother Hannah stays—if she stays, I want to stay." Ann did not know what Hannah would do, but she was certain that "her mother would die rather than leave her children."

Ann was obviously upset by the possibility that any decision might separate her from some part of her family, and she may have included the Smiths in that conception. "I cannot say now whether to stay or go. . . . [I]t is hard to be scattered so." These are the wrenching words of a child who had lost too many people: her family and friends in South Carolina, her father in Mississippi, and now, whatever she did, she was bound to lose someone she loved.

Ann's words made a particular impression upon Benjamin. In Smith's favor, the girl seemed to have felt herself free while living in his household in California, but the fact that she questioned her status in Texas indicated to Hayes that Ann, like all the other slaves, lacked knowledge about the circumstances of her life and relied almost blindly on Smith, the man who had been her master.

The interviews did not take long. Hayes had heard enough. His reaction was likely mirrored in the eyes of his two friends, the witnesses, and he returned to the spectacle of the courtroom where Smith and his lawyer waited at the defendant's table. Reporting on the outcome of the interviews, Hayes turned to his witnesses for affirmation. He then announced that he would render his verdict in the trial the following morning and adjourned court for the rest of the day. He had a long night's work ahead.

A sense of high drama undoubtedly pervaded when court was convened again on Saturday. Justice was about to be rendered. Moreover, the proceedings about to commence were a microcosm of the national divide over the issue of slavery that would, in just over five years, erupt into civil war.

Among those in the gallery may have been former slave Robert Owens who lived not far from the courthouse. Owens had worked for years to amass a sum of money representing his earthly worth, and, having purchased his freedom from his master, had left Texas for California. There he had begun again, saving every spare cent and many he should have used, until he had accumulated enough to buy the freedom of his wife and children whom he had left behind. Now Robert Owens and his wife, Winnie, stood in the courtroom and listened as a judge, whose accent bespoke his southern origins, began reading words that might swiftly accomplish what it had taken Owens years to secure: freedom.

> Now on this nineteenth day of January, in the year of Our Lord, one thousand, eight hundred and fifty-six, the said persons above named are brought before me in the custody of the Sheriff of said County, all except the said Hannah and infant boy two weeks old (who are satisfactorily shown to be too infirm to be brought before me), and except Lawrence, (who is necessarily occupied in

waiting on his said mother Hannah) and Charles (who is absent in San Bernardino County, but within said Judicial District) and Robert Smith, claimant, also appears with his Attorney, Alonzo Thomas, Esq. . . .

And it further appearing by satisfactory proof to the Judge here, that all of the said persons of color are entitled to their freedom, and are free and cannot be held in slavery or involuntary servitude, it is therefore argued that they are entitled to their freedom and are free forever.

And there they were: "free forever." Two words that swept away all doubt as to the legal status of Hannah, Biddy, and their children and simultaneously ushered in a veritable sea of uncertainty concerning the shape their lives would now take. If such moments had been recorded, what would we now be able observe in them? A mixture of relief and consternation on the assembled faces? Audible gasps or protestations, perhaps? Or merely the silence that sometimes follows in the wake of a startling event as minds struggle to assimilate what has occurred? Met with anything but silence, Hayes would have called the room to order and plunged forward in his reading of the decree, presenting his justifications for his decision:

And it further appearing to the satisfaction of the Judge here that the said Robert Smith intended to and is about to remove from the State of California where slavery does not exist, to the State of Texas, where slavery of Negroes and persons of color does exist, and is established by the municipal laws, and intends to remove the said before-mentioned persons of color, to his own use without the free will and consent of all or any of the said persons of color, whereby their liberty will be greatly jeopardized, and there is good reason to apprehend and believe that they may be sold into slavery or involuntary servitude and the said Robert Smith is persuading and enticing and seducing said persons of color to go out of the State of California, and it further appearing that none of the said persons of color can read and write, and are almost entirely ignorant of the laws of the state of California as well as those of the State of Texas, and of their rights and that the said Robert Smith, from his past relations to them as members of his family does possess and exercise over them an undue influence in respect to the matter of their said removal insofar that they have been in duress and not in possession and exercise of their free will so as to give a binding consent to any engagement or arrangement with him.

One hardly need guess the effect of these public accusations on Robert Mays Smith. It is a passage filled with scorn, insinuating that Smith's power over his slaves was hardly benign, but coercive. He had been judged guilty of keeping two women and their twelve children enslaved, not only "persuading and enticing" them to accompany his family to Texas, but also "seducing" them—a word charged, then as now, with a sexual connotation, and a word that Hayes ostensibly chose with intention. Hannah, as the judge would later write, was "a woman nearly white, whose children are all nearly so, one of whose daughter (of eight years) cannot easily be distinguished from the white race." Hayes's suspicions concerning miscegenation within the Smith family, though not a matter before his court, were not going to go unacknowledged. The fact that Smith may have had other undeclared "claims" over Hannah (and perhaps Biddy) had not escaped the judge's notice, and so it is hardly surprising that he would close his reading of the verdict with detailed instructions concerning the custody of the children, particularly the minor children under seventeen years of age.

Three of Hannah's minor children (Nathaniel, Jane, and Marion) and two of Biddy's (Ann and Harriet) were remanded to the custody of Sheriff Alexander, who was appointed a special guardian until other arrangements could be made. Martha, Hannah's two year old, was entrusted to her sister Ann.

Hayes further ordered that Hannah and her newborn (who were not in court that day); Lawrence (who was attending his mother); Charles (who was staying in San Bernardino, perhaps with his father); and Ann (Hannah's daughter) and her infant Mary, along with her sister Martha, all appear the following Monday, January 21, at ten in the morning, to receive his ruling in person.

Threading through this portion of Hayes's verdict is evidence of a subtle but discernible worry about Hannah, who "resides in [Smith's house] and is under his control." Given that Smith was now the declared loser in this matter and about to leave his courtroom feeling, to say the least, bruised and antagonistic, Hayes could not ensure that Hannah would learn of the court appearance scheduled in two days and, more important, would receive word that she and her children had been declared "free forever."

On Monday morning, however, as Hayes waited in the courtroom on his bench for Smith to appear with Hannah, his worst fears were confirmed. Those in attendance were probably Sheriff Alexander; a deputy or two; the court clerk; certainly Biddy and her older girls; and probably Robert and Winnie Owens, with whom Biddy, Ellen, and Ann were staying; as well as other free blacks—row upon row of seated and standing spectators, white and of color, eager to catch the final act of the habeas corpus trial.

Minutes went by. The door at the back of the courtroom did not open. Hayes would have considered the poor roads and Hannah's physical condition, and given Smith the benefit of the doubt. Perhaps Hannah had not recovered sufficiently to be brought into court, but, if so, Smith should have sent word by his lawyer or Sheriff Alexander. Eventually, however, it became clear to Hayes and to everyone else in the room that Smith was not coming—and neither, of course, was Hannah.

How differently Hayes had come to see Smith, a fellow southerner, since that first day of 1856, three weeks ago, when he had released Hannah to Smith's custody! How naive he had been to think that a man accused in open court of illegal and perhaps immoral behavior, not to mention a man owing the court costs for the trial in which he was so judged, would willingly return for more abuse.

That Smith might merely dodge another public appearance was not likely, however, the worst of Hayes's fears: Smith could already be gone, could have decided that, having lost Biddy and the children, he should leave with the three slaves still in his custody: Hannah, Lawrence, and this new baby. They could have headed out Saturday night or Sunday morning and by now be miles along the trail to Texas.

No use waiting any longer, entertaining dire thoughts about what had become self-evident. Hayes adjourned court until the following morning and ordered the sheriff to ride out to Smith's ranch and to bring Hannah and her children back into court. He could only hope he was not too late, that he would not find himself Tuesday morning again facing empty tables and a courtroom full of jeering and saddened spectators.

In the hours that ensued, Hayes would have found it difficult to think of much else but the whereabouts of Hannah, her infant, and Lawrence, the boy-child assigned to look after them. Clearly, the judge had miscalculated, but where exactly?

Assuming that Sheriff Alexander had delivered the message to Hannah that she and her children were free and that they had to appear in court Monday, Robert Mays Smith and his wife, Rebecca, would still have had several hours alone with Hannah to bend her sentiments. *She was free; therefore if she decided to go to Texas, the judge would be powerless to stop her.*

There was the matter of her minor children, of course, whom she would have to leave behind. Judge Hayes had made it clear to Hannah's daughter Ann during the interviews in his chambers that her mother and she (a mother herself) would forfeit their parental rights to their children should they decide to leave California. Ann had stated firmly that her mother would rather die than leave her children. But Hannah herself had not been interviewed: what if Ann or the sheriff or Smith had failed to convey that crucial information concerning custody of the children? What if Hannah did not understand that in choosing to accompany the Smiths, she would be choosing to remain with her lifelong mistress, Rebecca, forsaking her own children? Or, finally, what if Hannah did understand the consequences of her decision, but somehow the Smiths had persuaded her to make an unthinkable sacrifice?

In a newspaper article that he would later write about the trial, Hayes was adamant concerning this last scenario:

> Undoubtedly, those over 21 years of age can do what they please with themselves, and might be indulged their own caprice, as to their destination — IN THE ABSENCE OF FORCE OR FRAUD. It would not necessarily follow, that they could make their children the victims of such caprice. If a woman might deliberately surrender herself to slavery, she could not carry her offspring to that fate. It is the first grand thought of the Constitution — LIBERTY IS INALIENABLE!

Nevertheless, to a woman of color, thirty-four years old and not yet recovered from the birth of her eighth child, such abstractions as "inalienable liberty" might have been unfathomable. Hannah had belonged to the Dorns her entire life; how would she take care of her children by herself? Perhaps there were, as Hayes apparently suspected, other powerful ties between Hannah and the Smiths: perhaps she was related by blood to Rebecca or had, in fact, borne a child or two by Robert Mays Smith. For any one of many reasons, Hannah might have felt vulnerable and have been persuaded to acquiesce to the Smiths' wishes. Perhaps she was simply too tired, afraid, and confused to know what she should or should not do. Perhaps *indecision,* not its inverse, was the reason Hannah had failed to appear that day.

Sometime on Monday evening, Hayes would have received the welcome news that the Smiths had not left Los Angeles County. Hannah would have, after all, her day in court and hear the truth of her situation directly from the judge himself.

What seems most remarkable about Hannah's testimony is how little of it, or any of the events of January 22, is recorded. The gallery assembled in the courtroom would likely have been much the same as the day before: the judge, the court clerk, Biddy, the older girls, perhaps the younger children, free blacks, southern sympathizers, those supporting abolition, and an assortment of people seeking diversion. Probably, neither Smith nor Hannah had their attorneys present. Because the verdict had been rendered, there were no legal issues to resolve. All that was left to do, in this court in a state that outlawed Negro testimony, was to ask Hannah what she, a free woman, wanted to do and to ensure that her free choice was supported.

There were as many eyes as perspectives on what was about to occur. Biddy, watching the woman who had shared her life and bondage for almost nine years, who had delivered children into her waiting hands, would have known how difficult it was to appear in court before Smith and these white people—some for and some against freedom—watching.

Robert Mays Smith, standing beside Rebecca or seated alone at the defendant's table, would perhaps have been thinking of his wife's fierce attachment to her childhood slave, the woman he had been ordered to surrender; more likely, however, he was still nursing the fury over the accusations leveled at him in this courtroom the Saturday before.

Toby Embers may have been among those standing in the back of the room among the free blacks that morning. He would have seen Hannah through the eyes of a lover, a man who had fathered two of her children, who had already lost her once when she left Jumuba with the Smiths, and who now, perhaps, saw a chance to have her back.

Charles, Hannah's six-year-old son, perhaps stood beside his father, Toby. He had already been kept from Hannah for almost a month, only a bit longer than Hannah's other children, except Lawrence, who had been assigned to stay with his mother. All of them were likely anxious for even a glimpse of their mother; none of them had seen their new brother until the moment Hannah, with Lawrence at her side, walked into the courtroom.

Judge Hayes probably solicited testimony following the lines of his previous interviews with Biddy and the older girls. First, he would have told Hannah that she had been adjudged free, that as such she could go where she wanted, even if she wished to return to a slave state, as long as she was not being taken against her will, and the purpose of that day's questioning was to ascertain her true desires and intentions. He would also have informed her, as he had Biddy and Ann, that if she decided to go she could not take her children, as they were under the protection of the State of California and its laws and could not, as minors, be transported to a slave state. Hannah, thus, knew exactly what she was being asked and what she would forfeit by her decision to go.

Hayes's description of what took place in court that day is provocative. He mentions, first, Hannah's "silence," then her "hesitancy" and her "cold replies." The continuum of her responses, from silence to hesitancy to cold replies, is understandable, given her terror at being in court and her emotional distress. If she had not before understood the choice she was being called upon to make—leave Texas with the Smiths or retain custody of her children—she certainly did now. Yet Hannah hesitated—much to Judge Hayes's dismay and consternation. "[I]f she tell[s] the truth," he would write of her testimony, that she did want to accompany the Smiths, "a humiliating spectacle is exhibited."

The admission wrung from her and her agony at its expression deeply disturbed the judge. Others in the courtroom watching Hannah's examination and hearing her faint and fearful words would find her suffering unbearable and her decision irrational. There no doubt would have been protests from those in favor of her freedom and reactions from her waiting children until Judge Hayes's gavel silenced the courtroom.

If Hannah held her newborn during her testimony, Hayes might have let her keep it until the final moment, hoping the baby's weight in her arms might influence her. But now the worst had come to pass: Hannah had traded away not only her freedom for a migration into certain slavery, but her children as well. Hayes would have been all too aware of the dilemma he had created: he could not both free a woman and then compel her to act against her own stated wishes.

Hayes does not mention reactions of those in the audience, but we can well imagine some of them: Biddy and Ann's bewilderment, Toby Embers's outrage, Rebecca Smith's anguish—she had never meant for Hannah to lose her children. And what of Robert Mays Smith? Perhaps he felt momentarily triumphant—*I told you she wanted to go!* But more probably, like everyone else, he felt the weight of despair descending, felt the suck of the morass that was destroying everything he cared for—a morass not of his own making. The only reaction we can be sure of is Judge Hayes's: he felt sick. Having adjourned court, he watched Hannah and Smith walk up the aisle between the spectators toward the back door.

Perhaps the judge stewed all night, discussing the pros and cons with Emily, standing above Chauncey's small bed and wondering what it would take for him to leave his child, looking through his law books to find some exculpatory clause that would allow him to order Hannah to stay, then, at long last, accepting the consequences of the freedom he had declared for another human being.

But though Hannah was now free, had her *testimony* been also? That was the only remote possibility of redemption, it seemed: that Smith had in some manner frightened or intimidated Hannah to such an extent that she was willing to sacrifice her freedom and her children. What if, given a day to think over the consequences of her decision, she would change her mind? It was, Hayes knew, a long shot, but the only one he had. The next morning, he asked Sheriff David Alexander to ride out to the ranch again and to try to speak with Hannah away from the presence of the Smiths. All day on Wednesday, Benjamin awaited the sheriff's return.

Hannah's testimony could not stand; no one in his or her right mind would accept it. "The evidence, on the trial," Hayes would write, "does not tell precisely what influences have been brought to bear most upon [Hannah]. Some things point to actual duress; and, if a little bent by persuasion, the force of a feather might seal her lips."

If nothing else, Hayes intended to find that feather.

SIX

Getting to the Right State

I{T WAS DUSK WHEN THE PLANE} landed at the tiny airport in Augusta, Georgia.[1] The sky was full of ominous, heavy clouds, and I was already feeling anxious about the drive ahead when the young woman at the rental counter handed me the keys to a car. I asked for directions to Edgefield, South Carolina, and she tapped the air a few inches above the only map she had—of Georgia. "It's right up here. You can't miss it."

I knew better, so I asked her to draw the route. Another young woman at the counter knew a better way; her red line took off from the airport in a different direction. Her friend disagreed. By the time they finished, my map resembled an arteriogram.

Drivers in oncoming cars flashed their headlights. I twisted levers, poked buttons, then gave up and admitted to myself that I was going to drive across two states with my brights on. Rain started, lightly at first, then began falling in sheets. The wipers were too slow, then too fast. A sign appeared, then was behind me before I could read it. I turned off at the next exit, found a gas station, and ran through the rain with a bleeding map: "Edgefield?"

The attendant laughed. "Hell, you ain't even in the right state yet."

—

For months I had been searching all the census records for Texas after 1860, running down every Robert Smith that I came across and had finally traced the right one to Bexar County, Texas. Polite but unfruitful replies to my inquiries about him came from historical and genealogical societies, until a librarian from San Antonio, married to one of Smith's descendants, answered. Why yes, she wrote, a family history had recently been published about Robert Mays Smith, and that summer there had been a family reunion. She gave me the address of the woman who had written the family history.

I hesitated to contact her, imagining the tacit condemnation I might feel if someone told me they were researching slaves once owned by my ancestor. In my first letter, I merely said I was seeking information about Robert Mays Smith, had heard she had written a book, and asked to buy a copy. She wrote back, asking if I were a Smith descendant. As it happens, I have ancestors named Smith who once lived in Texas, so I trotted them out and, disingenuously, said that I did not know if we were related. I sent a check for a copy of the book and said, in what I tried to couch as an aside, that I was writing a book about Biddy Mason and other slaves once owned by the Smith family.

For several months, there was no reply. Then one day a large package appeared, containing a photocopy of the Smith family history, copies of supporting articles and documents, and photographs of Robert and Rebecca Smith in old age. The book was well done, recounting much about the ancestors of Rebecca Dorn, as well as detailing the lives of her many descendants. Ethel Klemcke, one of the two authors of *Robert Mays Smith: From South Carolina to Texas (the Long Way),* expressed her pleasure at my interest in her husband's ancestor and returned my check with a letter. All she wanted in return for her bundle of information was a copy of my book when published.

In one letter, Ethel mentioned that Robert had told a grandson he was from Edgefield, South Carolina, and to remember it because "[s]omeday someone will want to know."

Now, on a long, dark country road in Georgia, I wiped circles on the fogged windshield and peered past my brights into gloom, wondering how Robert would feel about the person fulfilling that prophecy.

I came into Edgefield late, and the town—not much more than a square with a courthouse and a few stores—was completely shut down. Not a soul anywhere. I walked around a while, looking for my bed-and-breakfast, with the sense I had stepped onto a movie set after everyone had gone home: the lighting and camera crews, the director and the players. No one to ask what kind of drama the darkened facades served.

I tried the door of a boardinghouse on the square and entered an old-fashioned lobby, with leather chairs and potted ferns. It was dimly lighted, but down the hall was a bright room where a long white table was laid out with place settings. I turned back to the lobby and took the staircase, calling as I climbed, "Hello! Hello!" At the top, I followed the sound of a television down one hallway then another until I came to an alcove. An old black-and-white movie was on—and no one was watching. Back in the lobby, I looked in the guest register for my name and realized I was at the wrong place—thank God.

In the center of the square was a monument—an obelisk dedicated to Confederate soldiers—a senator's statue, and a fountain flowing soundlessly. The courthouse, a building of great architectural beauty, designed, I later learned, in 1839 by Robert Mills, dominated the square. That altered-state feeling swept over me again. I thought about a trial in a Los Angeles courthouse a continent away, 137 years past, where the third act played out in 1856. This was the setting for the first act: Edgefield. I was here to try to learn what had happened long before the final curtain fell.

Following the road that had brought me into town, I found my bed-and-breakfast, but its windows were dark and its door locked. I knocked and hollered long enough; the night watchman came at last and let me in. The building seemed otherwise deserted, but I did not care: my room had a bed.

Most nights I ate from a gas station convenience store a few blocks from the bed-and-breakfast. One night, after a day of driving and research, I came in ravenous. I grabbed juice, barbecue on a bun, boiled peanuts, and a diet Dr. Pepper. The young woman behind the counter was African American, with the amber skin and golden eyes of Crista, a friend of mine. I asked if she was from Edgefield. She said yes.

"How long?"

She gave a little shrug. "My whole life."

"You like it?"

"It's quiet. Not much crime. Of course, there's always some crime, but nobody in Edgefield locks their door." She eyed me. "Why? You thinking of moving here?"

I said no, that I was there to research a book, and I was curious about what kind of town it was.

"It's all right."

"How big?"

"Small." She helped a customer. "The only thing," she said slowly, "is that there's old ways of looking at things."

"That's why I was asking about Edgefield," I said, and told her about my work: the African American women who were taken as slaves to Utah, then California, and freed in a dramatic trial. When I spoke about Biddy and Hannah, her eyes underwent a change. She listened intently. People came to the counter, and I stepped back.

"Are you in a hurry?" she asked. "It's interesting."

I was faint with hunger, but told her no.

"When was this?" she asked after the customers left.

"1856."

"How old are they now?"

"They're dead, both of them."

"What was her name, the one who lived here?"

I hesitated. She asked if that was personal. I said I was hesitating because Hannah had several names, depending upon who owned her. In Edgefield, it had been the Dorn family.

"There's some Dorns around here," the girl said, and she did not mean Caucasians. "Norman Dorn is on the council. He's in the book."

I told her that was helpful; the Dorn family's slaves would have taken the name of Dorn. Norman Dorn might be a descendant.

The young woman asked about tracing one's family back to Africa. We talked about that a while. It's hard, I said, but maybe doable, especially if her family had been in one place all the while. I advised her to start with her immediate family, make everyone write down everything they knew. I told her about census records and bills of sale for slaves. As we talked, people came and went, buying things. I asked her name: Jones.

"Jones!" I groaned; that would make research harder.

"Yes," she said. "It was a common slave name."

"I'm DeEtta, by the way."

"That's pretty," she said shyly. "It was nice to meet you."

And then my hunger spoke up again: I had to go, much as I wanted to stay.

⟶

"My Dorns may be different than yours," Norman Dorn said carefully on the telephone. I laughed and assured him the Dorns I was interested in were African Americans.

"You need to talk to my mama, then," he said. She was eighty-seven; her father had been a slave. He gave me her number and said what time it was best to call.

I phoned the next day when Mrs. Dorn was supposed to be up from her nap, but got Nan, her daughter. "My mama don't know nothing about no book," she said. "She's resting!" She hung up on me.

I called Norman back. He laughed. "I'll get you by Nan. You come up by school tomorrow afternoon, and I'll take you home to Mama myself."

Norman Dorn was a thin, spry man, in his forties, who taught eighth-grade earth sciences.

In the car, he told me about his years in the army and going to college up north.

"Why did you come back?" I asked.

He laughed. "I'm just a country boy. My idea of happiness is finding a stump in the woods and sitting on it."

A few minutes later, we pulled up to his mother's house. Around the small yard was a white picket fence. Attached to the front of the house was a porch that seemed to have been added as an afterthought. The house itself was a small one-room place, with a side addition, like the others along this stretch of road: former slave cabins, I supposed. The paint was old, oxidizing, but in the yard were flowers, pink roses coming into bloom.

Mrs. Dorn came out. She was a shy, petite woman, with a soft, sweet voice. She wore house slippers. She was almost blind from glaucoma—did not like following the doctor's orders for the eyedrops. She took the rocking chair on her porch; I sat on one of the two plank benches and waved good-bye to Norman.

Yes, Mrs. Dorn told me, her father had known slavery. His father was the white overseer who had taken advantage of his mother. Her maiden name was Youngblood; her mother had been an Atkins. All of her father's children by his first wife had gone to college, and she was supposed to go, too, but her father had died and it had not been possible. She had finished high school, though. Her husband's name was Gilbert Dorn. No, she did not know anything about his family, except he had been raised by his Grandma Mays. Her husband had died fifty years before, when she was thirty-seven. She had raised their three children on her own.

I was disappointed, knowing the afternoon would not add to what I knew about the Dorns. But a breeze carried the scent of roses to the porch, and I felt suddenly happy and content just to sit in the sun with a living person, away from dusty archives for a while.

Mrs. Dorn rocked herself gently as she talked. They had always had a garden, growing up, she said, a washtub in the backyard, hogs, and lamps instead of electricity. She had been out of Edgefield only once, on a trip to Augusta. She had never been to a beauty shop or worn makeup. During the hard years after her husband's death, her old invalid mother had cared for her children while she was a nanny for white families. There were doctors and judges still living in town whom she could point to and say, "I used to pull up his socks."

I mentioned Hannah and Biddy, how worried they must have been to choose freedom for themselves, wondering how they would feed their children. "Sure!" Mrs. Dorn said. She had also worked as a housekeeper; other opportunities were simply not available to her: "They wouldn't let me show other parts," so she "minded" and made her way as best she could, avoiding the "bad" whites, the mean ones she had to walk around, those who took advantage or who thought black people were just animals. "Sin-sick," she called them. But she would not let them make her hate.

After a time we went down to look at her garden. Mrs. Dorn had left her walking stick behind and leaned on my arm. We stood together at the fence while she pointed to her okra, her peas, her cabbage.

"When I plant seeds, I step on them," she said. "Don't hurt them none; only make them strong." She asked if I could see her footprints out there in the dirt.

It was getting chilly. Time to go. We walked out to the road together. There used to be nothing here, she said, but fields where she had picked cotton. But some things remain: a friend who had moved away was back, only a few houses away. It made her happy, Mrs. Dorn told me, when family and friends lived all in a row, right next to each other.

I smiled and thanked her for her time and her stories. She wished she could remember more: "If only I could show you what was in my mind!"

I held her hand and told her I did not want to be bossy, but I asked her to please use those eyedrops.

Norman Dorn had offered to come back for me, but I had told him I preferred to walk back to the bed-and-breakfast. The row of humble houses gave way to one-story dwellings with carports, then, along the main road, old mansions, many deserted, their windows cracked and leaves piling up on their porches.

Was Mrs. Dorn's husband a relative of Hannah or Biddy? I would probably never know. But what I was learning seemed just as important: this dusty road, Mrs. Dorn's house brimming with life and memory, and a little farther on, these empty, leaf-blown mansions.

Every morning a group of men met in the restaurant below the boardinghouse in Edgefield for coffee and conversation. By the time I arrived, a few would already be seated, farmers in overalls, used to rising with the sun. As the morning progressed, they were joined by men in work pants and jeans, and, later, by a man in a suit—the mayor, I thought, or maybe a judge.

One morning, a man got up from the communal table, said his good-byes, and on his way from the restaurant stopped at my table. He introduced himself. Sam C., dressed like my father did when he went hunting: work pants, a plaid shirt, and boots. He was a tall, solid, angular man, somewhere in his fifties, with grizzled black hair, blue eyes, and a quick grin. *Shrewd,* I thought, then waved the word away. He asked what I was up to.

I told him and asked if he could help me find the head of Sleepy Creek, explaining that I was looking for the place where John Dorn's family lived in the 1830s, which, according to a map I had gotten from the Tompkins Library, was on the west bank of the north branch of Sleepy Creek, close to its head.

Sam studied the map, started to give directions, then changed his mind. "How about I just take you?"

I was delighted. I bundled up my things, and we made our way to his truck. I was just about to step up into the cab when Sam cried, "Watch out!" I had stepped on a hill of red ants; some were already on my shoes. He took off his jacket and beat it about my legs, telling me how wicked fire ants could be.

We drove on the main road, then turned off onto a side highway, talking all the way. I asked what he did for a living. Sam said he owned trees. His wave took in several hills. He also collected log cabins—log houses he called them—buying them and the land they stood on, if possible; otherwise, buying the house alone, dismantling it, moving the logs to his own land, and rebuilding it there. He had five or six log dwellings. They were hard to find now, he said, and when you did find one, it was usually so cluttered or cut up that there was not much left of the original structure. He explained what to look for to determine whether an old log house was hiding under renovations: a shape and size of house congruent with log houses built in the nineteenth century, a certain placement of windows, or a particular way of attaching the chimney. He pointed out houses as we passed, leaning back to let me look, and soon I could recognize in a glance which houses had beautiful bones under plain skins.

Sam's family had been in Edgefield for generations. He had gone to college, earned a degree in English literature, and between college and becoming a landowner had been a schoolteacher. A wealthy, well-read redneck with an eye for architecture: I had to admit I was impressed by the dimensions to the man seated in the truck beside me.

He knew who lived in every house we passed, where their folks were from, what tragedies had transpired in their lives, and which families had intermarried. We stopped at the house of a friend whose wife, Sam said, was a Dorn—she might know something. His friend, he whispered, was ill. No one came to the door, and we were about to leave when a car turned in. They were returning from a funeral. Sam asked his friend how he was doing; his eyes said all we needed to know. I thought the friend's wife had the coloring of her ancestor, William B. Dorn, Rebecca's brother, whose portrait in the courthouse in McCormick showed him to be a small man with fair hair and gray eyes. Sam's friend thought we might find John Dorn's homestead by following the old gold-mine road. As we left, Sam C. shook his head sadly.

It was easy to see Sleepy Creek on the map, but to find it in the woods was another matter. Edgefield County is riddled with creeks, and even when we located the one we were looking for, we could not follow it. We came at it sideways, on a series of dirt roads, each higher up, closer to the creek's source.

The woods in late September were glorious. There were several kinds of pines and numerous hardwoods, their red and golden leaves just starting to shed. Sam was an excellent guide, knowing the names and uses of all the plants and flowers. Moreover, he was patient, pulling over whenever I saw an interesting plant, letting me get out, look closely, touch, and smell. We were beginning to relax with each other. After a while, Sam stuffed some chewing tobacco in his cheek, and spat in a can he kept under the seat as he drove.

In a section of woods managed by the National Forest Service, we got out and walked a dirt road because, Sam said, he did not know whether the culverts under the road would take the weight of his truck.

"This is it," he said at last and squatted beside the road. I followed his finger to a spot in the woods that was more glade than creek bed. Beneath overhanging branches, in a slight depression, was a wide bed of leaves. In the spring, Sam said, Sleepy Creek could be a torrent and showed me the culvert that directed it downstream.

So this was where the story that had taken over my life started: the place Rebecca's ancestors had settled when they came to America, where her family had lived for generations. Rebecca and Hannah's world. I looked around. I liked being here, in these woods, at this time of the year, with this man who was both knowledgeable and kind. I was pleased that we had found the head of Sleepy Creek together.

We went back to the truck to look for John Dorn's house—where it had been and where I hoped it still was. I was thinking that Sam was like the log houses he sought, his country-boy facade shielding the essence of the man.

At some point, we started talking about blacks. I do not remember how it happened. I never mentioned what I was writing about, but Sam may have heard about my visiting Norman's mother. Maybe it was just idle talking. He complained about the shiftless colored people, the ones who hung around the town square. He said he had talked to a realtor in Colorado about buying land out there, to get away from the "gnats and niggers." He was not a racist, he assured me. Things were "just different" down here.

I felt as though I had been slapped. In the few hours we had been together, I had come to like and admire this man. Now this. And had he learned anything about me in our time together? I guessed not. I wanted to swat him with his jacket and yell, "There are worse things around than a few red ants!" Instead, I was thunderously silent. He looked at me out of the corner of his eye and drove on.

At the Dorn homestead, I had expected ruins: a standing chimney, a few stones from the foundation, or rusting farm equipment. Instead, the house that sat on the west bank of the north branch of Sleepy Creek was someone's home, a remodeled farmhouse under which was definitely an old log house.

We had stopped on the side of the road, instead of turning in the driveway. I asked why. Sam said he thought the house belonged to a "colored family." Ah, the pejorative generic.

I almost laughed. "Would they mind if we asked to look at the house?"

Sam seemed nervous, edgy. Finally, he said he would run up and knock—and that is what he did, run, hands in his pockets, looking this way and that. He knocked, waited, then strolled back, obviously relieved the owners were not at home.

I got out of the truck and stood in the driveway to see the house better, the place where Rebecca had lived as a girl, where there had been an auction in which a woman named Hannah and her children were sold: October 26, 1846, in this season, in weather like this, here, 147 years ago.

I ran into Sam once after that day, on my way out of town. He walked me back to my car, warning me about stepping in the red ants.

"You too," I said. I thanked him again for our afternoon. We stood a moment at the car. I asked directions to the airport in Augusta, showing him the cryptic directions I had started with, coming to Edgefield. He made a few corrections and handed the map back to me. I got in the car. He leaned on the window, said good-bye, then stepped back. I started off the wrong way, and he waved me down. The last time I saw him, he was standing by the side of the road, hands in his hip pockets, looking after me with a quizzical expression, as if he wondered what went wrong.

At night in my room at the bed-and-breakfast in Edgefield, I would sit on the floor, eat a bag of boiled peanuts, and watch the Weather Channel on the television. Hurricanes blew up from the Gulf. Tornadoes ravaged the Texas Panhandle. The weather mirrored my despair. Sometimes when I got back to my room, I felt like a shade returning from the netherworld to ascertain how the living lived. The days were usually bearable, with interesting people to talk to and places to visit, along with the diversion of documents or notes to take. But at night in my room—and all those hotel rooms became utterly undifferentiated in my memory—I longed for someone to talk to, someone who knew me, to whom I could tell about the events of the day, who would be amused or impressed by my observations, or would laugh with me at what I thought funny. Nothing is lonelier than having a good story to tell and nobody to tell it to—except the weatherman on a flickering television screen. Robert, Rebecca, Benjamin, Hannah, and Biddy: these were my nightly entourage, the people who were real to me—but who unfortunately could no longer speak.

The hardest part, the saddest part, was that every morning I would look back at my half-rumpled hotel bed and realize that once again, needlessly, I had slept on my own side of the bed as if saving space for someone who was not there. And it was beginning to look as though I had come all this way, spent a great deal of money, devoted hours to nearly illegible records and blurred microfilm, and was soon to leave town, having learned nothing at all. Maybe that intuitive bump at the wall in Los Angeles had been nothing but imagination, and everything since, self-deception. Maybe the whole story began and ended in my unbalanced brain.

From the LDS Family History Center in Salt Lake, I had the box and package numbers for the probate record of John Dorn Sr., but, as I had learned on my first day in town, it was not where it was supposed to be in the archives of the Edgefield County Courthouse. I was beside myself. To come all this way and not be able to see John Dorn's will! I abandoned the courthouse and concentrated on the Tompkins Library, the research library on one side of the town square. I found a microfilm I wanted to read, but could not get the reel on the machine. The librarian helped, and I learned that the film was unreadable, almost black. In my journal for that night is a single word: "NADA!!!!"

The next morning, placated by a southern breakfast of sausage, eggs, and grits with lots of butter and black pepper, I returned to the Tompkins Library, lecturing myself on the need for patience and persistence. I again went through census records, maps, and family histories. Then there was no place else to look—I thought, until I saw the membership book of Little Steven's Creek Baptist Church. I opened the heavy cover, and ran my fingers down its yellowed pages until I found the entry stating that John Dorn and his wife—Rebecca's father and mother—had joined the church. I kept looking. In 1843, the church's total membership was 272: "Whites 182, Blacks 90." My finger stopped. "Sept. 9th. 1843 Rec'd for baptism . . . John Dorn Senr' Hannah."

Ah, Hannah, I knew I'd find you!

Little Steven's Creek Baptist Church stood in a large clearing with a line of trees marking the banks of an otherwise hidden creek. As I drove up, people were leaving the church—a meeting or a choir rehearsal—and getting in cars. When they were gone, I pulled in and parked beside the church, a simple white building with a proud steeple. The librarian at the Tompkins Library had helped me find a photograph of the church in the 1800s: unpainted, set high on an open foundation, with square

Little Steven's Creek Baptist Church, Edgefield, South Carolina, about 1840. Courtesy of the Edgefield Historical Society.

windows and no steeple. That was the church I now realized I had hoped to find. It was a tenacious illusion of mine that I could simply enter the past at will.

The windows were too high to peer into, but I made a few notes on a legal pad, tucked it under my arm, and turned to go. Then I thought of trying the front door. The latch clicked. The door opened.

A typical Baptist church. A center aisle, wood pews on either side, a plain pulpit, and, at the rear of the building, a balcony where the choir sang. I sat down on a middle pew not far from a side window. Hannah had been here, in this room. I stared up at the empty balcony as if I expected figures to materialize there. How had the invitation come? Did the white minister—Reverend Trapp—plead for "O Sinners to Come Home," or was that a later hymn? Would Hannah have made her way down from the balcony and up the center aisle, or had she been permitted to sit with John Dorn and his wife who saw her weeping and pushed her forward? Probably, she had been baptized in the creek nearby.

I stood, walked to the window, and found the cusp of trees bending over the creek beyond the clearing. The baptism had probably taken place in late September 1843, almost exactly this time of year, with leaves the same color as the leaves on those trees and the light the same autumnal hue. How old was Hannah in the fall of 1843? I consulted the judge's verdict in my folder on the pew. Hannah, thirty-four in January 1856, was probably born in 1821, making her twenty-two when she was baptized. Her eldest daughter, Ann, born in 1838, would have been four or five, and her son Lawrence, born in 1842 or 1843, was a baby or Hannah had still been pregnant with him. Returning to the window, I put my hand flat against the glass. Pregnant, I thought, and standing in waist-high water.

A distant yelping dispelled my reverie. A small spotted dog with pointed ears scampered across a field. Chasing him was a young black girl in a cotton dress and pigtails. I wondered if school was out, or if she was still too young to go. Suddenly, the little girl stopped running and now walked slowly, carefully, looking down. I wondered if she had lost something, then I saw the headstones and remembered the cemetery on the far side of the church. The little girl took a step here, a side step there. Perhaps she was trying to read what was on the grave markers. Her expression was both alert and distant, like a robin listening for a worm. She looked here, there, then called her dog. I watched them amble off.

I spent the next two days in panting pursuit of documents, following one reference after another like a woman possessed. At night in my upstairs room above the empty street, I would lie awake, thinking of questions for the next day. When the library opened in the morning, I was at its door. In the afternoons, I would go back to the courthouse and work my way through dusty probate records.

Late one afternoon, I sat alone on a bench in the little park in the center of the town square. Rain streamed from Sen. Strom Thurman's statue. Everyone else, including the birds, had sought shelter. Not me. In the courthouse records, misfiled, I had finally found it: John Dorn's probate folder. Besides his will, I had found the bill of sale for the auction of his estate and, in it, the entry: "Robert M. Smith Hanah & 3 Children 1210." Then I had shaken the folder containing the probate file, and out had fallen the nine slips of paper I had seen on microfilm back in Salt Lake City. I had balanced one ragged-edged slip on my hand—Frank, Hannah, child Nelson, Lawrence—as though it were a butterfly, lighting there for a magical instant. Was that slip what I was meant to see here in Edgefield, or was there something else?

It was almost time for the Tompkins Library to close, but, rain-drenched as I was, I went in. I asked if I could look up a couple of things. The librarian's computer was shut down, and her purse was on her desk. No one else was there. She was reluctant, but relented and asked if she could be of help.

I looked around for a straw to grasp and saw the old membership book of Little Steven's Creek Baptist Church. "I need to look in here one more time," I told her. "It will take me just one minute."

Carefully, I opened the yellow pages and skimmed them for—what? who? I saw Dorn names, notations about the behavior of slaves, then this entry: "Sabbath. Nov. 8th . . . Granted letters of dismission . . . to Bob and Hannah servants of the Estate of John Dorn Sr." The second Sunday after the auction, Bob, a slave bought by Robert Dorn, and Hannah, bought by Robert Dorn on behalf of Robert M. Smith, received letters of transfer of their church membership.

But Hannah could not read!—not according to Judge Hayes's verdict. What then did this document mean to her? Perhaps, I thought, in Hannah's view it was analogous to the passes that slaves had to carry when they were off plantation or away from their owners. Or perhaps, knowing she was leaving South Carolina forever, she wanted something of her old life with her. Perhaps the document, folded and carefully packed with her few belongings, was for her like Freedom Papers, something she could hold that offered solace in her present situation and hope for emancipation in God's kingdom.

I thought of a book, John Bunyon's *Pilgrim's Progress,* that I had had as a child and a single passage from it: "My marks and scars I carry with me, to be a witness for me that I have fought His battles."

"Closing time," the librarian said.

Outside it was dark. I thanked her for waiting.

"I didn't want you to leave Edgefield without finding what you came for. Did you find it?" She locked the door behind us, then stood beside me on the sidewalk.

"Maybe I did," I said.

My last morning in Edgefield. An early-morning drive through the county. Highway 378: misty woods, deer jumping across the highway.

At a store advertising "P-nuts," I stopped for directions to an obscure cemetery. The girl sent me to a house, "back of the store and up the hill."

A man in his sixties was standing on the porch as I drove up. I got out, introduced myself, and learned that he was the Mr. Holmes I was seeking. Mr. Holmes told me that his wife had died two weeks earlier. I apologized for bothering him, but he invited me up on the porch.

Across the driveway from the house was a great oak tree, the oldest in the county, Mr. Holmes said. He pointed to a stump beside the tree and said once it was equally grand, but it had been struck by lightning fifteen years ago. I watched his face as he stood looking at the tree and its lost companion. He seemed on the verge of tears. Some people, like some trees, I thought, belong in pairs.

I had chosen the right place to stop. Mr. Holmes knew all the cemeteries. For many years, he said, he had run a chain gang of prisoners that cleaned graves throughout the county. Two images instantly melded in my mind: a long coffle of slaves, weighed down with iron and men, mostly black men, in uniforms, moving together, working picks and shovels along a dusty red road. But the man watching them, the boss—the one holding a shotgun, the shouting, snarling white man—what did he have to do with this sad, sweet, wounded man on this porch? I could not merge the faces.

I felt a sudden wave of doubt, then fear. Maybe I saw only surfaces, masks. Maybe my whole life I had been seeing only the faces people presented to me or the faces I created from stories I made up—about total strangers like this man. Look at how I had misjudged Sam. Maybe there was another entire reality I knew nothing, or little, about. *White eyes, white eyes,* I thought. *You have been looking at the world through them your whole life. Yes, Robert Mays Smith, I was the one you expected to come looking for you. And tell me, what do I do with what I now know about us?*

Mr. Holmes watched me patiently. I asked about the burial places of the Dorns, and he directed me to a certain cemetery. He apologized for not taking me, saying he was standing out here, waiting for his daughter who was due from the city. As I drove away, I waved. Mr. Holmes on the porch moved his hand slowly back and forth.

Soon I was driving on private property, having turned off the highway onto a gravel road that petered out to dirt. On both sides of the road, there were open fields, with patches of woods, mostly spindly pines. I wondered if it was hunting season; if so, this was a dangerous place to be. The rain that sluiced my windshield on my drive to Edgefield had also created potholes in the red dirt road filled with water, but, as the road was narrow with banks on both sides, I had to drive through them. As I came over a rise and hit a large hole, I wondered how long I would wait for help if I broke an axle out here. I drove for what seemed like a long way and thought I had missed the cutoff. Then I saw a handwritten sign with the name of the family cemetery. I parked the car in a pullout, started walking toward the woods, then looked back to get my bearings. My white car was coated to the windows with bloodred mud.

The cemetery was set in a tiny clearing encircled by a copse of trees. In the few days I had been in Edgefield, the leaves had changed, lost color, become sere. Beneath the trees were a few gravestones, all old, mostly unreadable. Some markers were just rocks, one or two of dark pumice, the point being, I supposed, for survivors to be able to tell by the displaced stones where their loved ones lay. No one has been here for years, I thought. These were the old dead. Life went on; people forgot.

I knelt, then crawled, moving leaves from hidden stones, seeing sometimes a date, or a few letters of a name. On a small, eroded granite stone, I made out "Dorn." Beside it was a matching stone with similar markings. Was this Rebecca's father and mother? I had brought paper and pencil and now laid the paper against stone, used the side of my pencil, and traced lightly back and forth. Strange that a grave rubbing can pick up more than eyes can see, like a photograph emerging from a negative. This picture remained murky. The first names on both Dorn graves were unreadable, and I could make out only "18 . . ." I folded the rubbings and put them in my pocket.

Cross-legged, I sat with my back against a pine tree, and thought of the people I had met in Edgefield, and how they related to my book. Mingled with their faces were the other faces so familiar to me now: Robert, Rebecca, Benjamin, Biddy, and the assorted white and black children belonging to each of them. Hannah was the only one whose face I had not seen, but somehow I felt I knew Hannah. She was not a mask to me; I would have recognized her in any crowd.

And what would Hannah see, I wondered, if she were sitting here, in this quiet, almost holy glade, with its circle of shimmering trees? Would she be happy to be home? Would she be sad about the unreadable stones marking the graves of John and Rebecca Dorn? They had shared a lifetime. John Dorn Sr. may have been her father. How do you feel at the grave of a man who gave you life and then sold you as property? But I thought of Hannah as much wiser than me. Kinder, too. Perhaps kinder because wiser. I knew her, but so much of her was still a mystery.

Leaves drifted down from the surrounding trees. I thought of the leaves I had seen so long ago in California drifting across the photograph of Biddy Mason. What was it that falling leaves were supposed to represent in movies—the passage of time? But maybe time did not pass at all—maybe it was always here, all around us, keeping all of us together, like one single, ever present family. Maybe it did not matter whether we lived in South Carolina, California, Salt Lake City, Texas, Mississippi, or Seattle. Maybe it does not matter when we live, a hundred years ago, or in these troubled times. We could all still be here, in this place, in this moment.

A rising wind rushed through the trees, and eagerly I looked up.

SEVEN

The Promise

ON THURSDAY, JANUARY 24, two days after Hannah's traumatic public renunciation of her freedom and her children, Benjamin Hayes received the first good news he had had in almost a month. Sheriff Alexander, having returned from Smith's ranch, reported that he had successfully interviewed Hannah privately, away from Rebecca and Robert Smith. What a different woman she was from the one who had appeared in court and handed over her newborn son! She had not meant it at all, she told Alexander; she did not want to go to Texas with the Smiths, but wanted to stay in California and be with her children.[1]

Hearing this, Benjamin would have been jubilant—and perhaps a bit humbled. Hard as he was trying to see that justice was carried out, he had narrowly averted becoming a party to the *in*justice constantly percolating beneath the surface of this bizarre case. What if he had not followed his instincts and sent Sheriff Alexander on this errand? How many more generations of sorrow would he have unwittingly perpetuated? But perhaps the question that occurred to Hayes was how could he have doubted that Providence, so constant in his travels and travails, would not now be guiding him, guiding all of them?

"Free forever," he had said, and in those words, perhaps he had meant to deliver some recompense for the people he had owned himself—for Lewis, Grace, and the many others. But how close it had all come to flying back in his face because of one woman and the agonizing choice she seemed reconciled to make.

Hayes had sent Sheriff Alexander out for information, and now he asked him to go back to Jumuba and collect Hannah, without Smith this time, so that she could testify once more in open court on Friday morning. He set the time of her hearing with the clerk for ten in the morning, told the jailers to inform the children of their mother's imminent return, and, perhaps, sent word to Biddy.

On Friday, Sheriff Alexander would have taken a wagon to the ranch, knowing that Hannah, still recovering from childbirth, would not be able to ride. It was almost ten o'clock when the sheriff appeared in Hayes's chambers; the spectators in the courtroom would have already assembled. Hayes, thinking that Hannah was there to recant, to say that she wanted to stay in California with her children, would have had Hannah's children brought to court. He would have envisioned the day's proceedings culminating in a joyous and final reunion. But no such reunion would take place.

According to Sheriff Alexander's testimony, Hannah had requested that he speak with Judge Hayes, "before she would be brought into Court, and explain her situation." Hannah had told Alexander that morning that, before being brought before Hayes on Tuesday,

> she had been compelled by family of Robert Smith, and particularly by the wife of . . . Smith, that she would take an oath that she would state in Court that it was her desire to return to Texas. . . . She did not state distinctly whether Robert Smith compelled her to take said oath or not; the impression left on deponent by her statement is that his wife insisted upon her taking this oath. Now she wanted to tell me, as Sheriff, that such was not her real desire, but she wanted to stay in California and be protected by the law and the Courts.

But, having taken such an oath, Hannah told Alexander, she felt compelled to observe it, and would so again if she appeared in court that morning; she would tell Hayes that she wished to accompany the Smiths to Texas.

In a matter of five minutes, Hayes had once again been catapulted from hope into despair, and at the heart of that despair lay yet another of the painful ironies this case thrust upon him: outside his courtroom sat a woman in a wagon whose faith might, in fact, be stronger than his own, a woman who had taken a vow, who would not, could not, forsake it, regardless of the cost.

And now Hayes was the one with an impossible choice: bring Hannah into court and let her again say she wanted to go with the Smiths—a lie, though true to the vow she had taken—or let her go. How could he force her to say that she did not want to leave California or expose her as a liar for upholding an oath she seemed to hold sacred?

Hayes made his decision: he would not make Hannah testify again. Her testimony on Tuesday would stand. As the wagon left, taking Hannah away, Hayes might have watched from the window in his chambers, postponing the terrible walk to the courtroom.

By early Friday afternoon, the sheriff would have returned Hannah to the Smith encampment in Santa Monica, seemingly bringing the habeas corpus case to a close. Hannah would soon be leaving California—and her freedom and children. Biddy and the older of the girls, Hannah's Ann and Biddy's Ellen, along with the small children assigned to their care, Mary, Martha, and two-week-old Henry, had been placed in the residence of Robert and Winnie Owens, the free black family who had opened their modest home in the heart of Los Angeles to these needy friends.[2] The other children remained in jail, under the guardianship of the court, until Hayes found an appropriate placement for them.

In the camp in Santa Monica, Smith was readying his wagons for the departure for Texas along the southern route. The plan apparently was to leave the following morning, Saturday. But plans had seldom, and certainly not lately, panned out for Robert Smith. And when he could not be his own worst enemy, he seemed to be cursed with a host of people serving as understudies for the role.

Sometime on Friday, Smith had privately told A. J. Henderson, a deputy sheriff, that since the trial certain unidentified persons had offered to help him get his Negroes back "by force." Smith had not specified whether he had accepted the offer. But James M. Barnes, who had resided with the Smith family for a time, would soon shed light on the likely identity of these individuals, testifying that since the trial another of Smith's trail hands, Hartwell Cottrell, had said, "It was right Smith should have the Negroes."

Robert Mays Smith's three older boys had then chimed in, according to Barnes, saying:

> "[I]f their father had their grit, they would have the Negroes that were taken from them on habeas corpus lately. . . ." I understood them to allude to Hannah, Biddy, Ann, and Ellen. . . . [I]f they can get their consent, they intend to take them on this trip, and all are now in Los Angeles with the intention of looking around and feeling to see what the Negroes have to say in relation to going. [Smith] sold his cattle for $2,000 and has about $500 left.

The ambiguity of the "they" mentioned by Barnes is not clarified in the transcripts of the testimony that he was eventually called to give concerning these machinations, but could have included the teamsters Cottrell and Meredith, Smith's two older sons, and Smith himself. What is certain is that Cottrell and Meredith came to the Owens house sometime on Friday to confront Biddy and the older girls. They were drunk. After shopping for last-minute supplies, the men apparently stopped at one or more of the numerous saloons lining Los Angeles's dusty roads. By the time they arrived at the Owens's, their voices were raucous and their pounding on the door insistent.

Biddy was not home, but Robert Owens was there, along with Dr. A. H. Cooper who had perhaps come to have a look at Hannah's baby or to show his support. There may have been discussion between Ann, Ellen, and the men as to whether they should open the door, but in time someone did.

"[T]hey repeatedly asked Anna and Ellen to go," according to Dr. Cooper's account of the incident, "stating that the wagons were ready; that they were as free as any one; that the Judge had prejudged himself by not having discharged them; that Smith did not want to take them away to bondage, and was not going away, he wanted to have them as well situated as with him; if they wanted to go, they should go, and if anyone objected, let him come forward and they would show that they should go."

"Old man Smith has plenty of money," Cottrell reportedly said.

"Yes, and by God, he will see them out with it—he is not done with it yet," added Meredith. "[T]ell old Bob [Owens] if he has anything to do with it, not to have, or he will be sorry for it."

Cottrell's deposition following the confrontation directly contradicted the doctor's. He denied any intention to persuade Ann and Ellen to leave. "The family are all reconciled to the disposition that has been made of this matter by the Court," he said, adding that he and Meredith "merely wished to take them to see their old mistress, who is in bad health and wished to see them before leaving." He fingers Meredith as the man to blame for any misunderstanding: "I was out of the house when Meredith said, 'Old Smith will see them out,' and 'Old Bob will be sorry for it.' [H]e was drunk or would not have said it."

But in the next breath, Cottrell proved himself as undependable a liar as he was an accomplice. "I told the girls . . . that if they wanted to go to Texas as Mr. Smith had laid in provisions for them and they were free, they could go, according to law, as I thought—I did not say positively. I asked them to go out to the rancho—I don't think I asked them or urged them to go to Texas with us—if I did, I forgot it." That is to say, Robert Mays Smith's "reconciliation" to the court's disposition of the matter had not deterred him from buying supplies for the slaves he was supposedly leaving behind.

The most convincing evidence of Smith's involvement in the encounter at the Owens's home is revealed in Cottrell's testimony. First, he had told the girls that they were free and could go "according to the law." Then he made his explanation into an inducement. "I told them these words: 'The sheriff tells you to stay here; if you start it, it will be time enough for them to come forth and make his objections.'" Ann and Ellen, in other words, were being urged to follow Hannah's example, to exercise their "free" decision to go to Texas with the Smiths. It is a persuasive strategy that Cottrell and his sidekick, Meredith, could hardly have formulated on their own.

Owens and Dr. Cooper were likely instrumental in ending this first standoff, but it was not long before Cottrell was back again—this time with one of the Smith boys, probably William.

Later that day, according to Dr. Cooper, "Smith's son came and took out Ann and had a long conversation with her." Hannah's daughter Ann was seventeen years old and already a mother of two-year-old Mary. She had met Willy when he was ten and she was eight, having arrived with her mother and brother from South Carolina to join the Smith family in Mississippi. After the two years in Utah came California; the two had crossed into adolescence on the ranch on the Santa Ana River, and Ann had become pregnant there at fifteen. Perhaps Willy could not stand the thought of losing someone he had known half his life, or perhaps they were more than friends—perhaps Mary was his child.

Dr. Cooper became alarmed at some point during this second encounter at the Owens's, slipped out of the house, and ran to alert the authorities. He would have gone in a state of panic to Sheriff Alexander's office, telling the sheriff that Smith's gang was trying to coerce the older girls into leaving and had to be stopped. Sheriff Alexander would have agreed, but would have gone first to Judge Hayes's home, which, fortunately, was nearby, told him an abduction attempt was under way, and asked for orders to take the girls into protective custody. Because the Smith boy and the two teamsters were interfering with the court's placement of the minor girls and children in the Owens's home, Judge Hayes's agreement to the order was preordained. Biddy was presumably added to the order because she also resided in the Owens's house and was, therefore, in danger.

The unexpected and inspired addition to the order was the name of Hannah. Judge Hayes, heartsick at Hannah's imminent departure, realized—and Sheriff Alexander may have pointed it out or even insisted—that he now had an opportunity to include Hannah in the protective order. The argument in favor of her inclusion would have been that Smith, by his present actions or the actions of his agents, demonstrated that he was trying to take these people by force and that this behavior could be construed to apply to Hannah. The argument against adding Hannah to the order would have been that she had already stated in open court that she wanted to go. And although Benjamin knew it to be a lie, she had said it under oath. Force, therefore, was not legally a justification for taking Hannah into protective custody.

Pen in hand, however, the judge knew that without his addition of Hannah's name to the order, she might be gone by morning. He again weighed legal and moral outcomes, signed his name, and handed the paper back to the sheriff.

Biddy, the girls, and the children were quickly taken to the county jail and placed in the all-too-familiar cells. Charles, Hannah's six year old, was ordered into protective custody in San Bernardino County, where he had presumably been staying with his father, Toby. A posse went into the Santa Monica hills and returned with Hannah. On Friday night, long after dark, Hannah entered the jail, walked between the crowded cells, and finally—finally—embraced her children.

Arrests were made swiftly: Cottrell and Meredith, but not the Smith boy. Depositions were taken. Hayes, later reading a transcript of Cottrell's deposition, pronounced him "unscrupulous." A court appearance was scheduled for Monday morning, the obvious purpose of which was to implicate Robert Mays Smith in a kidnapping attempt. Cottrell was released pending the appearance in court Monday morning. His last words to the court were: "I am one of the teamsters; if I go home tonight we will start tomorrow," meaning Sunday. Apparently, the judge and sheriff hoped that with his teamster back in camp, Smith would decide to leave town that weekend, bringing this matter, at long last, to a close.

According to the court records, Robert Mays Smith "seemed to be content" with the execution of the protective orders.[3] But as had so often been true of this strange case, things were not what they seemed.

After giving his affidavit concerning the events of Saturday at the Owens's home, Dr. Cooper had been approached by one Joseph Clark around sunset. Cooper said that Clark demanded:

> [I] must go to _____'s shop and withdraw the affidavit brought by me in this case—that it must be settled that night on Southern principles, or I would suffer for it. I told him the affidavit contained the truth. He then said, "No one but a d____d abolitionist could have made it, and there is a gang joined here together to swindle Smith out of his Negroes." After much violent abuse, he

jumped off his horse, saying "You are a d____d abolitionist too, and I would as soon blow your brains out as not." He got his pistol half out—I stepped into the house. He then mounted his horse, saying "G_d d__n you, I will settle it with you before morning." He then rode away. The object was, I believe, to intimidate me from appearing as a witness.

Incredibly enough, after his release, Cottrell appeared at the jail on Sunday night with one of Smith's sons, likely Willy again, where Carpenter, the jailer, was keeping guard over Hannah, Biddy, and the children. "[T]hey brought a bottle of brandy for Ann," Carpenter reported, and "from their maneuvers, I believe they came to carry off some of the children."

―――

We can only imagine the desperation Robert Mays Smith was feeling on Sunday night, January 27. Only six months before, he had learned the Mormons were reclaiming his homestead on Jumuba. For months, he had tried to find a way to stay in California, including a pitiful attempt at hunting gold, but by November, he had begun making preparations to close the ranch. Leaving Jumuba had seemed as hard as anything he had ever done—but he had not known what was yet to come.

Now his life truly seemed a shambles. Having been involved in the beginnings of a new American faith, having known its leaders intimately, he was now considered an apostate. Having realized his dream of a ranch in California, having trusted men he considered spiritual brothers, he was now, thanks to them, homeless. Having been publicly scourged by a judge who shared his southern blood, he was now forced to choose between abandoning two women and a dozen children who had been part of his life or replacing them in the county jail. All Smith had to his name, really, was five hundred dollars and a bill for court costs. Thanks to the trial, they were already a month behind the scheduled departure for Texas and would pay the price trying to make it through the desert in the summer months.

When they returned from visiting the county jail late that evening, Willy and Cottrell might have been confronted by Smith for their stupidity and full of excuses for their behavior. It was all Dr. Cooper's fault, after all, for reporting them to the sheriff. *Hell's bells, they weren't trying to kidnap anyone, they was only asking!*

Although the Sunday-night visit to the jail may have been the Smith family's last-ditch effort to snatch some of their former slaves, it is equally possible that a lovesick young man was merely saying good-bye. The bottle of brandy given to Ann may have been a parting gift, a memento of their shared history. It is not difficult to imagine Willy, having undertaken his errand against his father's wishes or advice, standing forlorn outside a barred window.

Now that the two had returned from town, Robert Mays Smith had a decision to make. Tomorrow Cottrell would have to return to court. Robert himself would undoubtedly be summoned, if not arrested, and everything that had happened in the past few days would condemn him, whether he was guilty or not. It was time to go, but perhaps Smith hesitated. The memory of those faces at the barred windows would haunt all of them the rest of their lives. And if Smith had learned one thing in traversing a continent, it was that, for him, there was no turning back.

Even in winter, in California, the sun rises early. Robert saw the expectant faces around him and signaled for the wagons to roll.

On Monday morning, Judge Hayes found himself once more behind his bench, ready to hear testimony about the weekend's incredible events. Cottrell was nowhere to be found, but in response to his visit to the jail Sunday night, Hayes leveled a contempt charge against him for "attempting to induce two of said minors to leave the Sheriff's custody, etc."

But Cottrell would never answer to that charge. Sometime during the proceedings that morning or just after them, Judge Hayes received what could only have been welcome news: the Smiths were on their way to Texas.

EIGHT

Five Codas

Robert and Rebecca

O N MARCH 16, 1856, a special conference of the San Bernardino branch of the Church of Jesus Christ of Latter-day Saints was held. The *Deseret News* in Salt Lake would later report from its minutes: "The following persons were cut off from the Church by the unanimous vote of the conference." One person was charged with running off without paying his debts, but the offense of the other nine was "unchristianlike conduct." There is no elaboration available concerning the charge. The only clue may be President Charles Rich's advice to "all who wish to retain a standing in the Church, to live up to their covenants."[1] Listed among the names is Robert M. Smith. The expulsion might have simply been punishment for his failure to submit obediently to church authorities. Undoubtedly, there was bad blood between Smith and the brethren concerning the appropriation of Smith's property in San Bernardino. In addition, in the church's close-knit community, rumors might well have circulated about Smith's involvement in efforts to subvert the habeas corpus trial or the nature of his relationships with his former slaves and the parentage of some of their children. Although two women are included on the list of persons excommunicated—one named and the other referred to as "and wife"—Rebecca Dorn Smith is not mentioned in any way.

When or if he learned of the excommunication, Robert might well have felt the righteous vindication people sometimes do when seemingly victimized by circumstance again and again: *The world is a corrupt and formidable opponent; none of this is my fault.*

By March 1856, Robert and his party were well along the trail to Texas. According to *Robert Mays Smith: From South Carolina to Texas (the Long Way)*, a family history book, the trip through the desert Southwest was both difficult and dangerous.[2] Traveling with the Smith family were thirteen men Robert had hired as trail hands. They included Cottrell and Meredith, whose unscrupulous natures had recently come to the attention of Judge Hayes—and, of course, Robert himself. When speaking around any of the Smith children, Cottrell and Meredith were apparently wary, but an orphan boy whom the Smiths had let join their party overheard the men plotting: they intended to lead the Smiths into the desert and steal their cattle and horses, leaving the family there to perish. The boy's tale was almost unbelievable, but Robert and sons—four who would have been of age to be helpful in a fight—had to be ready. They kept themselves armed and waited for the men to make their move.

In the meantime, one of Cottrell's men attracted the unwelcome attention of a tribe of Indians. Returning to camp one day, he reported he had come upon an Indian woman swimming in a river. The woman had become frightened and fought him, and he had killed her—accidentally, he said. Retaliation for what was most likely a rape and a murder was certain. When the Indians came to the Smith camp, demanding to know which man was responsible, the company was at first mute. Eventually, though, one of the terrified children pointed out the perpetrator. The Indians took the man from camp, and he was never seen again.[3]

The Smiths moved on through the desert, fearing both the Indians tracking them and the men plotting among them. They were camped near Fort Yuma in the Arizona Territory when the latter encounter came. One of the ringleaders got drunk and began making threats. Nineteen-year-old Willy Smith drew on the man. Robert and his other sons covered the remaining trail hands. Robert told the men, twelve in all, to take their belongings and the stock that belonged to them and to clear out. Cottrell and his cohorts headed off, preceding the Smith party: Robert knew it was better to have this treacherous group ahead of him than coming up behind. But there was another advantage, as it turned out. Cottrell's company became a lightning rod for the long-anticipated Indian attack. One of his men was wounded, and the Indians stole the group's stock and forced the company back to the safety of Fort Yuma.

Smith and the few men who had remained loyal to his family went on. After Fort Yuma, they followed the Gila River Trail to Fort Thorn in New Mexico. According to one trail narrative passed down through the generations, the Smiths killed a head of their cattle for food. Indians trailing them asked for the entrails, eating them raw in front of the family. Joseph, who was then eight and a half years old, would remember seeing Indians holding the head of a rattlesnake, forcing it to strike a piece of fresh liver. They used the poison, he was told, for their spears and arrows.

From Fort Thorn, the Smiths followed the Rio Grande to El Paso, which was nothing but a village with a single store, then went along the river to Fort Quitman. In Texas, on the approach to Fort Davis, the Smiths themselves were finally attacked by Indians. At night, when everyone was bedded down except the men watching the herd, the Indians slipped in among the cattle. The men on horseback heard the restless animals and the whooping of the Indians, and were suddenly caught in a stampede. They managed to ride the cattle down, herd them up, and drive them for safekeeping into a cave in the Davis Mountains. They watched until sunrise, but the Indians never returned.

From Fort Davis, the Smiths traveled toward the unrelenting line of the Texas horizon until they arrived in San Antonio on June 26, 1856. In San Pedro Springs, on the outskirts of town, they made camp.

Compared to the mild climate and relatively civilized environment of southern California, Texas in the 1850s was a harsh country. Robert Smith homesteaded land on Salado Creek, then sold it and bought 160 acres a few miles farther west. For a while, his sons Elijah and Joseph had land nearby, but in a few years they wanted to leave. Robert bought their land, making him the owner of 431 acres. For his family's home, Robert built a two-room dog-run cabin. He farmed, made wagons, and hauled freight.

By 1860, Robert and Rebecca had again become guardians of Rebecca's insane brother Densley Dorn, and, perhaps as a consequence of taking on that burden, were given slaves by relatives in South Carolina, reportedly to replace the ones taken from them. The 1860 slave census for Bexar County, Texas, shows Robert and Rebecca with two slaves: a female, age twenty-one, and a male, age two.

During the Civil War, the older four Smith boys fought for the Confederacy. Robert and Rebecca cared for several of their grandchildren. One of them remembered his father speaking often of his mother, Rebecca, but never saying a word about his father, Robert. "His mother raised him up good. He always talked about his sweet mother, but he never did say anything about his father. We never did know why."⁴

After emancipation, the Smith slaves became servants. Children of uncertain parentage again appear in the family records. The 1880 Soundex shows that in the Robert Mays Smith household were a forty-year-old black woman, Emile, born in South Carolina, with sons Ciro, Robert, and Henry, all born in Texas, listed as Smiths. The ages of the woman and her oldest son confirm that they are the former slaves.

According to family history, Robert and Rebecca's older sons were the kind of notorious figures familiar in western lore.⁵ John, the first-born, was a drover on far-reaching cattle drives; became a friend of William "Buffalo Bill" Cody; served as a guide across the California desert; ranched in Medina County, Texas; and retired to San Antonio. William, the second oldest, was later called "Seco," after a creek he lived on. Seco Smith recounted the highlights of his life to a frontier printer who published his tales in periodicals and books. In one story, after a savage attack by Comanches in which he lost two friends, Seco decided to exact revenge on the tribe's chief. The chief took the scalp of one of Seco's friends, tied it to his spear, and shook it at Seco riding up the hill. Seco dropped from his horse, aimed over his saddle, and shot the chief through the heart and skinned him, making saddle strings and whips from his hide.

Seco Smith's drinking was also legendary. Once, after ending up drunk and disorderly in jail, Seco set fire to his clothing; when the jailer opened the cell, Seco rushed past him and jumped, half-naked, on his waiting horse. On another occasion, Seco's son accompanied his father into town, and when their business was done, Seco stopped by his favorite saloon. His son pleaded with his father to come home. "Pa, I'll give you everything I have if you will quit drinking, if you won't get drunk no more." Seco, glass in hand, looked down at the ten-year-old boy and said, "What the hell do you have?"[6]

When asked by a friend what she was going to do about William, Rebecca said that one day her prayers would be answered: before he died, Seco would change his ways. Indeed, toward the end of his life, Seco settled down and became a devout Methodist. He had three marriages—the last at age sixty-two to a twenty-five-year-old beauty—and sired a total of fifteen children.

Robert and Rebecca's other children were more reserved. Elijah, called "Lij" by his family, came home from the Confederate army, ranched for a number of years, and late in life became a cattle buyer. Sidney was an avid farmer, working in the fields after dark if the moon was up. Sarah Flora, Robert and Rebecca's only daughter, married a man who had served with her brothers in the war, had ten children in twenty-four years, and died of cancer at fifty. Joseph first married his brother Elijah's wife's sister, then, after her early death, the woman he hired as a housekeeper. Unlike his wild older brothers, he was known as a quiet, religious man. Robert Mark, Robert and Rebecca's youngest child, married a girl with Irish and Apache ancestry called Sally. He ranched and hauled freight, and lived near Fort Thorn for a time before returning to Texas, but spent his last years in Yuma, at the home of his daughter, Becky.

Rebecca became increasingly religious with age; Robert, however, found his solace in whiskey. In 1886, Rebecca left him and went to live with her children. In October 1886, she wrote that it was a comfort to know that he quit drinking after she was gone.[7]

There is a photograph of Robert Mays Smith in old age: he sits on a couch, beside Rebecca, facing the camera. His large, square hands are on his thighs, as if he does not know what to do with them. His knees are apart, and he wears old shoes. His jacket is tight across the chest, straining against a single button. Beneath his shirt can be seen the

Robert Mays Smith, Rebecca Smith, and son Joseph. Courtesy of Ethel Klemcke and Bob Weed.

collar of long underwear. His striped bow tie is incongruous. Robert's abundant hair is white and wild. His straight brows meet in a deep frown. His eyes, in their shadows, are surprisingly pale. His jaw is square, his mouth set in a firm line. His straight nose seems to have widened with age; the nostrils flare. His expression is intense, even ferocious; it is the face of a man haunted by grievances and overtaken with resentment.

Perhaps he felt time and history would eventually vindicate him: he told a grandson that he was born in Edgefield District, South Carolina, and to remember this fact because "[s]omeday someone will want to know."[8]

Robert Mays Smith died at seven in the morning, on Wednesday, October 28, 1891, at age eighty-six, in Atascosa County, Texas, while he was visiting his daughter, Sarah. He is buried in Rambie Grove Cemetery, fifteen miles southwest of San Antonio, near Somerset.

Rebecca, who had returned to her cantankerous husband three years before his death, supervised his burial. To the surprise of her children who had known her all of their adult lives as a devout Methodist, she requested that Robert be buried in Mormon Temple robes, which she had brought by covered wagon from California and for forty-five years had kept concealed, knowing that one day the fine white robe might, at the least, be useful.[9] However, it is possible that Rebecca, never formally excommunicated from the Church of Jesus Christ of Latter-day Saints, attached some significance to the garment, wishing that Robert in death might somehow be reconciled with his Mormon brothers.

Rebecca Dorn Smith survived Robert by eight years, living with her children and delighting in her grandchildren. The ill health imputed to her in her youth and middle years seems to have abated. She was never known as an invalid by any of her descendants.

One of her last letters, written on September 2, 1893, displays Rebecca's essence: sensitive, insecure, homesick, loving her family, missing her husband, doubting the world but never her Lord. She begins by praising one of her children's homes: "beautiful seanery . . . between two mountains. . . . The place is lovely to me, looks more like my childhood home than I have seen in all my travels. The first school I went to was in a valley . . . at the foot of the mountain. Looks so home like, brings back gone by days. . . . I feel I have been blessed in all my wanderings," she adds suddenly, then speaks of a trip between the homes of her sons:

> We left on Monday at 9 o'clock. . . . [I]t was cloudy and pleasant . . . rained a slow rain on us about ten miles . . . nothing to hinder travel. . . . I felt almost young. . . . As we traveled on, there were good houses, good fences to show that people lived there that were intelligent and industrious and of good taste. . . . Trees looked green . . . grass was dry, but plenty all over to make it lovely. . . . [T]rees looked like old apple trees . . . no underbrush to hide the beauty of the scene.
>
> I send my love to you. . . . [D]ont forget your family is sacred to me . . . never to forget.

She had intended to visit Robert's grave, "the sacred spot," she reports, but decided against it: "I felt it would be sad to me and I did not wish to bring to mind a fresh." She asks her children to overlook the mistakes in her letter. "I cant see very well. Tell the Children not forget me, kiss the two babys for me." In closing, she gropes through her disappointments for something tangible to leave her children—"Learn to put your trust in Jesus. He knows our weakness"—but confesses her "hope of rest when parting is no more." She ends by saying, "I have walked through the world, crave what the [world] never gave. . . . [There is] nothing real here."[10]

On September 29, 1899, at age eighty-nine, Rebecca died in Bexar County, Texas, and is buried beside her husband at Rambie Grove Cemetery.

Benjamin

Immediately after the habeas corpus case, Benjamin Hayes's main concern was his political future. Considering the adverse publicity generated by his championing the freedom of fourteen former slaves, Benjamin questioned whether he should run for reelection. In Sacramento, there was talk of impeaching him. His opponents were already, a full year before the election, uniting to defeat him. "Now we will beat Judge Hayes!" was their rallying cry.[11]

On September 11, 1857, Benjamin and his wife, Emily, took a long walk, returning from a friend's orchard with peaches and ripe figs. The next evening, they spoke of the upcoming election. Emily told him she did not want him to be a candidate again. She complained that campaigning depleted their finances. Benjamin said he did not know if he would run, but if he did, he would let donors pick up the bills. Regardless, Emily was adamant. If he chose to run, she warned, "I will start off for another country!" Benjamin thought she spoke "between jest and earnest," but that night Emily departed for a shore from which there is no return.[12] Her lungs, weakened from tuberculosis, hemorrhaged. Benjamin sent for Dr. Griffin, his brother-in-law and family physician, but there was nothing he could do. Within a few short hours, Emily was dead. She was thirty-six years old.

Benjamin Hayes had known his wife's health was precarious. Her cough, activated by almost any exertion, was a constant concern, but he had thought she was improving. Emily knew better. She wrote her sister about watching Chauncey at play, wild and healthy as a young deer: "It makes my heart ache when I think of leaving Chauncey—and I cannot expect to live to raise him."[13]

Benjamin was devastated by Emily's death. That night, Chauncey was taken to the house of Benjamin's sister Helena, wife of Benjamin Eaton, the first district attorney of Los Angeles, and Benjamin eventually went home with Dr. Griffin and his wife, Louise, another sister.

In the morning, he went to the Eaton house where he found Chauncey and his cousins enthralled with a litter of puppies. Benjamin took his son to the cemetery to show him where his mother would lie, next to his little sister, but four-year-old Chauncey wanted only to get back to the puppies. Benjamin returned home then and spent the day in Emily's rocking chair, thinking of his wife and making resolutions. He was comforted by recalling Father Raho's frequent comment about Emily: "If anyone will go to Heaven, she will!"[14]

Ultimately, Benjamin decided to run for reelection and won, despite the adverse publicity he had received because of the trial. His victory was a testament to his overall judicial reputation, the ability of voters to see beyond a single issue, and his retention of a few influential friends. On January 4, 1859, he was again sworn into office.

During the next years, Benjamin traveled throughout southern California in the course of his duties as a district judge. For protection, he carried a double-barreled shotgun and a Bowie knife. Benjamin took Chauncey with him as much as possible and missed him terribly when he began attending boarding school at San Paschal Rancho in present-day Pasadena. "When he goes away I hardly know what I will do. I must submit to it. So far, he has acquired no bad habits from his playmates on the streets. He is innocent, and good." But Benjamin's faith in a beneficent Providence was obviously shaken following Emily's death; upon hearing the tolling of bells, he wrote: "Is my little boy still living, or will the steamer bring me bad news?"[15]

Over the next few years, Benjamin's yearning for companionship was a recurring topic of his journals. He was caught by a Jewess's dark eyes, touched by the kindness of a married woman, and even responded to an old woman's coquetry. At forty-four years of age, he was, he confessed, still susceptible. His drinking increased; it dulled his pain, but introduced guilt. He who had started a temperance league in Missouri now drank occasionally to oblivion. In his book *Sixty Years in Southern California,* Harris Newmark noted that Hayes "was known as a jurist of high standing, though on account of his love of strong drink, court on more than one occasion had to be adjourned."[16] But Benjamin fought to stay sober, to find other solace for his sorrow.

His collecting of historical memorabilia, once an avocation, became an obsession. To record, to preserve, what was significant, to find meaning behind fact and event—these became the principles of his daily life and eventually his reason for living: he would turn his research into a single comprehensive history of southern California.

Meanwhile, the looming national conflagration—"May Heaven avert it!"—overshadowed his personal problems. On November 5, 1860, Benjamin Hayes noted his disenchantment with Abraham Lincoln's presidential election: "I voted for Douglass, both on the ground that he seemed to me to be the real nominee of the National Democratic Convention, and because his doctrine as to slavery in the Territories appeared to be the most practical way of settling forever this vexed question; so much for my vote."[17]

As the Civil War edged closer, Benjamin felt himself torn by conflicting loyalties. The man who had a few years before declared the inalienable liberty of a handful of slaves now reported he was fearful of the Emancipation Proclamation. "Never was there a revolution for juster cause," he declared to a friend. "The North I consider to be wrong on the vital issue," he wrote. "And the South is right, I think." "... But," he added, "my lot has been cast on the shores of the Pacific."[18]

The "juster cause" and "vital issue" apparently refer not to the question of slavery, but to the concept of states' rights. Benjamin Hayes, like many Southerners, thought it wrong for the North to impose its will upon a region fundamentally opposed to its dictates. "A few weeks only, we shall know our destiny. Myself born and educated on Southern soil, I observed with intense solicitude the course of Maryland—my mother!—and hardly with less interest, of Missouri, where my early manhood first met a kindly encouragement. If they secede, I am not the one who will have the ungrateful daring to impeach their patriotism, or suspect their righteousness."[19]

Yet Benjamin's sympathies continued to be tested. His family and friends were Southerners. Albert Sidney Johnston, who led Federal troops into Utah after the Mountain Meadows massacre, was Dr. Griffin's brother-in-law. Johnston later recruited a force of one hundred in the Los Angeles area and led them overland to fight for the Confederacy, where he was commissioned a brigadier general. He died at Shiloh. Benjamin came close to declaring himself aligned with the South: "I suppose any of my old acquaintances can imagine what is likely to be my course, if the worst comes to the worst." Yet he pleaded for "perfect freedom of opinion," accompanied by "forbearance, respect and moderation on all sides."[20]

In the 1863 election, Benjamin Hayes's opponent was Don Pablo de la Guerra who had demonstrated Southern sympathies, but, with the change in public sentiment, had become a staunch Unionist. Hayes, who had been called an abolitionist, now came under attack for being a Southerner. Caught in the national cross fire, Hayes could not and would not denounce the South, which had given him much of what he considered best about himself. "And still," he proclaimed, "I am for the Union." He knew he would be accused of sedition, but was adamant in his patriotism. "[I]t will be difficult for any man truthfully to record any act or sentiment of mine, inconsistent with fidelity to the Union."[21]

For Hayes, his personal views and his judicial record on slavery were not antithetical: "Whatever prepossessions a man may have on the political or social controversies of the day, no true sentiment of 'State Rights'—if he reflect well—will consent to the evasion and violation of the Constitution of his State; all should have pride enough to wish to keep unimpaired the integrity of his own Institutions."

Further employing the same logic, Hayes saw his support of the South and his belief in the Union as grounded on the same bedrock, namely, the Constitution of the United States. On this point, he made his stand: "I must leave to others to tell you how far I fulfill Thomas Jefferson's two requirements for office: 'Is he honest? Is he capable?' But it would be a false modesty, if I hesitated to declare myself plainly, as to his third test—'Is he faithful to the constitution?'"[22]

For the first time in his career, Hayes's alcoholism may have become an issue. His opponent could raise the specter of the inebriated judge fumbling as he tried to dispense justice. The charge was exaggerated. On rare occasions, Hayes's drinking prevented him from carrying out his judicial duties, but generally when he sat on the bench he was stone sober.[23] Moreover, he had recently stopped drinking altogether. But the reform had come too late to save his reputation.

Hayes seemed to sense he was fighting a losing battle, but he intended to wage it with honor, neither denigrating his heritage nor letting accusations of disloyalty go unanswered. Still, the barrage of criticism continued from both sides. He was deemed a "Copperhead," a Democrat who, by opposing vigorous persecution of the war, gave moral support to the South's rebellion. On November 5, 1863, after two terms as judge of the First District Court in California, Benjamin Hayes was swept out on the tide of anti-Southern sentiment. Of the thirteen district judges elected in 1863, only one "Copperhead" kept his office.

Without the comfort of a wife, the distractions of high public office, and the anesthesia of alcohol, Benjamin Hayes found himself ill-equipped to endure the years in which his country was engaged in what he considered "a fratricidal war." Sometimes he despaired. Once, on a beach with Chauncey, watching the sun sink into the ocean, he wondered if the sight might not be a metaphor for the fortunes of "our glorious Country." If it sank, he doubted that it would ever rise again. In a postscript to a letter, he reported stepping outside into a starry night: "How I wished I could hear a full band strike up the Star-Spangled Banner!" He noted that Maryland, the state of his birth, had given the anthem to the nation. "Tell your youngest granddaughter to sing it for you, and so may it inspirit each coming generation." He remembered his joy, having crossed the Nevada desert, when he came upon a village and found the flag "so gallantly streaming."[24] His fervent hope was that his own boy would grow up to cherish the song and to love the flag.

During the Civil War, known to Southerners as the War between the States, Benjamin Hayes's voluminous notebooks grew thick. He saved newspaper clippings of Lincoln's inaugural address, the Constitution of the Confederate States of America, the appointments of generals, and accounts of all the battles. The content of the clippings gradually changed with casualty lists, Sherman's scorching swath, the work of Catholic sisters among former slaves, and the South's devastation and suffering dominating the newsprint.

On April 15, 1865, while Dr. John S. Griffin, Hayes's brother-in-law, was paying a professional call on the Newmark family, a man ran by shouting that Abraham Lincoln had been shot. "Griffin, who was a staunch Southerner, was on his feet instantly, cheering for Jeff Davis," wrote Harris Newmark in *Sixty Years in Southern California*. "He gave evidence, indeed, of great mental excitement, and soon seized his hat and rushed for the door, hurrahing for the Confederacy." Newmark, realizing Griffin would be in jeopardy if he reached the street, forcibly held him back. Later, Dr. Griffin thanked him, acknowledging that his patient had saved him from certain death.[25] Hayes's sentiments on Lincoln's assassination are unknown. He was a devout Catholic and deplored violence, but he was also a Southerner with little affinity for the president. Southerners did not know at the time how Lincoln's death would greatly exacerbate the ruinous period known as Reconstruction.

Soon after the clippings reporting Lincoln's assassination in Hayes's notebooks appear articles concerning the war's end: General Lee's surrender to Grant at Appomattox Courthouse and his ride away on Traveler, Jefferson Davis shackled and taken prisoner. The Union had been saved, but at what cost?

In southern California, the years during and after the war were bleak. Then, as now, hard times trigger desperation and a concomitant rise in crime. Benjamin Hayes resumed his law practice in Los Angeles and found sufficient clients to support himself and his son. He moved frequently during these years, taking a suite of rooms in a boardinghouse, or staying in hotels.[26] The homes of his sisters took the place of his own; aunts, uncles, and cousins provided Chauncey with a sense of family.

Being an itinerant lawyer was by now a sideline; Hayes's main oc-cupation had become the collecting of historical materials. In scrap-books made from hollowed-out legislative journals, he pasted newspa-per articles on all aspects of California life, from native races, to mining, to social customs and political activities. On a daily basis, he recorded the times of sunrise and sunset and every detail of the weather: temperature, precipitation, wind direction, and unusual oc-currences. He was an amateur botanist, describing the plants he came upon. Besides newspaper clippings, he had important Catholic Church documents: San Diego mission books, a manuscript history by Father Lasuen, and a copy of an autograph manuscript by Father Junipero Serra. In 1852, an advertisement in the *Los Angeles Star* sought "a book giving an account of the Life and Missionary labors of Rev. Fa-ther Junipero Serra, and also a minute Chronicle of all the Missions in California." The prospective buyer of the book, which had been pub-lished in Mexico in 1787, said he was "a gentleman who is preparing a history of California from the earliest date."[27]

Benjamin also collected innumerable civic records. He had copies of all the important pueblo archives from 1829, records of the proceed-ings of military officials, correspondence between civic leaders, procla-mations by California governors, and reports of the most important civil and criminal trials. He saved materials relating to his former pro-fession, including articles about the English judiciary, and the pen-sioning and retirement of judges. In his notebooks were reams of pub-lished poetry, ranging from Shakespeare's sonnets and religious evocations to the maudlin and bawdy. Sometimes Hayes went far afield, preserving passages dealing with the sea, the creation of pearls, astronomy, Arctic exploration, Darwinism, life on other worlds, and comets, those "luminous strangers."[28]

As alluded to in his anonymous ad, this warehouse of materials was to serve as the basis for a California history, and he did manage some writing: accounts of his travels throughout the state and occasionally an article on an aspect of its past. However, the actual book, his *History of Southern California,* remained elusive. He thought about it constantly; what he could not do was begin.

In early 1866, while Benjamin was visiting the ranch of Don Ser-rano in San Diego, two young women rode up, one a beauty with flashing dark eyes. Her name was Adelaide. The guests later appeared on the porch; time passed, Benjamin noted, most cheerfully. Because it was New Year's, someone sang "Auld Lang Syne," and Benjamin Hayes bid adieu to the painful past. At siesta everyone slept, except Benjamin, who remained awake and restless, bewitched by the woman he had just met. Emily was the essence of the South, his past, whereas Adelaide personified California, his future.

On August 2, 1866, Benjamin married Adelaide Serrano, second daughter of Don Jose Antonio Serrano of San Diego. With thirteen-year-old Chauncey away at school, Benjamin Hayes began a new life in San Diego. Within a year, Hayes and his young bride had a daughter, Mary Adelaide. He served as local district attorney from 1866 to 1867 and as state assemblyman from San Diego from 1867 to 1868. Afterward, he resumed his law practice. Married to a daughter in an old and prominent family, Benjamin found life pleasant and colorful. Then tragedy struck again. On March 31, 1873, at age twenty-eight, his second wife died. The barely healed wound was ripped open again. "Emily! Adelaide!" he cried in his journal.[29] Once more Benjamin was left to raise a young child by himself.

On February 14, 1874, Benjamin Hayes celebrated his sixtieth birthday, although he looked much older. Two photographs of Benjamin Hayes warrant comparison. In one, taken just before leaving Missouri for California or shortly upon his arrival there, Benjamin is a young man, in his early thirties, his hair dark and parted in the middle, his face boyish with a poet's mouth, and beneath narrow, dark brows are pale eyes with a vulnerable, almost haunted expression. The other photograph, taken in the last years of his life, shows Benjamin Hayes as an old man: his hair thin, white, and receding; deep lines etched around the delicate mouth; a fringe of white hair beneath his chin; and eyes more hurt than haunted.

Nine days after his birthday occurred an event that changed the course of Benjamin Hayes's remaining years.[30] He and his seven-year-old daughter, Mary Adelaide, were living in San Diego, on Stockton Hill, in a hacienda overlooking the Presidio. Beside the porch were pear and olives trees, just beginning to bud. Adelaide had friends over, and the little girls scampered and tittered through the house's many rooms. What Benjamin saw that morning was a cloud of rising dust signaling the arrival of a carriage and unexpected visitors. And what visitors they were! The man striding up the steps was none other than

Benjamin Ignatius
Hayes, circa 1877.
From Benjamin Hayes,
Pioneer Notes.

Hubert Howe Bancroft, who, at age forty-four, was a prominent book
dealer, fledgling historian, and founder of a notable private library in
San Francisco. With him was his thirteen-year-old daughter, Kate, and
Mr. Oak, his assistant. Many times in their pursuit of historical materials, Hayes and Bancroft had crossed paths, and their meetings had always been enjoyable and stimulating. Bancroft was, in truth, the only
man capable of appreciating Hayes's collection. And now, here he was.

Bancroft told Judge Hayes they were on a tour of the southland and
hoped to avail themselves of this opportunity to see Hayes's splendid
collection. Benjamin invited the trio to stay for lunch and said afterward
he would gladly display his "scraps." Bancroft declined; he did not mean
to intrude and wished merely to make an appointment at a convenient
time, for now they were bound for Old Town to visit the archives of a

mission. Hayes encouraged them to return after lunch, then again watched from the porch as a cloud of dust rose and dissipated.

What motivated the visit was no real mystery: Bancroft's historical collection was the finest in California, but Hayes, in his twenty-five years of collecting, possessed documents, manuscripts, and records that Bancroft lacked. "This collection," Bancroft would later write, "was by far the most important in the state outside my own; and this, added to mine, would forever place my library, as far as competition in original California materials was concerned, beyond the possibilities." Bancroft recognized that the question was "how to transfer this rich mass of historical material to my library . . . notwithstanding the affection with which he who had labored over the work so long must regard it."[31] Hayes knew that Bancroft coveted his historical collection; what was puzzling was that Bancroft had not written to say he was coming. He soon learned why. Bancroft meant to ask for Hayes's collection and would have had to announce as much in a letter.

From the day in 1849 that Hayes had set foot on California soil, he had dreamed of a comprehensive history of southern California, a work that would describe it all: the sun, ocean, mountains, desert, plants, native races, missions, Spanish rulers, early explorers, pioneers, gold rush, advent of statehood, impact of the Civil War, and emerging cities. Toward that end, writing his encyclopedic book, Hayes had poured over newspapers; spent days in dusty, dim archives; transcribed court records; copied political documents; written down every story, myth, and legend told to him; cajoled heirs out of family heirlooms; and kept copious notes of his own travels. What had begun as a modest assemblage grew over the years into a vast warehouse. And the writing? Ah, the writing . . .

He had notes, of course, massive quantities of jottings, notebooks filled with ideas about how to do it, essays on structure and themes, lists of points to include, and references, yet, after all these years, the work itself was not begun. He had rationalized the delay by saying he still had to find certain essential documents, had things to tie up, connections to make. Although that may have had validity a decade earlier, by now, he realized, it had become an excuse. And Bancroft knew it.

Bancroft had often met Judge Hayes in San Francisco and knew that Hayes was familiar with his "literary doings," by which he meant gathering materials for his library. Now Bancroft had come to ask for

Hayes's collection, and was embarrassed because he knew what the request would imply.

When Bancroft returned later that day, Hayes escorted him, his daughter, and Oaks into the room that served as his study, but was actually a depository. The bookshelves were barely visible behind stacked boxes and piled tables. Bancroft described the chaos in the room: "There were some fifty or sixty scrap-books, besides bundles of assorted and unassorted scraps. All stowed in trunks, cupboards, and standing on book-shelves."[32] Hayes moved about the room, showing his journal of his 1849 trip to California and twenty-five years of newspapers, articles, letters, political speeches, documents of every description, court records, weather reports, geological studies, manuscript histories, mission books, and records of important civil and criminal trials, including transcripts of cases over which he had presided.

Bancroft's daughter, who was soon to depart for a boarding school in New Hampshire, served as her father's secretary during the meeting. Hayes noticed he was talking faster than she could write, so he slowed down and began interspersing stories between the items he enumerated. Later, in his memoirs, *Literary Industries*, Bancroft would describe Hayes's digressions:

> Fortunately for us, old men love to talk about themselves; so that while we were noting valuable facts he kindly filled the interludes with irrelevant matter, thus keeping us pretty well together. . . .
> Taking up one after another of his companion-creations, fondly the little old man handled them; affectionately he told their history. Every paper, every page, was to him a hundred memories of a hundred breathing realities. These were not to him dead facts; they were, indeed, his life.[33]

Bancroft was exuberant over what he saw. He said that, compared to the service Hayes had performed for his country, the world, and posterity by his historical efforts, his years of sitting upon a judicial bench and deciding cases was no more than "catching flies." Would Hayes have let the observation pass, or would he have told of at least one case in which his judicial decision transformed forever the lives of two women and their children? Bancroft himself, as an eleven-year-old boy in Granville, Ohio, had driven a wagon of runaway slaves on a leg of a journey from Kentucky to Canada.[34] Had he heard the story of the emancipation of Hannah and Biddy, he would have conceded that it, too, was noble work.

In the late afternoon, when the judge was no doubt spent, Bancroft finally broached the subject that was, he confessed, "nearest to his heart." "Judge," he said, "your collection should be in my library."

And there it was, the suggestion that would have made Hayes's spirit flail like an impaled butterfly: his history of southern California was never going to be written.

"Even if you should write your proposed history," Bancroft said, "the results, I fear, would be unsatisfactory to you." He would not, he said, know where to begin or end such a work. Bancroft had isolated the painful truth of the matter. Perhaps like a fantastic mirage, the completed book, his history of southern California, appeared before Benjamin's eyes once more. Then the image wavered and was gone.

"I shall never write my history," Hayes sadly conceded. "Time has slipped away."

Bancroft, his abundant black beard gleaming, leaned back in his chair and began a passionate discourse. He said the judge's collection belonged with his, that together they would make his library one of the greatest historical repositories in the world.

"I know that my material should be added to yours," Hayes said. "It's the only proper place for it, the only place I could bear to see it out of my possession."

Bancroft was effusive in his acceptance. Hayes stopped him. There was one last thing to do.

All his life he had been imprudent with money. He had come into a land of great resources, with endless possibilities for acquiring wealth. His friends had grown rich, purchasing land, buying up water rights, investing in timber, mines, freight routes, and railroads. His money had gone for books, maps, and manuscripts. Now his friends were land barons and captains of industry, and he was an old man, a widower, in declining health, with nothing to leave his young daughter or means to assist Chauncey at school. He could not let them suffer to save his pride. Benjamin Hayes did a thing he found deeply repugnant: he spoke of money.

"I would gladly give it to you," he said to Bancroft, "did not I need money so badly." He gestured toward the door through which his daughter and her friends could be seen playing. "I have to furnish bread for certain mouths." His shame was almost palpable. "It is not pleasing to me to make merchandise of such labors."

Bancroft said: "I do not ask you to give me your collection. I will gladly pay you for it, and still hold myself your debtor to the same extent as if you gave it. I appreciate your feelings fully." His own wife had died a few years earlier, and he too was a widower with a young daughter to think about.

Still Hayes hesitated. "It may seem a trifle to give up my accumulations for money," he said to Bancroft, "but it is not. It is the delivering, still-born, of my last and largest hope." Yet, he knew what he had to do. "I can't die and leave my materials to be scattered here. You may have them; and with them take all that I can do for your laborious undertaking as long as I live."[35]

Bancroft was overjoyed. "Not only shall I have the results of your labor up to this time, but your active aid and cooperation for the future. It is just such knowledge as yours that I am attempting to save." He had a whole list of activities on which he needed Hayes's help. He asked the judge to add to his collection while it was in Bancroft's library, exactly as if it were still housed in Hayes's home.

Thus it was, by his astute generosity, that Bancroft relieved Hayes of several burdens that day, not the least of which were worries about providing an inheritance for his young daughter and son. Hayes, thank God, did not know that Mary Adelaide would die in early womanhood, leaving Chauncey his only heir. Chauncey would go to law school and become, like his father, a judge, serving for many years as city judge of Oceanside, California.[36] In the meantime, however, with his son in law school, his daughter provided for, and his collection in good hands, Hayes could relax and do what he liked best: gathering artifacts of history and discerning how they fit together.

Bancroft, in turn, was astonished by the extent of Hayes's cooperation. "In transmitting to me his material, Judge Hayes seemed anxious that it should go forth, like a beloved daughter to her marriage, in its best apparel. And therein he proved himself a high-minded lover of history, ready to give himself, his time and best remaining thoughts to the cause." He "not only placed me in possession of all his collection," Bancroft wrote, "but gave me his heart with it. . . . He was pure-hearted and high-minded in every respect."[37]

J. Chauncey Hayes,
circa 1925. Courtesy of
the San Diego
Historical Society,
Photograph Collection.

During the following year, Hayes made several trips to Los Angeles, trying to use his influence to obtain resources for Bancroft. But time, they both realized, was running out. In 1876, Bancroft asked Hayes to "take up his residence at Los Angeles, and devote his entire thoughts and energies to securing for me the historical information which was so rapidly fading in that vicinity."[38]

In 1876, Los Angeles had embarked upon a boom period. Land values soared. The hills were dotted with homes. Streetcars appeared upon the streets. Sewers were constructed. In the downtown area, banks and other commercial buildings rose. The dusty pueblo was on its way to becoming a city.

Hayes never reflected in his journals upon the outcome of the trial that had so consumed him twenty years earlier, but in 1876 he would write, "In the Spring of 1850, probably three or four colored persons were in this city. In 1875 they number about one hundred and seventy five souls; many of whom hold good city property, acquired through their industry."[39]

It seems unlikely that he ever wondered about the fate of the defendant, Robert Mays Smith, who shared his loyalty to the South and his weakness for liquor—and one other thing neither would ever realize. Late in life, Benjamin Hayes, reflecting upon his travels, said if he had to choose the most perfect landscape in California, it would be a place he had seen on the Santa Ana River called "Gua-chama" by the local Indians and translated by Hayes as Jumua.[40] Jumua adjoined Robert Mays Smith's beloved ranch, Jumuba.

In that last year and a half of his life, Benjamin Hayes stayed at the Hotel Lafayette. The work he did during this period was invaluable. He examined the entire collection of original documents in the Los Angeles County Archives and wrote abstracts for all of them, made a complete index of all the papers, and hired two copyists to write out in full the most important documents. Because Hayes had been executor and legal adviser for several important estates, he was given permission to copy materials from their records. "I find a more kindly spirit, or greater confidence in me, growing up among the old native Californians," he wrote Bancroft. These old families gave him their personal and legal papers, and narratives of their memoirs. Shortly before his death, Benjamin Hayes achieved a coup, managing to obtain two large collections of documents, one containing a coveted diary by one of Los Angeles's first American settlers.[41]

Hayes also completed a writing project. In 1876, as part of California's celebration of the nation's centennial, Los Angeles public officials asked three men—Dr. Joseph P. Widney, Col. Jonathan J. Trumball, and Judge Benjamin Ignatius Hayes—to describe the founding and growth of Los Angeles County. On the Fourth of July, less than two months after having received the commission, the three historians presented their finished document.[42]

Benjamin's portion, book 2 of *An Historical Sketch of Los Angeles County, California*, covered the years 1847 to 1867, from the coming of Americans to the end of the Civil War. He described the changes that had come to Los Angeles County and the lives of men he had known intimately. Benjamin concluded the work with a paean to "one common country, under one Union—indivisible, perpetual!"[43]

Dr. Widney would later summarize his regard for the man who had been his coauthor, friend, and, during Benjamin's last illness, patient: "Knowing the man intimately as I did, I can unhesitatingly say that any statement made by him may be accepted as true, as far as human care and precautions can substantiate any historical statement."[44]

Judge Ygnacio Sepúlveda would later write of Benjamin Hayes:

> I saw him in the early days, manfully struggling with adversity, until fate smiled upon him and he reached the District Court bench; and then for many years I saw him preside in the District Court, which then embraced nearly all of Southern California. I see him now, the frail form, patient, quiet, indefatigable, pursing his vocation uncomplainingly and in silence, treating his friends with rare attachment and villifying [sic] not his enemies. . . . To him the sordid acquisition of means was nothing. With the poor he was sympathetic and liberal. His heart ever beat responsive to every noble appeal. He made an upright judge. As a lawyer he was learned. As a man he was unassuming, gentle, and good.[45]

August 2, 1877, Los Angeles, California. The city towers rose to meet a cloudless sky. Rolling hills descended into a sparkling sea. In his room at the Hotel Lafayette, Benjamin Hayes sat at a cluttered desk, studying old documents through a magnifying glass. From faded handwriting, he managed to decipher a word, then another, then . . .[46]

Benjamin Hayes would have considered it the best of deaths.

Biddy and Hannah

When it published Judge Benjamin Hayes's ruling concerning the habeas corpus trial on February 2, 1856, the *Los Angeles Star* noted, "The plaintiffs claiming their freedom were discharged, and, we learn, have hired themselves in different families in the city."[47]

This might well have been the last time history took notice of two extraordinary women as they slipped back into the obscurity that ordinary living tends to enforce. One of them, however, blazed a path meteoric in its significance, and the other whose life after the trial was less well known had a profound effect on the people around her.

In 1856, when Biddy was declared free, there were only a few black families in Los Angeles. Heading the most prosperous one was Robert Charles Owens—the man who had given shelter to Biddy, Ann, Ellen, and their young charges after the trial and had protected them from the threatening and coercive maneuvers of Robert Mays Smith's trail hands.

Shortly after arriving in Los Angeles in December 1853, Robert, known as Uncle Bob, performed manual labor and odd jobs; Aunt Winnie cleaned and washed clothes for white families. However, within a short time, Owens was buying and selling horses and mules. The large ranches near San Diego supplied him with wild livestock that he and his vaqueros broke and sold to settlers as well as the U.S. government, which awarded him a lucrative contract. By 1856, Robert Owens owned several lots on San Pedro Street and had opened a corral and started a livery stable.

Biddy may have met Robert Owens and his son on a visit to the Smith ranch to do business or when Biddy, Hannah, and the children accompanied the Smith family to the pueblo of Los Angeles to shop for supplies. Owens may have played a part in Biddy's decision to stay in California. Although Biddy, as she explained to Judge Hayes, was told by her owner that her legal status in California and Texas would be the same, either Owens or his wife could have contradicted this information and helped Biddy decide to stand her ground against Robert Smith. The Owenses obviously served as role models and provided support for Biddy (and Hannah indirectly) after the trial.

With a place to stay and work as a domestic to support her family, Biddy's life seemed to be moving toward stability. On October 16, 1856, nine months after the trial and the day after her eighteenth birthday, Biddy's daughter Ellen married Charles Owens, linking Biddy forever to this established and productive family. But less than a year after this happy nuptial, tragedy struck. On August 1, 1857, Biddy's fourteen-year-old daughter, Ann, died.[48] The cause is unknown, but she may have been a victim of the smallpox epidemics that visited the city every two years for several decades. The wagon sent to collect corpses was familiar enough to garner a nickname: Black Maria.

In 1859, Biddy's daughter Ellen had a child, giving Biddy her first

View of Los Angeles, 1857. From Benjamin Hayes, *Pioneer Notes.*

grandson, Robert. Another grandson, Henry, would be born a few years later.[49] According to the 1860 U.S. Census, "Bridget," age forty-five, born in Mississippi, was living with Charles and Ellen Owens. This seems to be Biddy: the discrepancy in age and place of birth could be explained by someone else, probably a member of the Owens family, giving information to the census taker.

This same year, a twelve-year-old black girl named Harriet Mason, born in Mississippi, is shown living with a black couple, Louis and Maria Green.[50] This is obviously Biddy's youngest, already working, helping bring in income, for it was during these years that Biddy herself began to be known by the surname Mason. One source has speculated that she took the middle name of Amasa Mason Lyman, the Mormon leader who had accompanied the southerners on their journey from Mississippi to Utah, and then on to California, but this seems to be a stretch at best.[51] The name probably had a deeper significance, as mentioned before: the name of her original owner in Hancock County, Georgia, or the name of a slave man she may have married.

As Biddy's new life continued to unfold, the influence of Judge Benjamin Hayes reasserted itself. It was Hayes who introduced Biddy to his brother-in-law Dr. John Strother Griffin. Griffin, a Virginian with a medical degree from the University of Pennsylvania, arrived in southern California in 1848 as ranking surgeon with Brig. Gen. Stephen Watts Kearny's Dragoons. In 1854, he resigned his commission and returned to California, where for the next forty-four years he

Mural showing Biddy Mason assisting Dr. John Strother Griffin. On walls of
Toland Hall, University of California Medical Center, San Francisco. The artist
was Boruch Barnard Zakheim, assisted by Phyllis Wrightson. Photograph by
Wesley Wong. Courtesy of the University of California, San Francisco, Archives
and Special Collections.

practiced medicine and became wealthy, investing in business and
speculating in land. Among his investments was the purchase of water
rights for Los Angeles and the acquisition of Rancho San Pasqual,
which became, in the 1880s, the city of Pasadena.[52]

In May 1859, Dr. Griffin was awarded a contract to provide medical services to the county hospital and jail. To assist in his general
practice, and with his new duties, Dr. Griffin hired Biddy, paying her
wages of $2.50 a day.[53] Biddy supplemented this income by midwifery
and through nursing during cholera and smallpox epidemics.

Although California was at a remove geographically from the Civil
War, its effects there were certainly felt. As Judge Hayes had learned
firsthand, the political sympathies of Southerners relocated in the West
were predictable and fervent. Biddy had been declared "free forever,"
but she knew that freedom for persons of color was qualified and that
there were many wanting to rescind the few rights she had. In 1860,
Biddy obtained a certified copy of the court order granting her freedom and reportedly carried it everywhere. The order was for her
probably analogous to the Freedom Papers carried by slaves in the

Deep South, guaranteeing them safe passage through watch points for runaways. On New Year's Day 1863 came the Emancipation Proclamation, granting freedom to slaves within the rebellious states, but there was little cause to celebrate as the country fell headlong into the ruinous war years.

The crises in California, as in the South, were both political and economic. Los Angeles entered a depression, brought about by three successive seasons of drought. Grass withered and stock starved, their carcasses littering the rangeland. Great ranches were mortgaged and then lost. Credit was refused to those who had, within recent memory, been cattle and land barons. Shopkeepers sold out if they could, or simply moved away. One local capitalist, holding notes bearing high interest, offered to peddle them for fifty cents on the dollar; he had few takers. For several years, not a cent was collected in taxes in the city.[54]

The end of the war only deepened the depression. The local military post closed, pulling its troops out. This had been one of the city's chief sources of revenue, and the effect was disastrous. More shops failed and foreclosures increased. Los Angeles seemed caught in an unending downward spiral.

Crisis, however, can create opportunity. Biddy Mason, now forty-eight years old, had been working and living frugally for ten years, and she was prepared when her chance came. On November 28, 1866, Biddy purchased, for $250, from William M. Buffum and James F. Burns, lots on Spring Street between Third and Fourth Streets.[55] (Burns had been a deputy sheriff during the time Biddy and the children were held in the county jail.) It was unusual for a person of color, and a woman at that, to own land, but one can imagine that Biddy, who had stepped into a courtroom thinking of herself as a person in bondage and out of it less than a week later as a citizen, understood better than most the power of and freedom in self-determination.

The house, its location considered out of town in those days, had a garden for food, herbs, and flowers, with privacy provided by a willow fence. Her children were told that this was to be their homestead, and whatever circumstances might befall them, they were to retain it always.

The homestead, though, was only the first expression of Biddy's ambition. She certainly had observed that constant displacement and loss of property had brought ruin upon Robert Mays Smith, whereas

Biddy Mason's first home in Los Angeles. Courtesy of the Golden State Insurance Company Records, Department of Special Collections, University Research Library, University of California at Los Angeles.

the fortunes of California's leading families and the prosperity of the Mormon Church were inextricably tied to landownership. Whatever the germ of her plan, Biddy Mason began to establish her financial security through real estate. In 1868, she purchased a second lot, on Olive Street, for $375. The following year, Los Angeles's first land boom began. In 1875, Biddy sold the northern half of the Spring Street lot for $1,500. In 1884, she sold part of the Olive Street land for $2,000. The proceeds were immediately invested in more land or into improvements to the land she already owned. Biddy replaced her frame house with a two-story brick building, living on the upper floor and renting out the lower floors to businesses eager to move into what had become a popular section of town.

By this time, Biddy had begun pursuing philanthropic interests. In 1872, she held a meeting in her home that was to lead to the formation of the First African Methodist Episcopal Church.[56] She paid the start-up costs of the church and later helped meet its taxes. Biddy started a day-care center, visited prisoners in jail, and paid grocery bills for people made homeless by California's recurring floods. "If you hold your hand closed," Biddy was known to say, "nothing good can come in. The open hand is blessed, for it gives in abundance, even as it receives."[57]

The great land boom in Los Angeles reached its peak in 1887. By the 1890s, Biddy's home was in a neighborhood of brick buildings, including the first black business block. Immediately south of her house were the Bradbury Building, the Stock Exchange, and the Grand Central Market. The land she had purchased for $250 was at the heart of the financial district.[58]

Just as Biddy systematically engendered economic independence, she worked to instill values in her family that would create intellectual independence. She encouraged Ellen, who had never learned to read, to attend school with her children. Mother and sons attended Jeremiah Sanderson's boarding school in Stockton, and when they came home, they worked.[59] Robert later told of performing day labor as a boy, working on a ranch, selling charcoal, and driving the wagon that watered down Los Angeles's dusty streets. While encouraging her grandchildren to acquire skills for survival, Biddy stressed understanding and tolerance. Robert called his grandmother his salvation. "She told my father he could not make a farmer or a blacksmith out of a boy who wanted to be a politician, and she was right."[60]

After the death of Charles Owens in 1882, Biddy's daughter Ellen married George Huddleston. Harriet, Biddy's youngest daughter, married twice, to W. H. Brown and a man named Washington. To her grandsons, Biddy was generous, giving them advice and financial assistance. In 1885, Robert Owens and Henry Owens started, with her help, a livery stable. In 1890, Ellen and oldest son, Robert, bought land for $7,200, which they would sell in 1905 for $75,000.[61]

In the UCLA Special Collections is a photograph of Biddy Mason, taken when she was in her fifties. She wears a dark dress that buttons down a ruffled front. At her neck is a big satin bow clipped with a square pin, silver perhaps, or bone. Her gaze is direct, unsettling. If not in her prime in terms of life span, this is certainly Biddy in the prime of her life achievements: her children raised, she is a homeowner, a businesswoman, a woman of great dignity and pride. She would live to be seventy-three, dying at her home on 331 South Spring Street on January 15, 1891, of "Chronic Difficulties with Nephritis." Included in her final estate was her original homestead, left in part to her grandsons, "in consideration of the sum of love and affection and ten dollars." Biddy's investments, left to and managed by her daughters and grandsons, were, in 1909, valued at $300,000.[62]

Biddy Mason. Courtesy of the Security Pacific Collection, History Department, Los Angeles Public Library, Los Angeles, California.

We cannot know which of her descendants Biddy Mason would have to thank for ensuring that she was remembered not only lovingly, but also accurately. Her marital status, originally shown as *S*, has been corrected to *W* for widow, and her race, shown as *M* for mulatto, has been crossed out. In its place, written with some insistence in ink, is the word *AFRICAN*.[63]

Like Biddy Mason, Hannah never referred to herself by the last name Smith, but perhaps because she resided in San Bernardino after the trial where the Smith family had been well known, others did associate that surname with her. Technically, however, she had never had one: an early white resident of Los Angeles, in recounting his experiences with its small African American community, mentions "Mrs.

Hannah (who had no family name)," and his reference to the trial makes certain he was speaking of Hannah.[64]

Hannah often visited her friends and, later, members of her family in Los Angeles, and she apparently lived independently in San Bernardino, either by assistance provided by the court, which continued the guardianship of her children, or by more direct intervention by Judge Hayes. A list of early San Bernardino physicians and midwives shows a "Hannah Smith" who was "for many years a midwife." A footnote in *Heritage of the Valley* mentions "Hannah Smith, the wife of Toby Embers, had belonged to Robert M. Smith. She was the midwife of the colony."[65]

There is no Hannah Smith on the 1860 U.S. Census for San Bernardino County, but listed as a head of a household is one "Hannah Suniley," or "Hannah Smiley," depending on the index.[66] From the names, ages, and birthplaces of her children, we can identify both as our Hannah. Confusion seems to have arisen from the handwriting of the census taker, which might be read either way: Smiley or Suniley.

The fact that a Smiley family was prominent in Edgefield District of South Carolina, attended Little Steven's Creek Baptist Church, was close neighbors of the Dorn family, and had social and business interactions with them suggests that originally Hannah might have been owned by the Smiley family. Perhaps after being declared free she took, for a time at least, the surname of her original owner. The name may also have belonged to her slave husband, Frank.

The mortality schedule for 1860 lists among the persons who died in San Bernardino during the year ending June 1, 1860, "Catherine Sunily, 6/12, Mu, Ca, d: Feb; Croup; sick 4 days."[67] Given the absence of any other Suniley or Smiley in San Bernardino at the time, it would appear that Hannah's ninth child, a girl named Catherine, died of croup after being sick only four days. The father's name is not listed.

In 1868, Hannah appeared with another name. In that year, on the twenty-sixth of June, "Hannah Embers" signed over "for natural love and affection," lot 7, block 5, in the city, to Charles Embers and Martha Embers, claiming she was the "widow of Toby Embers, deceased, San Bernardino County," and the land was hers, "having belonged to her husband and descending to her as homestead." There is no record of Hannah and Toby having actually shared a residence, and this is the only instance in which she is listed as Hannah Embers.

Although her status as Toby's legal wife is uncertain, Hannah would likely have had the interests of the children she bore with him in mind when Toby died. Confirming Judge Hayes's assertion that she was illiterate, Hannah signed the transference of the deed with an X.[68] The house Hannah inherited had a history of its own that is perhaps more representative of the injustices people of color in California experienced than might be implied by Biddy Mason's success.

Toby Embers, though free in California, continued to work for whites, including Daniel Thomas, his master since childhood, and Thomas's relatives. Occasionally, he was hired out, probably as a laborer, to other Mormon families. By 1857, a year after the habeas corpus trial, he had managed to save $150 with which to purchase a home, perhaps with Hannah in mind. In November of that year, Brigham Young ordered all members of the San Bernardino colony to return to Salt Lake Valley "as soon as possible in wisdom." The recall was prompted by the financial burden of the colony, the growing apostasy among its congregation, and rabid anti-Mormon sentiment rising from an incident that became known as the Mountain Meadows massacre. On September 7, 1857, a train of emigrants en route to California had been set upon by Indians near Mountain Meadows, Utah. Thirty-six members of the party were brutally murdered. When it was learned that the attack had been planned and led by a Mormon, blame was immediately attributed to all Mormons. The sudden exodus of the Mormons from San Bernardino dramatically depressed the price of land, and Toby's extravagant dream unexpectedly became a reality. On November 10, 1857, Toby Embers bought lot 7, block 5, within the city limits of San Bernardino.[69]

A year later, on November 11, 1858, Toby threw a party, perhaps a housewarming to celebrate the construction or remodeling of his home. "The black elite" was how the invitees were described in subsequent newspaper accounts, but considering the small number of blacks in San Bernardino at the time, this would have meant practically every person of color in town.[70] Surely among the guests were Toby's brother, Grief Embers; Grief's wife, Harriet; Charlie Rowan and Liz Rowan; and the mother of Toby's children and his beloved companion, Hannah.

Sometime during the evening, there was a commotion at the front door. Demanding entry were "a number of white sports under the leadership of one [Joseph] McFeely" who announced they wanted to "participate in the amusements." Intoxicated, swaggering, loud-mouthed, and rude, they forced their way in, looked around, and "unceremoniously interrupt[ed] the party-goers" by taunting, swearing, and grabbing women. Toby objected and ordered them out of his house. McFeely was incensed and ordered "a general house-cleaning." The fight that ensued was over quickly. The black men were outnumbered and fearful for the women with them; McFeely and his cohorts were probably armed. All of the guests were forcibly ejected from the house, and Toby was brutally beaten and thrown into the street.[71]

The next morning, Toby, with his face bruised and swollen, entered the office of James W. Wilson, a justice of the peace, who was also clerk of the First District Court, and said he wanted to swear out an assault complaint. Before Toby could finish, though, McFeely, flanked by his cronies, appeared at Wilson's office and asked to see the complaint. He read it over, refolded it, and handed it to Toby. He then took out a pistol, put the barrel to Toby's temple, and told him to eat the piece of paper.

One account says at that point Toby "paled." Another, trying to find humor in racist wordplay, says, "[T]he poor fellow turned as pale as nature would allow him. . . . [H]is pearly teeth chattered, ground the complaint at the rate of a grist mill."

James W. Wilson was "horrified," and "during these grim proceedings, he sat with sealed lips, ashen pale face and bristled hair . . . afraid to interfere . . . lest he too would be made to dine on court records."

"The unnamed black resident of San Bernardino left the Court of Justice further humiliated and denied any redress of his grievances," claimed one report.[72] And that might have been true if it had been any other man. Toby, however, went back to court.

Perhaps Hannah and Biddy's successful trial played a part in Toby Embers's tenacious belief in the judicial system, and, ironically enough, Toby narrowly missed appearing before Judge Hayes himself. Unfortunately, according to court records of the case, on November 6, 1858, Hayes had adjourned court until the next regular session, citing his inability to attend.[73] Perhaps Hayes's alcoholism had begun to interfere with his duties.

On November 11, 1858, Toby's witnesses—Mr. and Mrs. James W. Wilson, Dr. B. Barton, Horace Rolfe, and William Osgood—gave depositions and, in February 1859, a grand jury indicted Joseph McFeely for "assault with intent to inflict bodily harm," according to the court transcripts. A warrant for McFeely's arrest was not issued until June 7, 1859, but two days later the local sheriff brought him in.

On June 10, 1859, the case of *People vs. Joseph McFeely* came to trial. After hearing the testimony of the prosecution's witnesses, the jurors asked why Toby Embers had not been called to testify. As Judge A. D. Boren informed them, "The court is of the opinion that a colored person may file a complaint but not testify in open court." Boren's ruling was consistent with the same California law that had prevented Biddy's and Hannah's testimonies three years earlier, but it doomed Toby Embers's case.

In their deliberations, the jurors struggled over the apparent contradiction in the instructions given them by Boren: they had been told to be judges of the facts—and the facts were plain—but owing to the law against Negro testimony, they were unable to hear Toby's accusation. After debating, the jury was apparently deadlocked. In the court record is a piece of paper: "We the jury disagree. Moses Morse, Foreman, San Bernardino June the 10." The jurors were ordered to reconsider, and two days later, on June 12, 1859, they returned with a predictable verdict: "We the jury find the Defendant not gilty [*sic*]." On the back of this paper stating the verdict is an almost illegible sentence: "Dam[n] your, your damning Heart." Beneath that writing are two signatures, neither of which belongs to the jury foreman, Moses Morse. Below the names is another line: "To the People of the State of California." What this document with its unexpected additions seems to indicate is that some of the jurors, forced to comply with California state law, wanted to register dissent from and indignation at an unjust law.

In 1859, when he lost the trial, Toby Embers would have been about sixty. The image of a man of that age, or any age for that matter, being forced to chew and swallow a legal complaint is not "rather humorous," as described in *Black Origins of the Inland Empire*, but it does, as the book says, "illustrate how precariously blacks lived."[74]

A month after he received title to Toby's land from his mother, Charlie Embers married, then eventually left his wife and moved to Arizona where he worked as a cook in a mining camp and married a Mexican woman. In 1870, Charlie was listed as delinquent in paying the taxes on the property he had inherited from his father. The same year, Charlie's first wife, Jane, and his daughter, Eliza, are shown in the federal census as living in Los Angeles, next door to Biddy Mason.[75]

A Charles Embers served as a private in Company D of the Twenty-eighth United States Colored Infantry during the Civil War, but it is not known if this was the Charles Embers who was Hannah's son. In the 1930s, Charlie Embers was among the former slaves interviewed by WPA writers and, by his references to San Bernardino, can be positively identified as Hannah and Toby's son.[76]

In 1870, Hannah's daughter Martha is shown as living with Toby's brother, Grief, and his wife, Harriet Ambrose, and is listed as their niece. (To a census taker, unfamiliar with southern dialect, "Embers" might be heard as "Ambrose.") Martha and her brother Charlie were listed as Toby's children in the probate record of Harriet Embers and apparently inherited land from their aunt. When she was sixteen or seventeen, Martha married Israel Beal, who became a prominent citizen of Redlands, California. In her later years, Martha said she often heard her people laugh, remembering the terror they had felt on reaching California and learning they were no longer slaves. They did not know how they would live, and begged their former owners to take them back to a slave state.[77]

Hannah's daughter Ann married Manuel Pepper, a cowboy employed at Robert Owens's stables, and they had several children. When Manuel died, Ann married Henry Daniels. In the 1890 U.S. Census for Los Angeles, Ann is listed as a widow, identified as a laundress, and shown living in the household of her son, "Manwell Pepper."[78]

Hannah's daughter Jane Smiley married George Goins in Los Angeles in 1862. In 1867, in Los Angeles, Nelson Smiley or Smilley married Juana Biggs, the daughter, probably, of Peter Biggs, the former slave who had first greeted Benjamin Hayes on his arrival in Los Angeles.[79] The fates of Lawrence, Marion, and Henry are unknown.

After 1868, when she deeded Toby's land over to Charlie and Martha, Hannah vanishes from the historical record. She was forty-four years old. At that time, her daughter Ann was married, as were Jane and Nelson. Charlie was to be married within a month, and Martha would be married in two years. Hannah's oldest son, Lawrence, born in 1842, was twenty-six, Marion sixteen, and Henry twelve years old.

There are several plausible explanations for Hannah's seeming disappearance. She may have died. Yet, there is no will or record of probate, and the transfer of land has no mention of infirmity. Perhaps she remarried and her whereabouts are thereafter disguised by a new surname. Yet, "Hannah" by any other surname does not show up in the lives or households of any of her known children.

Perhaps Hannah, with most of her children grown and Toby dead, decided to leave California at last. Perhaps she returned to South Carolina. But if her intention was to find Frank, the father of her first three children, she would have gone to Texas where Rebecca's brother Robert Dorn had moved in 1850, taking with him his slaves, including Frank and Hannah's brother.[80] Perhaps Frank had been part of the incentive the Smiths had offered in persuading Hannah to lie in Judge Hayes's courtroom.

In 1860, Rebecca's brother Robert Dorn was living in Caldwell County, Texas. In 1880, two Frank Dorns, identified as black or mulatto, lived at the same address in Caldwell County: the older one was forty-seven and was born in South Carolina; the younger one was thirty-six and was born in Mississippi. The older Frank may have been Hannah's husband and the father of the younger Frank, although there is some discrepancy in the ages. The elder Frank is shown to have a wife named Susan; if this Frank Dorn was Hannah's husband, he did not wait.[81]

Of all the possibilities, this is, of course, the most satisfying to imagine: that Hannah, whose young family was torn apart by the drawing of a slip of paper, might have found a way back to where she started: Edgefield, South Carolina. A place where the name Hannah was all a person needed.

NINE

The Letter

FOR SEVERAL YEARS, I had known that Benjamin Hayes's papers were housed in the Bancroft Library on the campus of the University of California at Berkeley. I have a brother, Marshall, also a writer, who lives in San Francisco. In the spring of 1996, I cajoled Marshall into going through Benjamin Hayes's *Scraps,* as his notebooks in the Bancroft Library are called. I was seeking no specific documents. I just felt something might be there. Marshall did a good job, and found a few things; I was pleased and insisted on paying him. Even so, I kept hearing a voice—intuition or something more mysterious—calling me, saying I needed to visit the library myself.

For a few months, I resisted, fearing self-deception, not wanting to offend my brother, and having the ubiquitous excuses of little time and no money. Finally, I gave in. I called my brother, gave him a song and dance about wanting to expand on his research, and asked if I could crash for a week in his spare room. Marshall, my mellow-tempered brother, did not feel criticized or questioned, or, if he did, he accepted my obsession. At any rate, he said, "Sure." I consulted the credit limit on my last credit card, found a fare that hovered between my credit balance and the amount I could charge, and caught a night flight down from Seattle.

—

The next morning I rode BART, the underground subway, from San Francisco to Berkeley. As the doors opened and closed at the stops, I imagined that once again I was traveling through the stations of other people's lives. When I emerged from the underground train, I climbed the stairs and met the summer heat full-face. I had suspected it already in Oakland when the train arose from its tunnel and ran alongside houses, stores, and skinny trees, their curled leaves dangling like tiny, parched possums.

A few minutes' walk later, I entered the Bancroft Library: a great open room, its walls lined with bookcases, oak card catalogs near the entry, and a central kiosk where the reference staff received request slips for the rare books and manuscripts kept behind locked doors. Books were brought out to patrons and placed beside them on the tables. I wondered how they remembered who had requested which book, but they always did. At the other tables—the alignment reminded me of lunch tables at a school cafeteria—sat people intent upon their own projects. Many had fortresses of stacked books, and within those scholarly walls they tapped on laptops. A few, like me, took notes by hand on legal pads or in notebooks. It was so quiet I heard the scratching of the pen of a man who sat two tables away. Occasionally, I heard the rattle of wheels as the staff rolled in carts filled with books to be distributed.

I had chosen to come to California in the hottest month of the hottest year in San Francisco's recent history. I learned soon enough that the air-conditioning in the Bancroft Library had failed and that the tall windows in the reading room did not open. For three days, traveling back and forth between San Francisco and Berkeley, I spent all hours the library was open going page by page through the 138 volumes of clippings that constitute Benjamin Hayes's scrapbooks. Mold and mildew permeated the old papers; I am allergic to both, and I sneezed frequently and ferociously in the quiet research room. The acid in the newspapers ate at the flesh of my fingertips. The temperature inside had reached an unbearable ninety-five degrees.

I looked around the room one last time and accepted that I had come on a fool's errand. Between the heat, my afflictions, and the frustration of finding nothing, I was ready to book a flight home.

But then, that voice: *Don't. Stay.*

Page by page, I started back through the Hayes collection. The library staff, grown weary of trotting out separate volumes, had granted me the privilege of examining the books by the cart, some thirty volumes at a time. What would they think had they seen me, holding my hand over a row of books, like a diviner seeking the pull of water? I reached for volume 14.

It was a letter, a note really, just 3-1/2-by-5-1/2 inches. I had missed it before either because it was so inconspicuous or because it was hidden by the end of an article. The letter had been written by Hayes to a man named Jack Hinton.

> An interesting reminiscence occurs to me at the moment. In the year 1854 [*sic*], at Los Angeles, with "public opinion" against me, I tried the case of fourteen Negroes, claiming the protection of the writ of *Habeas Corpus.* I discharged them, as entitled to freedom. I was denounced as—an abolitionist! For declaring a simple proposition of *law*—for granting a clear constitutional right! Even at Sacramento, I was "damned" (so Gov. Downey informed me.)
>
> A month passed: one day my little boy [fell] from a buggy, under the heels of the horse; one of these same poor Negro women, whom Providence placed nearby, rushed under the very wheels, and snatched him from death! If a Judge could be repaid, for any duty performed by him—what do you think can be the measure of my reward, in such circumstances? If, dear Jack, you had a boy—and one only—you would feel as I do; and yet your kindness of heart easily will teach you what must be the lively gratitude of a father who has escaped from such a danger. This incident has always seemed to me one of the most singular in my "brief career." B.H.[1]

I felt suddenly as if Benjamin Hayes and I were together in his room in the Hotel Lafayette where he spent the last days of his life,

Sept. 20th 1863 –

To F. Hinton (Fort Yuma.)

"An interesting reminiscence occurs to
me at the moment. In the year 1854, at
Los Angeles, with "public opinion" against
me, I tried the case of fourteen negroes,
claiming the protection of the writ of Habeus
Corpus. I discharged them, as entitled to
freedom. I was denounced as — an
abolitionist! For declaring a simple
proposition of law – for granting a clear
constitutional right! Even at Sacramento,
I was 'damned' (so Gov. Downey informed
me.) A month passed: one day my
little boy from a buggy, under the
heels of the horse; one of these same
poor negro women, whom Providence
placed near by, rushed under the
very wheels, and snatched him from

death! If a Judge could be repaid, for any duty performed by him — what do you think can be the measure of my reward, in <u>such</u> circumstances? If, dear Jack, you had a boy — and one only — you would feel as I do; and yet your kindness of heart easily will teach you what must be the lively gratitude of a father who has escaped from such a danger. This incident has always seemed to me one of the most singular in my "brief career."

B. H.

P.S. I have buried the "big-bellied bottle"; and they have saved "Rosin the Bow!" — for a later ceremony of that kind.

Letter from Benjamin Hayes to Jack Hinton concerning the rescue of Chauncey. Courtesy of the Bancroft Library, University of California at Berkeley.

surrounded by books, clippings, and letters. I could see Benjamin turn from the papers on his desk and hold the letter out to me. *So much was gone. I thought I might lose everything. But then I realized it, you see: I had already been given a miracle, my blessing. My only son was alive because she was there to save him. She was there because I had prevented her from being taken to Texas.*

A few minutes earlier, I had felt hot. Now I shivered.

I knew enough about Benjamin's life to identify his friend "Jack Hinton, as we call him," Benjamin wrote in his diary, alluding to a previous identity in which Jack Hinton had been Abraham T. D. Hoornbeck of Rondout, New York. But Hinton had shed that name and its identity to enlist in the United States Army for the Mexican War, and, after coming west, had gained wealth as a merchant in Fort Yuma and San Diego, somehow earning the friendship and deep respect of Benjamin Hayes. Hayes's drinking, which had become worse, was both a campaign issue and a growing concern to his friends. In Benjamin's diary for 1863 he noted that Hinton often wrote friends in Los Angeles "to inquire if the Judge has been drinking!"[2] In the fall of 1863, with his country on the verge of war and his own reelection prospects dimming, District Judge Benjamin Hayes wrote his friend a letter so short it is almost a jotting, like a note meant to capture a dream dissolving upon waking.

⁓

The date of the incident can be pinpointed to a day in February 1856. "A month passed," Benjamin says, apparently referring to the end of the trial when he rendered the verdict on January 19.

District court convened on the third Mondays of March, July, and November in Los Angeles; of April, August, and December in San Diego; and of February, May, and October in San Bernardino. One month after the verdict would have been the weekend between Friday, February 14, and Sunday, February 16. To be in San Bernardino in time for the opening of district court on February 17, the third Monday of the month, Benjamin would have had to leave Los Angeles on Sunday, February 16. The carriage accident probably occurred, then, on Saturday, February 15, 1856. The Friday before, February 14, 1856, was Benjamin's forty-first birthday. If Chauncey had been rescued from death on his father's birthday, Benjamin (ever on the lookout for examples of Providence) would surely have mentioned the coincidence.

On Saturday, likely in the afternoon, Benjamin, Emily, and Chauncey, who would be three years old in April, would have left their house for a buggy ride. Horses were Chauncey's delight. Since he was born, his father had been taking him for rides, Chauncey seated before him in the saddle, and Benjamin's hand steadying his son's small body. The buggy was probably a light carriage, a four-wheeled vehicle that can be pulled by a single horse—Benjamin mentioned only one— with a single seat for two people, or two adults with a child seated on one of their laps. Perhaps the buggy ride was both a way to please Chauncey—"A promise to a child must never be broken," Benjamin wrote in his diary—and an opportunity for Benjamin to show himself about town after the difficult trial and a month of insults and recrimi- nations.[3]

The Hayeses' house, rented from Benjamin S. Eaton, who was mar- ried to Benjamin Hayes's sister Helena, was on a hillside a few blocks behind the courthouse and county jail. Benjamin wrote that he and Emily lived in this house "from Jan. 1, 1856, til April 13, 1857." One of the joys afforded by the location of the house was the Catholic cemetery on a high hilltop nearby, which he and Emily referred to as "our garden," because they often went there to gather wildflowers.[4]

With Emily seated beside him and Chauncey on her lap, Benjamin would have driven the buggy down the hillside, past the jail and the courtroom, and then into Plaza Square. Friends would have hailed the three of them; former friends would have averted their gazes. Ben- jamin might have been distracted from either, worrying that the rising dust might bring on Emily's cough and that that night he would again sit on the bed beside her and watch for traces of blood on her lace handkerchief.

On Saturdays, Plaza Square, the hub of Los Angeles, would have been a spectacle of activity and color, a study in contrasts: women in black mantillas entering the great dim cathedral, farmers driving produce-laden wagons, cowboys on horseback heading for favorite sa- loons, farm girls leaning out of brothel windows, men who had come to California with dreams of golden nuggets, pleading for a coin—and a black woman on her way to the house where she worked as a domestic.

Only ten months earlier, Benjamin and Emily had buried their second child, the newborn Sarah. Whatever gratitude they might have been feeling for a fine spring morning and their vibrant son was gone in an instant. Chauncey, breaking free from his mother's arms, was falling forward, over the footboard, through the reins, and beneath the buggy.

Within the confines of the celebrated Bancroft Library, a scene from a century and a half earlier replayed in slow motion: A boy tumbles from a wagon. A woman screams. People on the sidewalk pivot. Through the dust-choked air, we see a woman turn, but things are happening too fast. Perhaps she sees the judge, but there is no time for calculation. There is a child in the street about to be trampled, and her entire body knows only one thing: *Protect him. Run.*

One step, two, then she is on her knees, her eyes and mouth full of dirt, grabbing the baby, yanking him toward her and away from the second set of wheels.

By the time Benjamin could have reined and set the brake, Emily would have already been out of the wagon and running back toward a mound on the road—a shape too big for such a little boy.

Who was alive.

The woman had curled herself around Chauncey, trying to comfort him. When she looked up, Benjamin stared back in disbelief at the familiar face.

I held the letter in my hand, but it did not tell me what I most wanted to know: was it Biddy or Hannah?

Perhaps had Benjamin named her, he would have felt compelled to explain her story to Jack Hinton. Perhaps, after seven years and overwhelmed by his own troubles, that was how Benjamin thought of them—"poor Negro women"—as if their separate identifies had blurred into a single image: a slave in a homespun dress standing next to a plantation porch, her feet bare, her young face already stern and resigned, her bearing as straight and dignified as a caryatid on a Greek temple.

Benjamin had not named her, but I knew who it was: a woman who would never have a proper surname, who would hand over her newborn son before she would break a vow made before God, who would throw herself without thinking beneath a carriage to save a child.

Logic aside, my heart answered the question for itself and without a doubt: Hannah.

⁓

I wish I could say that my epiphany about racism, standing in the wings of that stage when I was fourteen, had instantly made me into the woman I still hope someday to be. After that night, I became instead a teenaged girl too impatient to finish high school who had a six-month-old baby on her hip before she was twenty-one. Fortunately, Catherine's birth had coincided with Columbia University offering me a fellowship to attend its graduate film school. The apartment in New York I had found would not be available for a month, so I decided to store my belongings, except for a few clothes and diapers, and head south until school started.

At the ticket window in Grand Central Station, I asked the agent the price of a ticket, passenger class, to Virginia Beach, Virginia. Behind me a woman with gray hair protested. "You can't go all that way with that baby on your lap." She paid for a sleeper for the two of us. In the night, I reached over Catherine asleep beside me, raised the shade, and watched for Virginia.

The earliest photograph I have of myself is as a toddler on Virginia Beach. I stand, bald-headed in a sunsuit, a shovel dangling from my hand, interrupted in my digging by my father, behind the camera, calling my name. There is a trace memory of him saying, "Here comes a biggie!" as I am lifted above a wave rushing in. The water swells, and then I watch it tumble to shore and sprawl across white sand.

After a painful year, I supposed I was going back to Virginia Beach to remember how to ride out crests and troughs.

We arrived without reservations on Labor Day weekend. NO VACANCY as far as the eye could see. I walked from one hotel to another, carrying Catherine, a bag with her things, and a suitcase. Dusk was approaching. It began to rain. The last address on my list was a few blocks off the beach. It was a small boardinghouse, with white siding, front porches on both of its two floors, and a blooming rhododendron bush. I opened the screen door and knocked. For a long while, there was no answer, then an elderly woman with long, unkempt gray hair came to the door. A witch interrupted in her diabolical work, I thought. Mrs. Humber leaned on her cane and asked what I wanted.

"A room," I said, "for three weeks."

She let me into her parlor. "What you doing out in a storm with that baby?" she demanded.

I said I could not find a room.

"No wonder. No one wants to rent a room to a single woman without a wedding ring." I told her I was newly divorced.

She humphed in disbelief and disapproval, "with a squalling baby to boot." She lifted my coat to look at Catherine. "Although she is a pretty thing. . . . No, I can't do it. Folks would complain, move out."

I thanked her, stood, swaddled the baby as best I could, and started out. Behind me the cane hit the floor.

"Come back here, you fool!"

All that month, I played on the beach with my daughter. We cuddled against warm sand or blanketed ourselves against the afternoon breeze. I taught her to love the water; I lifted her above the waves.

Often in the evening, after Catherine had gone to sleep, Mrs. Humber and I would sit together in the parlor, Mrs. Humber enthroned in her oak chair, me in a rocker. And so, I was a witness on the rainy night three soldiers came looking for a room. One of them was black. It was 1964—everything segregated still, while the country fought and fomented over civil rights.

"I can't do it," Mrs. Humber said. "Maybe it's wrong, but I've never rented a room to a Negro, and I can't start now, although if I were going to do it for anyone, I would do it for you. My son was a soldier and he died on a beach in Italy, and I've never been able to place a flower on his grave. But no, I can't do it. Everyone would move out. My neighbors would disown me. No, I just can't. I won't."

I rocked Catherine and watched. The soldiers thanked Mrs. Humber, stood up, and walked toward the front door. Out of the corner of her eye, my landlady looked at me.

"Did I do right?" she asked.

"No, ma'am," I said. "You did not."

She turned full-faced and glared at me. The cane rapped wood. "Come back here!"

And that night, Mrs. Humber desegregated her hotel.

Decades passed. My wounds healed. My daughter thrived. Over time, I earned three college degrees, but in many ways grew no wiser for them. I forgot all about Mrs. Humber: how ready and true our instincts for good can be, what power a single person acting on impulse—or even on second thought—can wield.

In the Bancroft Library, with a tiny letter on the table in front of me, I sat with my raw fingertips pressed together. I was remembering how once years ago I had reached for a wall. I was thinking that Hannah and Biddy had reached back.

EPILOGUE

Coming to Rest

[S]oon we shall die and all memory of those five will have left the earth, and we ourselves shall be loved for a while and forgotten. But the love will have been enough; all those impulses of love return to the love that made them. Even memory is not necessary for love. There is a land of the living and a land of the dead and the bridge is love, the only survival the only meaning.

—Thornton Wilder, *The Bridge of San Luis Rey*

BETWEEN THE LIVING ROOM and the kitchen in my small rented house in Seattle once hung a curtain of threaded white seashells. As an ornament, it was totally impractical: the only bathroom is not adjacent to the single bedroom—as the logic of convenience would suggest—but located on the other side of the house and accessible only by passing through the kitchen. A dozen or more times a day, then, I had to push through the curtain. Given the wear and tear, I did not expect it to last long, but, as long as it did, I knew I would enjoy it, this sheet of sound that mimicked the music of shells tumbling in waves, that slid against my face, making me conscious of passage, of being in the physical world.

The rivulets of rain streaming off the overhang at the curb at the airport in Seattle reminded me of my partition of shells. Behind me, blurry in the afternoon rain, were Seattle's gray-blue hills. My raincoat, also gray-blue and mottled with faint purple flowers, was damp from the short time I had waited beside the airport shuttle to get my bag and pay the driver. Now, at the curbside check-in, I wondered whether I should shed the coat and stuff it inside a suitcase or carry it with me on the plane. I was curiously reluctant to let it go. Rain is usual even in summer in Seattle, and a raincoat is always appropriate, but I was on my way to Texas. The hills in Texas, I knew, would be a brittle brown and yellow, hazy behind waves of heat. A raincoat would be superfluous, even silly. I felt disturbed by the difference between where I was and where I soon would be, and my seeming indecision over something as simple as a coat. Once again, I seemed to be straddling landscapes and a widening chasm within myself.

"Wait," I told the clerk at the airline counter. I took off my raincoat, shook it, folded its sleeves and collar, and maneuvered the resulting roll into a plastic bag. Four plums, which had been in the bag, went into a side pocket of my purse. I was chilled and missing the raincoat even before I lost sight of my suitcase, being trundled along by the conveyer belt.

The woman seated beside me on the plane chattered about llamas she had recently transported to Montana to keep them from dying in the Texas drought. "Llamas are amazing animals, you know," she said. "They always have twins."

I was glad she was talkative. Without her, I might have spent the entire flight alone with my apprehensions, staring at the porridge of clouds outside. They seemed almost solid, and I imagined myself stepping out barefooted upon them. Perhaps I could sustain my belief for a few steps before plunging like a brick through thick, wet fog. I had promised myself I would use this time to write my speech, but that was not happening. I wondered if the refugee llamas were missing their home as much as I already did mine.

Night had fallen in Texas. The lights below were a constellation that had settled on a dark field. The voice on the intercom welcomed us to San Antonio and reported the ground temperature was 105 degrees. As I walked toward the terminal, the heat increased with each step until I felt that I had entered an oven.

Following our letters to one another about Robert Mays Smith's descendants, Ethel Klemcke and I had exchanged phone calls. "I hope you don't mind my asking," she finally ventured, "but several of our relatives wonder, are you black?"

I was startled, my feelings a jumble of amusement, suspicion, and fear. "No, ma'am," I had said—but why so firmly?

"Not that it would have mattered," she added without a beat.

Now walking down the jetway, I replayed that moment, thinking about my response, alternatives to it, pondering their outcomes. All I could be sure of at the moment was that I had been invited to speak at the Smith Family Reunion in Texas, and that, waiting at the gate, would be Bill Klemcke and his grown son.

On a trip to Alaska, the Klemckes had stopped in Seattle, and I had met them at their motel near the airport. Bill, a pilot in World War II, still had a flier's lanky stature, but his body had thickened with age and now was solid as a tree trunk. During his working days, he had been a mechanic for a petroleum company. I kept inadvertently calling Bill "Bob," the diminutive of Robert, seeing in Bill's brown eyes the same piercing blue intensity of his great-great-grandfather's eyes. Ethel was a sturdy-built woman of medium height, with short, pale hair. She was stern and seemed shrewd, but under these qualities I sensed vulnerability.

Much of our time together was spent in the cramped quarters of my Ford Escort. Bill, folded like a marionette to fit into his seat, diagnosed the squeal emanating from my car as a problem with my brakes and suggested I have them relined. In the driveway of their motel, we took pictures. My photograph with Bill in a red baseball cap standing beside me, his hand on my shoulder, had been on my bookcase for a year. Now he stood before me again, and stooped to embrace me—his body as lean and hard as I remembered—then introduced me to his son.

We rode through the night with the air-conditioning on high. The windows were sheathed with shades that shut out the searing Texas sun by day. We talked, but our conversation was like a creek in darkness flowing over unseen stones. They told me we were in hill country, but I could not see hills. I thought of the game in which you let yourself be blindfolded and led through obstacles by a stranger. I wondered who was leading whom, and which of us had to do the trusting.

The Bandera Motel was indistinguishable from hundreds of other motels built along America's highways in the 1950s: three floors with walkways with railings in front, picture windows covered by drawn drapes, an adjoining restaurant, and a fenced swimming pool, its water an eerie cerulean blue in this drought-choked landscape. The Klemckes had rented a room for me adjoining theirs on the lower floor; other Smith relatives were scattered throughout the motel. It seemed ironic: my only tie to these dozens of living Smith descendants, utter strangers to me, were Robert and Rebecca, a couple long dead whom I felt I knew enough, nonetheless, to claim as kin. Bill deposited my suitcase in my room, turned on the air conditioner, then took me next door to see his wife. Ethel and I hugged like old friends.

Back in my room, the air was icy. Once again, I felt isolated, as though sunk at a great depth in the ocean in a bathysphere, sealed off from everyone and everything familiar. I looked around at the all-too-familiar appointments—a double bed, a desk, a mirror over a dresser, a minirefrigerator, and a closet with bare hangers, hastily filled and hastily stripped—that had become metaphors for the dislocation I felt in my travels. *This is what I have been doing for ten years: waiting to resurface.*

In the nightstand by the bed was a Gideon Bible. I thought of Hannah's vow, her hand on a Bible proffered by her mistress, Rebecca, promising to say she wanted to go with them, promising to lie.

The woman in the mirror seemed weary. I returned the Bible to its drawer, lifted the suitcase to the bed, and emptied it methodically. Inside the plastic bag, my raincoat was still damp, but warm. I shook it out and hung it at the end of the closet, apart from the other clothes. The plums in my purse were dusty and drab, but like the coat, they spoke *home*. I washed them in the bright, sterile bathroom, polished them with a face towel, and set them on a washcloth on the washstand.

Still life with cheap linen.

In the top drawer of the desk would be motel stationery on which I could draft my next day's speech. Or not. Perched on the edge of the bed in my nightgown, I channel surfed until I found something that would qualify as an educational diversion, and bit into the first purple-gold plum. On the television screen, in fifty-year-old black-and-white footage, was Jesse Owens, his dark body taut and lean, striding through his victory lap around the Olympic stadium in Berlin.

In the morning, after breakfast, Bill and Ethel, who coordinated the yearly reunions, filled the trunk of their car with signs and other supplies. On the outskirts of town, we turned from the highway onto a gravel road leading to a warehouse. Bill stopped at the turnoff and hung a sign: SMITH FAMILY REUNION. "They should see that," he said, but Ethel questioned the legibility of the letters' size.

The door to the warehouse was locked. Bill and Ethel argued about who was responsible for the door and what had happened last year. The heat of the day had already begun collecting in asphalt under our feet. A single tree stood between the warehouse and the road.

"What kind of tree is that?" I asked. After breakfast, after spraying our shoes and pant cuffs with insect repellent to keep off ticks and chiggers, we had taken a short walk along the river behind the motel. I asked the names of several trees and plants. Bill told me about the cedar trees used to make shakes before tastes in roofing changed.

"Scrub oak," Ethel answered, as though intent on beating Bill to the punch in a game-show playoff. A truck turned off the highway and came up the gravel road. A man with a cowboy hat jumped out, apologized for oversleeping, and opened the padlocked doors.

Inside was a big, empty room with a kitchen and bathrooms along the rear wall. Folded metal tables and chairs leaned against a side wall. Bill, Ethel, and I lugged them to the center of the room and arranged them in rows. People began coming through the doors, closed against the rising heat. Electric fans were placed around the room. As soon as the tables at the front of the room had been draped with plastic tablecloths, baskets, covered pots, plates, platters, and bowls of food covered them. Bill and another man worked on setting up the microphone and sound system on a raised platform in front of the room. I looked at my watch. Ethel told me the speeches would take place after lunch.

Men in jeans stood near the front door of the warehouse, talking about the drought and comparing it to past droughts. They discussed the price of feed and debated how long they could sustain their herds. Robert Mays Smith, I thought, would have been comfortable here.

Ethel took me around, introducing me to relatives; one hundred and ten had made the gathering. The youngest was an infant of eight months; the oldest, Bill's mother, was ninety-four. She told me she had once spent a night in Seattle because by mistake she had boarded the wrong plane. I met a young couple who had an expensive metal detector that they used to find bullets and buttons from the Civil War.

Many asked about the paternity of Biddy's and Hannah's children. Were any of them Robert Mays Smith's? The expressions on their faces ranged from prurient interest to shame to glee.

"Both Biddy and Hannah had their own love stories," I said, "but the paternity of some of the children is in doubt."

"I knew it," said one man, slapping his knee.

In one family cluster, someone explained how watermelons were kept cold when he was a child in the horses' water trough. "But we had to stop 'cause the coons kept stealing them."

I felt my jaw drop open, but the conversation continued as though nothing unusual had happened. Maybe I had misunderstood; maybe he had meant *raccoons.* Could a raccoon lift a watermelon? The back of my neck felt hot and stiff. Ethel and I moved on.

Several people wanted me to understand that most southerners treated their slaves well, and many, "who would have starved if we had just turned them out," stayed on with their owners after emancipation.

I was tempted to point out that Biddy Mason had managed to become extremely wealthy without her master's largess, that her estate easily exceeded the value of the estates of any of their ancestors. But I held my tongue; I was the guest of honor in name only: it was the power of Biddy's and Hannah's stories that had any chance of making a difference here. My job, I thought, was not to undermine them by causing ill will.

At lunch we ate barbecue, beans, potato salad, peach cobbler, three kinds of pies, melon, and pineapple upside-down cake. People sat in family groups, but moved between the tables to speak to other relatives and to catch up on a year's news. After an hour, people began clearing their paper plates, then got themselves a cup of coffee or a soda, and settled expectantly in metal seats.

The first speaker was a woman who had returned from a trip to Germany where she researched the European ancestors of Rebecca Dorn. She presented charts and slides of villages along the Rhine River. I tried to focus on her presentation, but my attention was swamped by anxiety: I was next.

Ethel was helped onto the makeshift stage by Bob Weed, who coauthored the Smith family-history book with her. He fumbled with the microphone, adjusting it to Ethel's height. She smiled broadly and welcomed everyone, moved quickly through announcements about newsletters, sign-up sheets, and other reunion business, then introduced me and asked me to come forward.

Ethel presented me with a glittering rhinestone pin that said TEXAS, earrings in the shape of the state, a certificate proclaiming me an honorary citizen, and an autographed copy of *Robert Mays Smith: From South Carolina to Texas (the Long Way)*. She smiled and backed away.

I thanked Ethel and the entire family for the gifts and the invitation to be with them. My voice, piped through the sound system and trapped by the concrete walls, sounded dull, metallic. I looked around the room at the upturned faces. "Thornton Wilder's novel *The Bridge of San Luis Rey*," I heard myself say, "is the story of five travelers who come by different routes to meet a common fate on a fragile bridge. It is a story I thought of often during my research about another group of five people who found themselves confronting one another in a California courtroom a century and a half ago."

I briefly outlined my process of discovery over the past few years: the trips to California, Utah, Mississippi, Georgia, and South Carolina. As I was talking, my travels unwound like a movie in my head, a chronicle not only of the physical journeys I had undertaken, but of the interior journeys as well. I told the people seated in the room about Benjamin Ignatius Hayes, a southerner and former slave owner who had to judge this case and his own past. I mentioned Biddy's colorful history, the theory that, before she was a Smith slave, she had been married to a Cherokee chief. I told them about Rebecca and Hannah's relationship and how I had found the entry about Hannah's baptism in a faded record of Little Steven's Creek Baptist Church. I talked about

Biddy and Hannah and the children held in jail for twenty-one days. I told about a mother compelled to take what she believed was a holy vow and nearly forced to give up her children, including a two-week-old baby. For a moment, I saw recognition in the eyes of the audience, parents most of them, who could understand what it meant to lose a child, and I realized that they had forgotten that I was speaking of a black woman.

In the stillness, I saw Ethel look at her watch, and I knew I had to bring my speech to a close. "What is a family?" I asked. "Isn't it people who have lived together and shared experiences? By that definition, Robert and Rebecca, Biddy, Hannah, and all their children constituted a single family." Robert Mays Smith's defense was that these women and children of color were not his slaves and that he was not forcing them to accompany him to Texas, I said. He claimed they were members of his family and were going with them voluntarily. "The essential element for a family is love. It is what binds us to each other and to our ancestors. It is why you have this family reunion each year, why you are here today."

Before me, a crowd of faces with expectant bright-blue eyes. I wished the other faces were there as well. It was what I had been missing all along: the descendants of Biddy and Hannah. "I believe that Robert Mays Smith believed that these women of color and their children were part of his family, that it was a bond, rather than bondage, between them. But the women and children may have felt another way. There is a white truth and a black truth and a greater truth that encompasses us all. Only now, after all these years, it may be possible to seek that greater truth. I hope you like my book."

Ethel patted my back.

Bill said, "I didn't know you were going to say all that."

Bill's son smiled and shook his head. "You chickened out," he said.

I wondered if he meant my dodging the paternity question regarding Biddy's and Hannah's children or my soft-pedaling the issue of racism. "Read my book," I said.

A little girl wanted my autograph. "Sure, honey, but I don't know what you're going to do with it." She told me her name, and I wrote out inscriptions to her and her sister. She said she was going to put it in a stained-glass window. I burst out laughing. "I have to work my way up to stained glass," I said.

The Texas hill country in August in this year of drought had an unreal aspect, a kind of hallucinatory distortion that set everything at a distance and at the same time made it as subjective and intimate as a dream. I leaned my cheek against the car window and surveyed the passing landscape: khaki-colored hills; rock houses set on hilltops or in folds between hills; parched fields with scrubby, infrequent trees; and, closer to the road, fences laced with fuzzy weeds called grandpa's whiskers. Here and there, a cactus. Beside the road was the winding Medina River, a mere trickle in its bed of exposed stones. I thought of a shed snakeskin, an empty, translucent coil.

In the front seat of the car, driving, was Bill; Ethel was beside him. They pointed out places we passed, but I hardly heard them. I ached with love for these people, and I was afraid. They had trusted me. They had opened their lives to me, unlocked the doors, let me look through the linen before they washed and strung it on a line. Among the flapping sun-soaked shirts and petticoats, I had seen a few shadows whipped by the wind. The car stopped and a door was held open.

Bill and Ethel had chosen to stop by a cemetery where several family members are buried. The cemetery was on three sides of Oak Island Methodist Church, a square white building. Inside the church, a service was being held. A choir sang. I worried about being in the cemetery, but Bill and Ethel assured me it was all right. We walked in separate circles, looking at names and dates.

One grave, an old grave, was laid out at an odd angle, breaking the pattern of the other headstones. Bill offered the local theories about the grave's odd placement: either Joseph Smith, Robert and Rebecca Smith's son, promised his wife, Elizabeth, that he would bury her with her head facing a certain direction, or he buried her hurriedly, realized his error, and did not want to disturb her further by digging her up again or did not care enough to do it. The contradictory explanations intrigued me as did the woman's anomalous alignment. Even in death, some of us seemed destined not to fit in.[1]

I remembered another church, an empty one in Edgefield, South Carolina, and how I had stood by a window, watching a little black girl chase her dog across a cemetery, another cemetery, older, southern, silent. I wondered about the triangulation of a writer reluctantly keeping a rendezvous, an anonymous woman buried at an exceptional angle, and a child of color romping over forgotten graves.

The next stop that day was Oak Rest Cemetery where another of Robert Smith's children had been buried. William Seco would always be Willy to me—a young man, a teenager, standing on a porch in California pleading with a dark-skinned girl to wake her baby, napping in the house, to bring her and come with him, to please come with him.

Ethel, who had bad knees, stayed in the car. I followed Bill into the cemetery. The heat was so intense that everything was bleached out, like an overdeveloped photograph. Gravel crunched beneath our feet. Bill pointed out Seco's grave, but I avoided it. I could not accept that Willy was buried there, so far from his youth, from the person he might have been. On our way out of the cemetery, I noticed a recent grave, that of a teenager, heaped with mementos: bouquets and strewn flowers, glass jars filled with unfurling letters from high school friends, stuffed animals, puzzles, games, a toy car, and, on the border of the plot, a message spelled out in agates: "We miss you." I wondered whether it was worse to die young, beloved and full of potential, or to outlive one's dreams or sense of certainty.

The last stop was in Somerset at Rambie Grove. Both Bill and Ethel got out, and I followed them in. Rambie Grove was a family cemetery of the Smith-Klemcke clan, although now Hispanic families brought their family members there, presumably because they did not have to pay for burial plots as they did in San Antonio. The Hispanic—most people here said *Mexican*—graves had ornate crosses and colored carvings and were heaped with flowers. Benjamin Hayes would have liked these gay graves. In his diary, he remarked about a Spaniard who, instead of consoling him on the death of his daughter, exclaimed with a smile: "Now, friend, you have an *angelito* in Heaven!" Benjamin had returned the smile, because, he wrote, the man spoke the truth.

The section of the cemetery where Robert Mays Smith and his wife, Rebecca, were buried was fenced in, originally to keep cattle out, but now to separate the family plot from intrusion by latecomers. Most of the fence was simple chain-link, but part was wrought iron, beautifully worked. The patch of land was seared from heat and drought. Bill and Ethel told me that in spring it was covered with tiny daisies. I would have liked to see it then, but, no, I liked it better now, in the white-hot summer heat, with twisted trees and curled leaves and a resilient cactus with tiny red flowers reaching through the fence.

We paused at a concrete grave, made, I was told, in the depression by itinerant grave diggers. Entombed within were a Smith son and his wife. Originally, the twin mounds were embedded with shells, but the shells were long gone, leaving only impressions that I traced with my fingertips. Then, a few steps farther on, we were there: Rebecca's and Robert's graves.

The tombstone was surprisingly new, a polished granite replacement erected by a descendant, decorated with a passage of Scripture. Ethel backed up to take a picture of me by the tombstone, wearing sunglasses and a baseball hat. I was surprised by how shy I suddenly felt. I had imagined having a moment alone by the graves without people watching. What had I imagined I wanted to say to them?

I'm sorry, but I do hold you accountable.

A moment later, perhaps sensing my mood, Bill and Ethel moved away to read inscriptions on other graves. I focused on the passage of Scripture on Robert and Rebecca's tombstone: "Blessed are the pure in heart for they shall see God."

What a thing to choose for the grave of slave owners! But the truth was I felt as guilty for judging them as I would have had I not. *Blessed are the pure in heart. . . .* Was any of us, ever? Wasn't the best I could offer just a prayer over them for all of us?

In another part of the cemetery, Ethel and Bill stood together over a grave, fairly new. I knew from Bill's shaking shoulders, before he took off his glasses and wiped his eyes, that he was crying. Coming up behind them, I read the dates and recognized that this was the grave of their son who had drowned when he was eighteen. Ethel and I both put a hand on Bill's hard, warm back.

—

It was two years later, on a visit to California, that I said the last of my good-byes. It was a conscious pilgrimage undertaken on a hot, muggy day, one more like Atlanta than Los Angeles. An efficient urban breakfast. A bus through Chinatown and then the Hispanic neighborhoods. A sign: ARTICULOS RELIGIOSOS Y ESPIRITUALES. Off at the stop for Evergreen Cemetery on Boyle Heights.

Overcast day, air like mist, fogged in, not foggy. The cemetery gates were open, but I was too early for the office. Behind the building were three workmen. I asked one if he could direct me to Biddy Mason's grave.

"Biddy?"

I told him about the ceremony erecting the headstone. He listened without comment. I was not sure if he understood. I asked if there was an index to people buried at Evergreen Cemetery. Yes. I asked for a copy.

"It would," he said, "stretch from here to San Francisco."

I stuttered: "Of course . . . the cemetery started in 1877 . . . all those dead people." I asked if he could look up the location of Biddy's grave—and Hannah's.

"Hannah?"

"Her sister," I said, lying, just wanting to find them.

"Her last name?" I wrote two: Embers, Smiley.

"Her married names," I said. Endless explanations or little lies; would they ever end?

The workman went away with my piece of paper, disappearing through a back door.

I waited. Birds called between bushes. I studied the tall, bearded pines. What did they remind me of? Grandfathers? Sentries? My attention was caught by a geranium growing against a Japanese tombstone. Japanese graves, simple and elegant, row after row, each with a name in English and Japanese characters. On the back of each tombstone were more characters, prayers perhaps.

The Hispanic man reappeared, with two pieces of paper: the names I had given him and a little map with a number. He showed me Biddy's grave on the map, then pointed it out on the hillside, between pine and magnolia trees. Now he remembered: at the Biddy Mason ceremony there had been television cameras. He could not find Hannah under Embers or Smiley.

No Hannah.

I thanked him and started off.

It took me a while to locate grave no. 320. Biddy's tombstone, with the shape and simplicity of a Japanese headstone, looked new.

Biddy Mason
August 15 January 16
1818   1891
Former Slave
Philanthropist
Humanitarian
Founding Member
First African Methodist
Episcopal Church
1872
Los Angeles, California

The back of the marker was slick and blank. The only prayers would be mine. I laid my hand on the curve of the stone, wishing it were her shoulder. Wishing for them both. Where was Hannah?

Unmarked stones and simple slabs all around. I pushed away caramel-colored magnolia leaves and found three initials. Not hers, not any of hers. No Hannah. But did I really want to find her here?

Journeys do not necessarily end when you reach a destination; sometimes you just choose to stop. In the cemetery where Biddy Mason was buried, I realized I had come to that stopping place. At Biddy Mason's wall in Los Angeles in 1992, I had peered over my glasses at a mistake on an otherwise lovely memorial installation and made a commitment to help a small truth surface and had been shown something infinitely larger. There were so many things I had not learned, much about these people and their story that would always remain a mystery, but I knew it was time for this particular journey to be over.

I came upon the broken halves of a monument piled against a tree, then other remnants: a lovely stone scroll with a rose on its crest, a base with a slot where the headstone had broken off. Stones without names or dates, just roles and relationships: *Mother. Our Papa. Our Boys. Beloved Sister.* A child, aged six years, eight months, who died in Detroit in 1889: *Come to Heaven.*

Against the headstone of a Japanese woman was a Polaroid snapshot of a baby pulling up, probably for the first time. Mother or grandmother? I wondered. Sixty when she died. A photograph to show Grandma what she missed.

I wanted to return to Biddy, but I had wandered too far in the cemetery. I was disoriented; probably I would not find her again. I turned in a circle, and then I saw it: the magnolia tree, a lone southern landmark, showing me the way.

APPENDIX

Permission to publish Judge Hayes's verdict in the habeas corpus case was given by the University of California, Los Angeles, Department of Special Collections, Charles E. Young Research Library, where it is found in the Golden States Insurance Company Records. The verdict was previously published in Delilah Beasley and M. N. Work's "Documents: California Freedom Papers" and in Beasley's *Negro Trail Blazers of California*.

STATE OF CALIFORNIA
COUNTY OF LOS ANGELES   ss.

> Before the Hon. Benjamin Hayes,
> Judge of the District Court of the

> First Judicial District State of California,
> County of Los Angeles.

In the matter of Hannah and her children Ann (and Mary, child of Ann), Lawrence, Nathaniel, Jane, Charles, Marion, Martha, and an infant boy two weeks old; and of Biddy and her children, Ellen, Ann and Harriet, on petition for habeas corpus. Now on this nineteenth day of January, in the year of Our Lord, one thousand, eight hundred and fifty-six, the said persons above named are brought before me in the custody of the Sheriff of said County, all except the said Hannah and infant boy two weeks old (who are satisfactorily shown to be too infirm to be brought before me), and except Lawrence, (who is necessarily occupied in waiting on his said mother Hannah) and Charles (who is absent in San Bernardino County, but within said Judicial District) and Robert Smith, claimant, also appears with his Attorney, Alonzo Thomas, Esq. And after hearing, and duly considering the petition for habeas corpus and the return of claimant thereto, and all the proofs and allegations of the said parties and all the proceedings previously had herein, it appearing satisfactory to the Judge here that all the said persons so suing in this case to-wit: Hannah and her children, and Biddy, and her said children are persons of color, and that Charles, aged now six years, was born in the Territory of Utah, of the United States, and Marion (aged four years), Martha (aged two years), Mary, daughter of the said Ann, and aged two years, and the said infant boy aged two weeks, were born in the State of California, and that the said Hannah, Ann, Lawrence, Nathaniel, Jane, and Charles as well as the said Biddy, Ellen, Ann, and Harriet have resided with the said Robert Smith for more than four years, and since some time in the year of our Lord one thousand, eight hundred and fifty-one in the State of California; and it further appearing that the said Robert Smith left and removed from the State of Mississippi more than eight years ago with the intention of not returning thereto, but of establishing himself as a resident in Utah Territory, and more than four years ago left and removed from said Utah Territory with the intention of residing and establishing himself in the State of California, and has so resided in said last mentioned State, since some time in the year of our Lord one thousand eight hundred and fifty-one. And it further appearing by satisfactory proof to the Judge here, that all of the said persons of color are entitled to their freedom, and are free and cannot be held in slavery or involuntary servitude, it is therefore argued that they are entitled to their freedom and are free forever. And it further appearing to the satisfaction of the Judge here that the said Robert Smith intended to and is about to remove from the State of California where slavery does not exist, to the State of Texas, where slavery of Negroes and persons of color does exist, and ~~is~~ established by the municipal laws, and intends to remove the said before-mentioned persons of color, to his own use without the free will and consent of all or any of the said persons of color, whereby their liberty will be greatly jeopardized, and there is good reason to apprehend and believe that they may be sold into slavery or involuntary servitude and the said Robert Smith is persuading and enticing and seducing said persons of color to go out of the State of California, and it further appearing that none of the said persons of color can read and write, and are almost entirely ignorant of the laws of the state of California as well as those of the State of Texas, and of their rights and that the said Robert Smith, from his past relations to them as members of his family does possess and exercise over them an undue influence in respect to the matter of their said removal insofar that they have been in duress and not in possession and exercise of their free will so as to give a binding consent to any engagement or arrangement with him. And it further appearing that the said Hannah is thirty-four years, and her daughter, Ann, seventeen, and all her children, to-wit: Lawrence (aged from twelve to thirteen years), Nathaniel (aged ten to eleven years), Jane (aged eight years), Charles (aged six years), Marion (aged four years), Martha (aged two years), and said infant boy of Hannah, aged two weeks, as well as Mary (aged two years), daughter of said Ann, are under the age of fourteen years and so under the laws of the State of California, are not competent to choose a guardian for themselves; and it further appearing that the said Biddy is aged thirty-eight years, and the said Ellen is aged seventeen years, and the other children of Biddy, to-wit: Ann (aged from twelve to thirteen) and Harriet (aged eight years), are under the age of fourteen years, and so by the laws of the State of California are not competent to choose a guardian for themselves. It further appearing that the said infant boy two weeks of age of Hannah is of tender age and must be kept with his said mother, Hannah, the same is accordingly ordered and said infant boy is entrusted to his said mother hereby, and is ordered to appear with him before the Judge—here at the Court House, in the City of Los Angeles, on next Monday, January [21], 1856, at ten o'clock, A.M., of said day, if her health should permit and if not, as soon thereafter as may be practicable, of which the Sheriff of Los Angeles is thereby notified to notify her, the said Hannah, and whereof the said Robert

Smith, being now in the Court, has notice, it appearing that she resides in his house and is under his control, and the said Mary, child of Ann, appearing to be of tender age, is entrusted to the said Ann, to be brought before the Judge here at the time and place aforesaid, to be dealt with according to the law of which the said Ann and the said Robert Smith have notice here and the said Martha, being of tender years, is entrusted to the said Ann, her sister, to be brought before the Judge here at the time and place aforesaid to be dealt with according to the law of which the said Ann and the said Robert Smith here have notice and the said Hannah and Ann are appointed Special Guardians respectively of the children so hereby entrusted to them, and notified that it is their duty to obey all lawful orders of the Judge here or of some competent Court touching the premises, and the further hearing in this case as to the said Hannah, and the infant boy and her children, Lawrence, Charles, Mary and Martha, is adjourned until said last mentioned time at the Court House of the City of Los Angeles, and it is further ordered that the said Nathaniel (aged from ten to twelve years), Jane (aged eight years), Marion (aged four years), all children of said Hannah, and said child Ann (aged seventeen), and Harriet (aged eight years) are committed to the custody of the Sheriff, of Los Angeles County, David W. Alexander, Esq.; as Special Guardian until the further order of the Judge, here or of some other Judge or Court of competent jurisdiction to appoint General Guardians, of aforesaid children last mentioned and the said Sheriff will leave in full liberty and discharge the said Biddy and her child Ellen, (aged seventeen years), and the said Ann, only being required to obey the said orders hereinbefore made to appear before the Judge here in manner and form aforesaid, and it further appearing that the said Charles is absent in San Bernardino County, within said Jurisdiction District. It is ordered that Robert Clift, Esq., Sheriff of said county, be and is hereby appointed Special Guardian of said Charles, and as such duly authorized and required to take said Charles in his custody, and him safely keep in such manner that the said Charles shall not be removed out of the State of California, but shall abide the further order of the Judge here or other Judge or Court of competent Jurisdiction touching his Guardianship. And it is further ordered and adjudged that all costs accrued in the case up to the present date and in executing the present order of the Judge here as to the production of said Hannah and her said infant two weeks old, and said Lawrence, Martha and Mary, before the Judge here as aforesaid, shall be paid by the said Robert Smith.

Given under my hand as Judge of the First Judicial District Court of the State of California, on the 19th day of January, A.D. 1856, at the City of Los Angeles.

BENJAMIN HAYES
District Judge

NOTES

Introduction: Coming to the Wall

1. Articles about the artworks about Biddy Mason's homestead and life include: "Biddy Mason Place: A Passage in Time"; Patricia Leigh Brown, "A Wall Running Back into History"; Gregory Crouch, "Early Black Heroine of L.A. Finally Receives Her Due"; Judith Freeman, "Commemorating an L.A. Pioneer"; J. H. Gillette, "Power in Place"; and Dolores Hayden, "Biddy Mason: Los Angeles, 1856–1891." Hayden was one of the first writers to doubt that Biddy and Hannah were sisters. She mentions one source saying they were sisters, then says: "Mason's descendant, Linda Cox, in a personal communication to this author, March 1989, said the family is unclear about the relationship, but thinks Hannah was at most a half-sister. No contemporary accounts list her as a sister." She also notes: "Given the attention to family relationships at the trial, it is significant that Hannah is not called Biddy's sister here" (148).

Chapter 1: The Dream

1. James E. Wooley and Vivian Wooley, *Edgefield County, South Carolina, Wills, 1787–1836*, 206–7. Robert Mays Smith's Mormon records show his parents as John and Sarah Smith. The Dean will implies his mother was Sarah

Dean. In the Dean cemetery in the northern portion of Edgefield County, not far from the grave of William Dean (1765–1830), there is a marker showing S. Smith, deceased Jan. 3, 1807. If Robert's mother died when he was young, he may have been raised by his maternal grandparents.

2. Probate Record of John Dorn, Sr., Edgefield County Courthouse, Edgefield, S.C.

3. Orville Vernon Burton, *In My Father's House Are Many Mansions: Family and Community in Edgefield, South Carolina*, 86.

4. Bernard DeVoto, *The Year of Decision, 1846*, 83.

5. Wallace Stegner, *The Gathering of Zion: The Story of the Mormon Trail*, 5.

6. The story may be apocryphal, but not impossible. The timing of Biddy's reported running away from Hancock County, Georgia, going to the Cherokee Nation, and winding up in Hinds County, Mississippi, where her first child, Ellen, was born in 1838 is the same period as the expulsion of the Cherokees on the Trail of Tears. But if Biddy had been either married to a Cherokee or held as a Cherokee slave, her descendants would seemingly have passed that story down, although it should be noted that some accounts of the heritage of her children, particularly her first daughter, Ellen, do mention possible Cherokee ancestry.

7. Ralph Betts Flanders, *Plantation Slavery in Georgia*, 67, 68.

8. B. Gordon Wheeler shows Biddy "surviving hunger and thirst and attack by Indians and her owner, Robert Smith, a Georgia redneck who believed his ownership of Biddy entitled him to sexual favors, forced or not" (*Black California: The History of African-Americans in the Golden State*, 71). Joan Swallow Reiter says, "At thirty-two Biddy set out with her three daughters, Ellen, Ann and Harriet, the two younger daughters, it has been claimed, fathered by Smith" (*The Women*, 138). Dolores Hayden says, "In addition to being Smith's slaves, some of Hannah's children may have been his own offspring, or perhaps Cottrell's" ("Biddy Mason," 90). The difficulty is that, barring genetic testing of the descendants, there is no way to know whether Robert Mays Smith fathered any children by Biddy and Hannah, and, even if he did, the circumstances or relationships between him and the women cannot be known.

A remote possibility for Biddy's husband is "a black man by the name of Mason" who was baptized by John Brown on Apr. 21, 1844, at the same time as members of the Bankhead family (John Zimmerman Brown, ed., *Autobiography of John Brown, 1820–1896*, 46). In 1846, the Mississippi Mormons were asked to send a party to Council Bluffs, and five volunteered their slaves. Brown reports on a horrible trip: "It finally turned cold and we had a very severe time of it. The negroes suffered most." After they reached the Bluffs, "Bankhead's negro died with the winter fever" (72). No Bankhead slave named Mason is shown on the 1850 Utah census, although their other slaves are listed by name.

9. Benjamin Hayes, "Suit for Freedom," *Los Angeles Star*.

10. Burton, *In My Father's House*, 150–51.

11. Membership book of Little Steven's Baptist Church, Sept. 9, 1843, Tompkins Library, Edgefield, S.C.

12. *Edgefield Advertiser,* June 10, 1846, Tompkins Library, Edgefield, S.C. Quoted in Carlee T. McClendon, *Edgefield Death Notices and Cemetery Records,* 58.

13. Probate Record of John Dorn Sr.

14. Ibid.

15. *Edgefield Advertiser,* Oct. 7, 1846.

16. Inventory of Sale, Probate Record of John Dorn Sr.

17. Probate Record of John Dorn Sr.

18. Ibid.

19. Ibid.

20. Ibid.

21. Mary Boykin Chesnut, *A Diary from Dixie;* quoted in Burton, *In My Father's House,* 187.

22. Leonard J. Arrington, *Brigham Young: American Moses,* 110, 111.

23. J. Z. Brown, *Autobiography of John Brown,* 47.

24. Stegner, *Gathering of Zion,* 30, 38.

25. Arrington, *Brigham Young,* 123–25.

26. Leonard J. Arrington, "Mississippi Mormons," 46.

27. Edith Klemcke and Bob Weed, *Robert Mays Smith: From South California to Texas (the Long Way),* 3.

28. Ibid., 5.

29. Hayes, "Suit for Freedom," *Los Angeles Star.*

30. J. Z. Brown, *Autobiography of John Brown,* 88.

31. Ibid., 96.

32. Ibid., 93.

33. Ibid., 92, for example.

34. Ibid., 97.

35. Ibid., 96.

36. Ibid., 97–98.

37. Stegner, *Gathering of Zion,* 197.

38. Brown, ibid., 100.

39. Arrington, *Brigham Young,* 157; Stanley B. Kimball, *Heber C. Kimball: Mormon Patriarch and Pioneer,* 180–81. Stegner says there were "923 wagons and something over 2,400 people" (*Gathering of Zion,* 199). The more exact numbers are derived by adding the totals for each of the companies, but these differ according to recorder.

40. Juanita Brooks, ed., *On the Mormon Frontier: The Diary of Hosea Stout,* 317; Stegner, *Gathering of Zion,* 200; Arrington, *Brigham Young,* 159.

41. Brooks, *On the Mormon Frontier,* 326.

42. Ibid., 327.

43. Arrington, "Mississippi Mormons," 46–51.

44. Kate B. Carter, *The Story of the Negro Pioneer,* 2.

45. Ibid.

46. See Jane Manning James's biography in ibid. Her *Autobiography* is in the LDS Church History Department, Salt Lake City.

47. "Record of the First Group to Enter the Valley," 81.

48. For biographies of slaves of the Mississippi Mornons, see Carter, *Negro Pioneer.*

49. Kate B. Carter, "From the Journal of Parley Pratt," 197; Arrington, *Brigham Young,* 183.

50. Carter, "Journal of Parley Pratt," 198–200.

51. William B. Smart and Donna T. Smart, eds., *Over the Rim: The Parley P. Pratt Exploring Expedition to Southern Utah, 1849–50,* 82, 137.

52. Stegner, *Gathering of Zion,* 13.

53. Kate B. Carter, "Eliza Marie Patridge Lyman," 235.

54. *Seventh Census of the United States,* 1850, Utah Territory.

55. Arrington, *Charles C. Rich,* 160–61.

56. Ibid., 159. The diary of Mary Ann Rich, wife of Charles C. Rich, is rich with details of the hard desert crossing (LDS Church History Department, Salt Lake City).

57. Arrington, *Charles C. Rich,* 165.

58. Arrington, in his chapter "The Settling of San Bernardino," gives the best overview of the purchase and financing of the ranch for the Colony (ibid., 153–83).

59. Robert Smith's son William "Seco" said that when the family moved to California, they "arrived at the Santa Ana River about where San Bernardino now stands. Here Father stopped and Father established a ranch which he sold out after a time and we moved near to Los Angeles" (Klemcke and Weed, *Robert Mays Smith,* 12). George W. Beattie and Helen Pruitt mention "Robert M. Smith, who later made his home on Jumuba" (*Heritage of the Valley: San Bernardino's First Century,* 186). Jumuba, originally an Indian encampment, became a Spanish rancho. Beattie and Pruitt also give the history of Jumuba (67–68). Its location is south of the Santa Ana River, near Colton, California, not far from the present freeway intersection.

60. Arrington, *Charles C. Rich,* 165.

61. Ibid., 173, 188.

62. Ibid., 171.

63. Arrington discusses the land dispute (ibid., 195–96). Arda M. Haenszel says explicitly that Jumuba was one of the areas the Mormons wanted ("Jumuba: From Indian Huts to Condominiums").

64. There is disagreement as to when Smith's term as counselor ended. Klemcke and Weed say, "During a meeting of the leaders of San Bernardino on Apr. 8, 1855, Robert M. Smith was still listed as counselor to William Crosby" (*Robert Mays Smith,* 11). The May 14, 1856, entry by the colony clerk refers to "RM Smith, one of the High Council" (California Mission, "San Bernardino Branch Historical Record, 1851–1856," LDS History Department, Church Archives, Salt Lake City). Smart and Smart contend that "in subsequent conferences, on April 6, 1852, and April 8, 1855, Smith and the

others were sustained in the same positions. Robert M. Smith continued as a counselor through 1856" (*Over the Rim,* 240). Arrington argues, "In May, 1853, Lyman and Rich released Bishop Crosby and his counselors and ordained Nathan C. Tenney bishop of the settlement, with Orrin H. Carter and I.S. Harris as counselors" (*Charles C. Rich,* 178).

65. California Mission, "San Bernardino Branch Historical Record, 1851–1856," May 14, 1856, LDS History Department, Church Archives, Salt Lake City.

66. Ibid., Aug. 18, 1855.

67. Ibid., Sept. 29, 1855.

68. Burton says that in 1860, Dorn was the wealthiest person in Edgefield District, "whose goldmine alone was valued at over a million dollars" (*In My Father's House,* 67). Willie Mae [Gilchrist] Wood quotes the *Greenville (S.C.) Southern Patriot's* account of the wedding of William Burkhalter Dorn, fifty-six, to Martha Jane Rutledge, sixteen (*Old Families of McCormick County, South Carolina, and Dorn Families of Edgefield, Greenwood, and McCormick Counties,* 190–91).

69. California Mission, "San Bernardino Branch Historical Record, 1851–1856," Tithing Ledger, pp. 54–55, LDS History Department, Church Archives, Salt Lake City.

70. On June 26, 1868, Hannah conveyed the property she had inherited from Toby Embers to "Charles Embers and Martha Embers, her children by said Toby Embers" (San Bernardino County Archives, San Bernardino). In Harriet Embers's probate file, Charles Embers and Martha Embers Beal are listed as relatives and specifically named as children of Toby Embers (Probate Record no. 34, in ibid.). None of Hannah's other children is mentioned. It may be that the other children Hannah had after commencing a relationship with Toby Embers—including Marion, Henry, and Catherine (see chap. 8, n. 67, below)—had all died prior to 1868, but no record of their deaths has been found.

71. California Mission, "San Bernardino Branch Historical Record, 1851–1856," Dec. 25, 1855, LDS History Department, Church Archives, Salt Lake City.

Chapter 2: White Woman Running

1. This chapter—I realized later by going back through my journals—blends two visits to Los Angeles: the first, in 1992, was for a week after the riots following the Rodney King trial, and the second, in 1995, was for three days during the O. J. Simpson trial. Because both visits had for me the same overtones of fear and hostility, I left them together in the book in the same way they had merged in my memory.

2. Eleanor Munro, *On Glory Roads: A Pilgrim's Book on Pilgrimage,* 6, quoted in *Home/Stead,* by Susan Elizabeth King.

Chapter 3: The Writ

1. Benjamin Hayes, *Pioneer Notes from the Diaries of Judge Benjamin Hayes, 1849–1875*, 175. Both Robert Curry Owens ("My Grandfather," typescript, 1930, University of California, Los Angeles, Department of Special Collections, Charles E. Young Research Library) and Delilah L. Beasley (*The Negro Trail Blazers of California*) mention Smith's encampment in the Santa Monica hills.

2. Michael A. Normandin, "The Journey of Life: A History of Benjamin I. Hayes and His Family between 1791 and 1871," 11–12. Harold Eaton, a descendant of John Hayes, gave me information about the death of Mary Hayes (recorded in Cathedral Records of Baltimore, now in Maryland Archives) and the number and names of her children.

3. Hayes, *Pioneer Notes*, 140.

4. Ibid., 103.

5. Ibid., 174.

6. Ibid., ix; Normandin, "Journey of Life," 42.

7. Hayes, *Pioneer Notes*, 86.

8. Ibid., 17.

9. Ibid., 13.

10. Ibid., 14.

11. Ibid., 32.

12. Ibid., 17, 33.

13. Ibid., 41.

14. Ibid., 43.

15. Ibid., 52, 72.

16. Ibid., 71. Harris Newmark provides more information on Biggs (*Sixty Years in Southern California, 1853–1913: Containing the Reminiscences of Harris Newmark*, 137–38).

17. Hayes, "Emigrant Notes, San Diego, CA, 1875," Feb. 6, 1850, Bancroft Library, University of California at Berkeley, BANC MSS C-E 62.

18. Hayes, *Pioneer Notes*, ix, 76–78.

19. Ibid., 75.

20. Ibid. Benjamin became a slave owner briefly when his father-in-law died, dividing his slaves among his heirs, including daughter Emily. Information provided by Hal Eaton, John Hayes's descendant.

21. Hayes relates Emily's diary of her trip west via the Panama Canal (ibid., 80–86).

22. Hayes, "Emigrant Notes."

23. Hayes, *Pioneer Notes*, 88.

24. Hayes, *Pioneer Notes*, 93.

25. Ibid., 95, 105.

26. Ibid., 89, 93.

27. Ibid., 91, 141.

28. Ibid., 125.

29. Ibid., 94.

30. Ibid., 101.

31. Ibid., x, 123.

32. Rockwell D. Hunt, "History of the California State Division Controversy," 39–40.

33. Hayes, *Pioneer Notes*, 105.

34. Ibid., 104, 106.

35. Ibid., 125, 129.

36. Hayes, "Suit for Freedom," *Los Angeles Star.* His opinion specifically names the sheriffs from the two counties.

37. Kate Bradley Stovall says, "Biddy Mason was the first to doubt the many promises of freedom made by her master" ("Negro Women in Los Angeles and Vicinity: Some Notable Characters"). This is probably a true description of Biddy's feelings as reflected by her later statement to Judge Hayes: "I always feared this trip to Texas since I first heard of it." However, Biddy did not say, as she well could have at that time, that she told anyone of her feelings or alerted one of the two sheriffs. Anita King states: "News of Biddy's plight reached Los Angeles members of the Executive Committee of the Colored Convention, a group of successful blacks. . . . A writ of habeas corpus was issued against Smith" ("Pioneer Vignettes"). This is unlikely considering that these men are not mentioned in any of the documents or accounts of the trial. Dolores Hayden credits Robert Owens and Elizabeth Flake Rowan with notifying the local law officials ("Biddy Mason," 89–90). It may have been a combination of people raising the alarm, but I feel that Toby Embers had the most to lose and would have been involved.

38. Hayes, *Pioneer Notes*, 132.

39. The story of the removal of Biddy, Hannah, and their children from the Smith camp is told in Owens, "My Grandfather," typescript, 1930, University of California, Los Angeles, Department of Special Collections, Charles E. Young Research Library; and Beasley, *Negro Trail Blazers.*

40. Hayes, "Suit for Freedom," *Los Angeles Star.*

41. Newmark, *Sixty Years,* 189.

42. Henry W. Splitter, "Los Angeles in the 1850's, as Told by Early Newspapers," 117.

43. Stovall, "Negro Women."

44. Hayes, "Suit for Freedom," *Los Angeles Star.*

45. Although Hayes says in "Suit for Freedom" in the *Los Angeles Star,* "At Chambers on Habeas Corpus," he says "in court" within this article and also within the subsequent article (also named "Suit for Freedom") in the *Sacramento Daily Democratic State Journal.* It appears that the original hearing was held in his chambers, but the actual trials were held in open court. Another reading of "At Chambers" is that the habeas corpus case was not heard during the regular session of the district court; therefore, it was heard at the judge's discretion.

46. Hayes, "Suit for Freedom," *Los Angeles Star.*

47. Ibid.

48. Charlotta A. Bass, *Forty Years: Memories from the Pages of a Newspaper,* 115.

49. The undated *New York Times* article is in Benjamin Hayes, *Scraps,* Bancroft Library, University of California at Berkeley; letter to Jack Hinton in ibid., 14:106; Hayes to Benjamin D. Wilson, Wilson Papers, Henry E. Huntington Library, San Marino, Calif.

50. Hayes, "Suit for Freedom," *Los Angeles Star.* Except where noted, the rest of this chapter's quotes and text are taken from this source.

51. James A. Fisher, "The Struggle for Negro Testimony in California, 1851–1863." Rudolph M. Lapp, in *Blacks in Gold Rush California,* also discusses the obstacles to testimony.

Chapter 4: Meeting Mississippi

1. Lester E. Bush Jr. and Armand L. Mauss, eds., *Neither White nor Black: Mormon Scholars Confront the Race Issue in a Universal Church,* 12–13.

2. Ibid., 65.

3. Ibid., 15.

4. Ibid., 223–24.

5. Ibid., 225.

6. Eudora Welty, *The Optimist's Daughter,* 169.

7. The holograph of Jane Elizabeth Manning James's *Autobiography* is in the LDS Church History Department, Salt Lake City. Robert Lang Campbell's "Journal of Southern Exploring Expedition," is in ibid. Campbell's journal is one of the main documents for *Over the Rim.*

8. Estate of John Dorn, Edgefield County Archives, Edgefield, S.C., box 54, pkg. 2249; John Dorn, will, Will Book D, June 16, 1846, pp. 285–87, in ibid. Family History Film 162265, in ibid. (also available on microfilm through LDS branch libraries).

Chapter 5: The Verdict

1. Hayes, "Suit for Freedom," *Los Angeles Star.* All of this chapter's quotes and text are taken from this source.

2. Hayes's choice of witnesses to the interviews is interesting. Don Abel Stearns came from Massachusetts, went to Mexico, became a Mexican citizen, moved to Los Angeles, married a daughter of the wealthy Bandini family, became involved in transportation, and soon was a wealthy cattleman and rancher. James B. Winston was a doctor from Virginia, proprietor of the Bella Union Hotel, and a civic activist. He, too, was married to a Bandini daughter.

Chapter 6: Getting to the Right State

1. To preserve their privacy, I changed the names of the men I call Sam C. and Mr. Holmes in this chapter.

Chapter 7: The Promise

1. Hayes, "Suit for Freedom," *Sacramento Daily Democratic State Journal.* Except where noted, this chapter's quotes and text are taken from this source.
2. In the *Los Angeles Star,* Hayes wrote that they were placed in custody of the sheriff. In the article in the *Sacramento Daily Democratic State Journal,* Hayes quotes a witness who testifies about "the house of Robert Owen, a colored man, where the petitioners had been placed by the Sheriff."
3. Hayes, "Suit for Freedom," *Los Angeles Star.*

Chapter 8: Five Codas

1. Klemcke and Weed, *Robert Mays Smith,* 11.
2. Ibid., 14–15.
3. Ibid., 198.
4. Ibid., 221.
5. Ibid., chaps. on John Dorn Smith and William "Seco" Smith.
6. bid., 57.
7. Ibid., 24.
8. Letter to author from Ethel Klemcke.
9. Klemcke and Weed, *Robert Mays Smith,* 16.
10. Ibid., 25–26.
11. Hayes, *Pioneer Notes,* 166–68.
12. Ibid., 169.
13. Hayes, "Emigrant Notes," Apr. 17, 1855.
14. Hayes, *Pioneer Notes,* 167, 172.
15. Ibid., 265–66, 197.
16. Newmark, *Sixty Years,* 46–47.
17. Hayes, *Pioneer Notes,* 243.
18. Ibid., 253.
19. Ibid., 255.
20. Ibid., 256.
21. Ibid., 254.
22. Hayes, "Suit for Freedom," *Los Angeles Star;* Hayes, *Scraps,* 14:119.
23. Newmark, *Sixty Years,* 46–47.
24. Hayes, *Pioneer Notes,* 254, 226, 255 (two quotes), 256.
25. Newmark, *Sixty Years,* 337.
26. Hayes, *Pioneer Notes,* 176.
27. William B. Rice, *The "Los Angeles Star," 1851–1864: The Beginnings of Journalism in Southern California,* 51.
28. Hayes, "Emigrant Notes"; Hayes, *Scraps,* vol. 30, *Chance Studies.*
29. Hayes, "Emigrant Notes."
30. Hubert Howe Bancroft, "Historic Researches in the South."
31. Ibid., 481.
32. Ibid., 479.

33. Ibid., 484.

34. Ibid., 471, 479.

35. Ibid., 482.

36. Hayes, *Pioneer Notes*, x. Normandin's *Journey of Life* also follows John Chauncey Hayes's life.

37. Bancroft, "Historic Researches," 509.

38. Ibid.

39. J. J. Warner, Benjamin Hayes, and J. P. Widney, *An Historical Sketch of Los Angeles County, California: From the Spanish Occupancy, by the Founding of the Mission San Gabriel Archangel, September 8, 1771, to July 4, 1876,* 82.

40. Hayes, *Pioneer Notes*, 277.

41. Bancroft, "Historic Researches," 511. Bancroft says: "At the time of his death Judge Hayes was deep in two large collections of documents which he had shortly before obtained, one from Mr Alexander, son-in-law of Requena, and the other from Coronel, the former containing the valuable diary of Mr Mellus" (527).

42. Warner, Hayes, and Widney, introduction to *Historical Sketch*, dated July 4, 1876.

43. Ibid., 121.

44. Ibid., 1936 ed., 4.

45. Hayes, *Pioneer Notes*, xi.

46. Marjorie Tisdale Wolcott, editor of Hayes's *Pioneer Notes*, mentions his "eventually returning to his former home at the Hotel Lafayette in Los Angeles, where he died at the age of sixty-two, on August 4, 1877" (ix).

47. Editorial comment on Hayes, "Suit for Freedom," *Los Angeles Star*, 2.

48. Beasley, *Negro Trail Blazers*, 110.

49. Ibid.

50. *Eighth Census of the United States*, 1860, Los Angeles County.

51. Hayden says this theory about her middle name was put forth by Barbara Jackson in an unpublished paper presented at a symposium sponsored by the Power of Place ("Biddy Mason," 91).

52. Newmark's *Sixty Years* has many entries relating to Griffin. For the purchase or lease of water rights, see 365–66; for the acquisition of Rancho San Pasqual, see 237.

53. Beasley, *Negro Trail Blazers*, 90, 109.

54. Newmark, *Sixty Years*, 328.

55. The growth of Biddy Mason's real estate fortune is chronicled in Beasley, *Negro Trail Blazers*, 90, 109–10; and Stovall, "Negro Women." See also Hayden, "Biddy Mason."

56. Hayden, "Biddy Mason," 97.

57. Sue Bailey Thurman, *Pioneers of Negro Origin in California*, 47.

58. Stovall, "Negro Women."

59. Beasley, *Negro Trail Blazers*, 110.

60. Owens, "My Grandfather," typescript, 1930, University of California, Los Angeles, Department of Special Collections, Charles E. Young Research Library.

61. Beasley, *Negro Trail Blazers,* 110; Stovall, "Negro Women."

62. Biddy Mason, death certificate, Hall of Records, City of Los Angeles, Los Angeles County Archives; Biddy Mason, will, Golden States Insurance Company Records, University of California, Los Angeles, Department of Special Collections, Charles E. Young Research Library (a printed guide to the papers is available); Stovall, "Negro Women."

63. Biddy Mason, death certificate.

64. Bass, *Forty Years,* 115–16.

65. Beattie and Pruitt, *Heritage of the Valley,* 186.

66. *Eighth Census of the United States,* 1860, San Bernardino County.

67. Mortality Schedule, in ibid.

68. Conveyance of Property between Hannah Embers and Charles Embers and Martha Embers, June 26, 1868, in ibid.

69. Arrington, *Charles C. Rich,* 207; Index to Deeds, 1854–1926, San Bernardino County Archives, San Bernardino.

70. The party, its disruption by McFeely and thugs, and the subsequent complaint, humiliation, and trial are described in Byron R. Skinner, *Black Origins in the Inland Empire,* 46–47; and Luther A. Ingersoll, *Ingersoll's Century Annals of San Bernardino County, 1769 to 1904,* but they do not mention Toby Embers by name. The full account can be found in the trial record of *People vs. Joseph McFeely,* Nov. 9, 1858, San Bernardino County Archives, San Bernardino.

71. Skinner, *Black Origins,* 46.

72. Ibid., 47.

73. Hayes, Nov. 6. 1858, San Bernardino County Archives, San Bernardino.

74. Skinner, *Black Origins,* 46.

75. *Tenth Census of the United States,* 1880, Pima County, Arizona Territory; George Rawich, ed., *The American Slave: A Composite Autobiography,* 17; Delinquent Tax List, San Bernardino County, from the *San Bernardino Guardian,* Feb. 1, 1873, San Bernardino County Library, Heritage Room, San Bernardino. Embers's first marriage to Jane Thompson on July 20, 1868, is recorded in Marriages, Book A, 1855–1870, San Bernardino County Archives, Archives.

76. See National Parks Service, Civil War Soldiers and Sailors System, at http://www.itd.nps.gov/cwss/. Rawich, *American Slave,* 17.

77. *Ninth Census of the United States,* 1870, San Bernardino County; Probate Record of Harriet Embers, San Bernardino County Archives, San Bernardino; Beattie and Pruitt, *Heritage of the Valley,* 186; Skinner, *Black Origins,* 63–65.

78. *Eleventh Census of the United States,* 1890, Los Angeles County.

79. Marriage licenses, Jane Smiley to George Goins, 1862; and Nelson Smiley to Juana Biggs, 1867; both in Hall of Records, City of Los Angeles, Los Angeles County Archives.

80. *Seventh Census of the United States,* 1850, Free and Slave Schedules, Tishomingo, MS.

81. *Eighth Census of the United States,* 1860, Free and Slave Schedules, Caldwell County, Tex.; *Tenth Census of the United States,* 1880, Caldwell County, Tex.

Chapter 9: The Letter

1. Hayes to Hinton, Sept. 20, 1863, in *Scraps*. There is a postscript to the letter: "P.S. Have buried the 'big-bellied bottle,' and they have saved 'Rosin the Bow!'—for a later ceremony of that kind." It apparently refers to Hayes's decision to stop drinking and to a festive experience he and Hinton had shared.

Hayes's reference to public reaction against him after the trial is supported by a letter written on Feb. 12, 1856, to influential friend Benjamin Wilson: "I send you a copy of the opinion filed by me in the case of some colored persons lately tried before me, and *notes of the evidence*. I am anxious to have the whole of this printed in a Sacramento paper, *In justice to myself*, the evidence was not printed here—and the newspaper publication being made merely to satisfy the public mind here, does not contain the whole of the opinion and Waite's little 'Star' rather limited me for room. I do not think this would take more than *two columns of the Sacramento Union, or State Journal*, or San Francisco *Herald*. I would not like to have the opinion abridged. Will you confer the favor on me to see if your influence can get it printed in one of these papers—however, do not let it be known that I have written you on this subject. If they did not charge more than $25.00 in case they want pay, I will pay it. I am a little afraid of *misrepresentation*, in regard to this case, particularly as the evidence was not printed. *Interest* yourself, my dear Don Benito, in this matter, and you will oblige me exceedingly. . . . I am truly yr friend, Benj. Hayes" (Wilson Papers). Hayes's offer to pay to have the full account published shows the pressure he was under. He wrote Wilson again on Feb. 22, 1856 (ibid.). The article, with accompanying notes, was subsequently published in the *Sacramento Daily Democratic State Journal*, Feb. 19, 1856.

Benjamin Davis ("Don Benito") Wilson was one of southern California's leading citizens who married into an influential Spanish family. See John C. Macfarland, "Don Benito Wilson." Don Benito and his wife were grandparents of Gen. George S. Patton.

2. Hayes, *Pioneer Notes*, 209, 204.
3. Ibid., 131.
4. Ibid., 174, 175.

Epilogue: Coming to Rest

1. This is how I remember the conversation about the odd alignment of the grave. In the family history, *Robert Mays Smith*, there is a different explanation, verified with Ethel Klemcke: Elizabeth Hester Smith, young wife of Joseph Smith, Robert and Rebecca's sixth child, died of blood poisoning in 1879, leaving behind four young children. "Joseph had her grave dug at the Oak Island Methodist Church near Somerset, Bexar Co. TX. When they arrived with the body it was discovered the grave had been dug north and south. There was nothing to do but proceed with the burial" (200).

BIBLIOGRAPHY

Manuscript Sources

Bancroft Library, University of California at Berkeley.
Edgefield County Archives, Edgefield, S.C.
Edgefield County Courthouse, Edgefield, S.C.
Hall of Records, City of Los Angeles, Los Angeles County Archives.
LDS History Department, Church Archives, Salt Lake City.
San Bernardino County Archives, San Bernardino.
San Bernardino County Library, Heritage Room, San Bernardino.
Tompkins Library, Edgefield, S.C.
University of California, Los Angeles, Department of Special Collections, Charles E. Young Research Library.
Wilson, Benjamin D. Papers. Henry E. Huntington Library, San Marino, Calif.

Census Schedules and Tax Records

First Census of the United States. Head of Households, 1790. South Carolina.
Second Census of the United States, 1800. South Carolina.
Third Census of the United States, 1810. Edgefield, S.C.
Fourth Census of the United States, 1820. Edgefield, S.C.

Fifth Census of the United States, 1830. Edgefield, S.C.

Sixth Census of the United States, 1840. Edgefield, S.C.; Hancock County, Ga.; Hinds County, Monroe County, and Tishomingo County, MS.

Seventh Census of the United States, 1850. Los Angeles; Free and Slave Schedules, Tishomingo, MS; Utah Territory.

Eighth Census of the United States, 1860. Free and Slave Schedules, Bexar County, Tex.; Caldwell County, Tex.; Los Angeles County; Mortality Schedule, San Bernardino County.

Ninth Census of the United States, 1870. Arizona Territory; Bexar County, Tex.; Edgefield County, S.C.; Los Angeles County; San Bernardino County.

Tenth Census of the United States, 1880. Bexar County and Caldwell County, Tex.; Edgefield, S.C.; Los Angeles County; San Bernardino County; Pima County, Arizona Territory.

Eleventh Census of the United States, 1890. Los Angeles County.

1852 California State Census. Available at the National Archives, Pacific Region; 1000 Commodore Dr.; San Bruno, CA 94066.

Tax Records. Franklin County, MS, 1841. Mississippi State Archives, Jackson.

Other Sources

"Anti-Slavery Case in Los Angeles." *New York Times,* n.d. In Benjamin Hayes, *Scraps,* the Bancroft Library, University of California at Berkeley.

Arrington, Leonard J. *Brigham Young: American Moses.* New York: Alfred A. Knopf, 1985.

———. *Charles C. Rich.* Provo: Brigham Young University Press, 1974.

———. "Mississippi Mormons." *Ensign* (June 1977): 45–51.

Arrington, Leonard J., and Davis Bitton. *The Mormon Experience: A History of the Latter-day Saints.* Urbana: University of Illinois Press, 1992.

Atchley, Tom. *Early Black History of the San Bernardino Valley.* San Bernardino: San Bernardino County Museum Commemoration Edition, 1974.

Bancroft, Hubert Howe. "Historic Researches in the South." In *Literary Industries: A Memoir,* 478–529. Vol. 39 of *The Works of Hubert Howe Bancroft.* San Francisco: History Company, 1890.

Bass, Charlotta A. *Forty Years: Memories from the Pages of a Newspaper.* Los Angeles: C. A. Bass, 1960.

Beasley, Delilah L. *The Negro Trail Blazers of California.* Los Angeles: Times Mirror Printing and Binding House, 1919.

Beasley, Delilah L., and M. N. Work. "Documents: California Freedom Papers." *Journal of Negro History* 3 (1918): 50–54.

Beattie, George W., and Helen Pruitt. *Heritage of the Valley: San Bernardino's First Century.* Oakland: Biobooks, 1951.

Beller, Jack. "Negro Slaves in Utah." *Utah Historical Quarterly* 2 (Oct. 1924): 122–26.

Berrett, LaMar C. "History of the Southern States Mission, 1831–1861." Master's thesis, Brigham Young University, 1960.

Berwanger, Eugene H. *The Frontier against Slavery: Western Anti-Negro Prejudice and the Slavery Extension Controversy.* Urbana: University of Illinois Press, 1967.

"Biddy Mason Place: A Passage in Time." *International Review of African American Art* 9, no. 1 (1990): 42–43.

Bitton, Davis. *Guide to Mormon Diaries and Autobiographies.* Provo: Brigham Young University Press, 1977.

Bond, J. Max. *The Negro in Los Angeles: A Dissertation.* Los Angeles: University of Southern California, 1936; San Francisco: R and ER Research Associates, 1972.

Bowman, Lynn. *Los Angeles: Epic of a City.* Los Angeles: Howell-North Books, 1974.

Bringhurst, Newell G. *Saints, Slaves, and Blacks: The Changing Place of Blacks within Mormonism.* Westport, Conn.: Greenwood, 1981.

Brooks, Juanita, ed. *On the Mormon Frontier: The Diary of Hosea Stout.* 2 vols. Salt Lake City: University of Utah Press, 1964.

Brown, Hallie Q. *Homespun Heroines and Other Women of Distinction.* Schomberg Library of Nineteenth-Century Black Women Writers. New York: Oxford University Press, 1998.

Brown, John Zimmerman, ed. *Autobiography of John Brown, 1820–1896.* Salt Lake City: Stevens and Wallis, 1941.

Brown, Patricia Leigh. "A Wall Running Back into History." *New York Times,* Dec. 7, 1989, Living Arts section, pp. B5(N), C3(L), col. 1.

Bunch, Lonnie G. *Black Angelenos: The Afro-American in Los Angeles, 1850–1950.* Los Angeles: California Afro-American Museum, 1988.

Burton, Orville Vernon. *In My Father's House Are Many Mansions: Family and Community in Edgefield, South Carolina.* Chapel Hill: University of North Carolina Press, 1985.

Bush, Lester E., Jr., and Armand L. Mauss, eds. *Neither White nor Black: Mormon Scholars Confront the Race Issue in a Universal Church.* Midvale, Utah: Signature Books, 1984.

Campbell, Eugene. "A History of the Church of Jesus Christ of Latter-day Saints in California." Ph.D. diss., University of Southern California, 1952.

Carter, Kate B. "Eliza Marie Patridge Lyman." In *Treasures of Pioneer History,* ed. Kate B. Carter, 12:213–84. Salt Lake City: Daughters of Utah Pioneers, 1953.

———. "From the Journal of Parley Pratt." In *Heart Throbs of the West,* ed. Kate B. Carter, 12:195–206. Salt Lake City: Daughters of Utah Pioneers, 1951.

———. "Mississippi Saints." In *Our Pioneer Heritage,* ed. Kate B. Carter, 2:421–76. Salt Lake City: Daughters of Utah Pioneers, 1968.

———. *The Story of the Negro Pioneer.* Salt Lake City: Daughters of Utah Pioneers, 1965.

Chesnut, Mary Boykin. *A Diary from Dixie.* Ed. Ben Ames Williams. Boston: Houghton Mifflin, 1949.

Coleman, Ronald G. "A History of Blacks in Utah, 1825–1910." Ph.D. diss., University of Utah, 1980.

"Courthouses of Los Angeles County." *Southern California Quarterly* 41, no. 4 (Dec. 1959): 345–75.

Crouch, Gregory. "Early Black Heroine of L.A. Finally Receives Her Due." *Los Angeles Times,* Mar. 28, 1988, sec. 1, col. 5.

DeVoto, Bernard. *The Year of Decision, 1846.* Boston: Houghton Mifflin, 1942.

Finkleman, Paul. "The Law of Slavery and Freedom in California, 1848–1860." *California Western Law Review* (San Diego) 17 (1981): 437–64.

Fisher, James A. "The Struggle for Negro Testimony in California, 1851–1863." *Southern California Quarterly* 51, no. 4 (1969): 313–24.

Flake, S. Eugene. *James Madison Flake: Pioneer Leader and Missionary.* Bountiful, Utah: Wasatch, 1970.

Flanders, Ralph Betts. *Plantation Slavery in Georgia.* Chapel Hill: University of North Carolina Press, 1933.

Freeman, Judith. "Commemorating an L.A. Pioneer." *Angeles Magazine* (Apr. 1990): 58–64.

Gillette, J. H. "Power in Place." *Historic Preservation* 42, no. 4 (July–Aug. 1990): 44+.

Goode, Kenneth G. *California's Black Pioneers: A Brief Historical Survey.* Santa Barbara: McNally and Loftin, 1974.

Haenszel, Arda M. "Jumuba: From Indian Huts to Condominiums." *Odyssey* (San Bernardino) 6, no. 4 (Oct.–Dec. 1984): 50–53.

Halliburton, R., Jr. *Red Over Black: Black Slavery among the Cherokee Indians.* Contributions in Afro-American and African Studies, no. 27. Westport, Conn.: Greenwood, 1977.

Harris, J. William. *Plain Folk and Gentry in a Slave Society: White Liberty and Black Slavery in Augusta's Hinterlands.* Middleton, Conn.: Wesleyan University Press, 1985.

Hayden, Dolores. "Biddy Mason: Los Angeles, 1856–1891." *California History* 68, no. 3 (fall 1989): 86+.

———. *The Power of Place: Urban Landscapes as Public History.* Cambridge: MIT Press, 1995.

Hayes, Benjamin. *Pioneer Notes from the Diaries of Judge Benjamin Hayes, 1849–1875.* Ed. Marjorie Tisdale Wolcott. Los Angeles: N.p., 1929.

———. "Suit for Freedom." *Los Angeles Star,* Feb. 2, 1856, p. 2.

———. "Suit for Freedom." *Sacramento Daily Democratic State Journal,* Feb. 19, 1856, p. 2.

Hinckley, Edith Parker. *On the Banks of the Zanja: The Story of Redlands.* Claremont, Calif.: Claremont College Press, 1951.

Holcomb, Brent H. *Marriage and Death Notices from Baptist Newspapers of South Carolina.* Spartanburg, S.C.: Reprint Company, 1981.

Hunt, Rockwell D. "History of the California State Division Controversy." *Historical Society of Southern California* 13, no. 1 (1924): 37–53.

Ingersoll, Luther A. *Ingersoll's Century Annals of San Bernardino County, 1769 to 1904.* Los Angeles: L. A. Ingersoll, 1904.

Inghram, Dorothy. *Beyond All This.* N.p., 1983.

"Israel Beal, Early Resident, Dies in Injury." *Redlands (Calif.) Daily Facts,* May 11, 1929.

Jenson, Andrew. *Encyclopedic History of the Church of Jesus Christ of Latter-day Saints.* Salt Lake City: Deseret News, 1941.

Jung, C[arl] G[ustav]. *Memories, Dreams, Reflections.* Ed. Aniela Jaffé. New York: Pantheon Books, 1973.

Katz, William Loren. *The Black West.* 3d. ed. Seattle: Open Hand, 1987.

Kimball, Stanley B. *Heber C. Kimball: Mormon Patriarch and Pioneer.* Urbana: University of Illinois Press, 1981.

King, Anita. "Pioneer Vignettes." *Essence* 6, no. 6 (Oct. 1975): 42.

King, Laura, and P. Angell. "Women of the Mormon Battalion and Mississippi Saints." In *Heart Throbs of the West,* ed. Kate B. Carter, 2:65–87. Salt Lake City: Daughters of Utah Pioneers, 1951.

King, Susan Elizabeth. With historical writing and research by Dolores Hayden and Donna Graves. *Home/Stead.* Los Angeles: S. E. King and the Power of Place, 1989.

Klemcke, Edith, and Bob Weed. *Robert Mays Smith: From South Carolina to Texas (the Long Way).* Wolfe City, Tex.: Henington, 1988.

Lapp, Rudolph M. *Blacks in Gold Rush California.* New Haven: Yale University Press, 1977.

Lyman, Albert R. *Amasa Mason Lyman: Trail Blazer and Pioneer from the Atlantic to the Pacific.* Delta, Utah: N.p., 1957.

———. *Francis Marion Lyman, 1840–1916: Apostle, 1880–1916.* Delta, Utah: N.p., 1958.

Macfarland, John C. "Don Benito Wilson," *Historical Society of Southern California Quarterly* no. 31 (1949–1950): 273–90.

Matthews, Miriam. "The Negro in California from 1781 to 1910: An Annotated Bibliography." N.p., n.d.

McClendon, Carlee T. *Edgefield Death Notices and Cemetery Records.* Columbia, S.C.: Hive Press, 1977.

Mooney, James. *Historical Sketch of the Cherokee.* Nineteenth Annual Report of the Bureau of American Ethnology. Pt. 2, pp. 14–548. Washington, D.C: Government Printing Office, 1900.

Moore, Frank. "With a Grain of Salt." *Redlands (Calif.) Daily Facts,* Feb. 6, 1975.

Moore, Frank, and Bill Moore. "With a Grain of Salt." *Redlands (Calif.) Daily Facts,* Oct. 24, 1962.

Munro, Eleanor. *On Glory Roads: A Pilgrim's Book on Pilgrimage.* New York: Thames and Hudson, 1987.

Newmark, Harris. *Sixty Years in Southern California, 1853–1913: Containing the Reminiscences of Harris Newmark.* Ed. Maurice H. Newmark and Marco Newmark. Los Angeles: Zeitlin and Ver Brugge, 1970.

Normandin, Michael A. "The Journey of Life: A History of Benjamin I. Hayes and His Family between 1791 and 1871." Master's thesis, University of San Diego, 1993.

Perdue, Theda. *Slavery and the Evolution of Cherokee Society, 1540–1866.* Knoxville: University of Tennessee Press, 1979.

Rawich, George, ed. *The American Slave: A Composite Autobiography.* Supp. ser. 2. Vol. 1. Westport, Conn.: Greenwood, 1979.

Reiter, Joan Swallow. *The Women.* Old West Series. Alexandria, Va.: Time-Life Books, 1979.

Rice, William B. *The Los Angeles Star, 1851–1864: The Beginnings of Journalism in Southern California.* Ed. John Walton Caughey. Berkeley and Los Angeles: University of California Press, 1947.

Robertson, Ben. *Red Hills and Cotton.* New York: Alfred A. Knopf, 1942.

Skinner, Byron R. *Black Origins in the Inland Empire.* San Bernardino: Book Attic Press, 1983.

"Slavery in California." *Journal of Negro History* 3 (1918): 33–54.

Smart, William B., and Donna T. Smart, eds. *Over the Rim: The Parley P. Pratt Exploring Expedition to Southern Utah, 1849–50.* Logan: Utah State University Press, 1999.

Splitter, Henry W. "Los Angeles in the 1850's, as Told by Early Newspapers." *Historical Society of Southern California Quarterly* 31 (1949): 114–18.

Starr, Kevin. *Inventing the Dream: California through the Progressive Era.* New York: Oxford University Press, 1985.

Stegner, Wallace. *The Gathering of Zion: The Story of the Mormon Trail.* New York: McGraw-Hill, 1964.

Stovall, Kate Bradley. "Negro Women in Los Angeles and Vicinity: Some Notable Characters." *Los Angeles Daily Times,* Feb. 12, 1909, Lincoln Centennial edition, sec. 3, p. 4.

Thompson, Richard. *Pioneers of San Bernardino Valley.* San Bernardino: San Bernardino Pageant, 1976.

Thurman, Sue Bailey. *Pioneers of Negro Origin in California.* San Francisco: Acme Publishers, 1952.

Wallis, Brian. "Public Art Marks Historic L.A. Site." *Art in America* 78, no. 6 (June 1990): 207.

Warner, J. J., Benjamin Hayes, and J. P. Widney. *An Historical Sketch of Los Angeles County, California: From the Spanish Occupancy, by the Founding of the Mission San Gabriel Archangel, September 8, 1771, to July 4, 1876.* Los Angeles: Louis Lewin, 1876.

Weaver, John D. *Los Angeles: The Enormous Village, 1781–1981.* Santa Barbara: Capra Press, 1980.

Welty, Eudora. *The Optimist's Daughter.* New York: Vintage, 1990.

West, Ray B. *Kingdom of the Saints: The Story of Brigham Young and the Mormons.* New York: Viking Press, 1957.

Wheeler, B. Gordon. *Black California: The History of African-Americans in the Golden State.* New York: Hippocrene Books, 1993.

Wilder, Thornton. *The Bridge of San Luis Rey.* New York: Perennial Classics, 1998.

Williams, David. *The Georgia Gold Rush: Twenty-Niners, Cherokees, and Gold Fever.* Columbia: University of South Carolina Press, 1993.

Wood, Joseph S. "The Mormon Settlement in San Bernardino, 1851–1857." Ph.D. diss., University of Utah, 1967.

Wood, Willie Mae [Gilchrist]. *Old Families of McCormick County, South Carolina, and Dorn Families of Edgefield, Greenwood, and McCormick Counties.* Vol. 1. McCormick, S.C.: W. M. G. Wood, 1982.

Wooley, James E., and Vivian Wooley. *Edgefield County, South Carolina, Wills, 1787–1836.* Greenville, S.C.: Southern Historical Press, 1991.

ABOUT THE AUTHOR

DeEtta Demaratus was born in Batesville, Arkansas; moved frequently
during childhood; and attended numerous schools. She dropped out of high
school, graduated from the University of Washington, attended Columbia
University's graduate film school, and graduated from Rosary College's Villa
Schifanoia in Florence, Italy.

Her writing credits include plays and published articles on history, art,
and politics. She has also worked as a screenwriter. She lives in Seattle,
Washington.

The author and her daughter at
Virginia Beach, 1964.

Author photograph:
Savanah Kent/Bohemian Nomad
Picturemakers